Teachers **Develop** Teachers **Research**

Papers on classroom research

and

teacher development

general editors

Julian Edge and Keith Richards

HEINEMANN

Heinemann English Language Teaching

A division of Heinemann Publishers (Oxford) Ltd
Halley Court, Jordan Hill, Oxford OX2 8EJ

OXFORD MADRID ATHENS PARIS FLORENCE
PRAGUE SÃO PAULO CHICAGO MELBOURNE
AUCKLAND SINGAPORE TOKYO IBADAN
GABORONE JOHANNESBURG PORTSMOUTH (NH)

ISBN 0 435 24056 0

First published 1993

Dedication

This book is dedicated to those participants at the TDTR Conference whose contributions are not recorded here. Most particularly, it is dedicated to Alison Birch, who was always there even when we were not, who knew what to do when we did not, and who, when we wondered whether we could manage to … frequently already had.

Acknowledgements

We want to thank Eryl Griffiths and Katie Head for their work in the preparation of the conference, and all the conference team at Aston for helping things to run so smoothly. Thanks also to Chris Hartley at Heinemann for his immediate and continuing enthusiasm for this publication.

Printed and bound in Great Britain by
Thomson Litho Ltd, East Kilbride, Scotland

95 96 10 9 8 7 6 5 4 3 2

Contents

◆

TDTR: Conference as catalyst

Julian Edge & Keith Richards

Aston University

◆

This paper has two purposes. Firstly, as an editorial voice, it introduces and links this selection of papers from the Teachers Develop Teachers Research conference held at Aston University from 3-5 September 1992. Secondly, it records the professional and personal development occasioned for the authors by the planning, running and aftermath of that conference. As a consequence of our reaching out towards these two purposes, writing this paper also continues our development. Thus, to borrow from the title of Bridget Somekh's workshop, do one and one make three.

The paper is written in four parts. The first offers a little historical perspective and takes us into the opening plenary sessions; the second and third introduce the remaining conference papers; the fourth reflects on and articulates our own sense of development.

PART 1

The Teacher Development Special Interest Group (TD SIG) of the International Association of Teachers of English as a Foreign Language (IATEFL) issued its first newsletter in 1986, with three aims listed on the first page:

1 To promote individual and institutional awareness of the importance of Teacher Development.
2 To enable and encourage all categories of teacher to take more responsibility for professional and personal evolution throughout their careers.
3 To encourage the provision of facilities for Teacher Development which do not already exist.

In his opening editorial, Adrian Underhill brought together the themes of personal responsibility and self-development in the question:

How can I develop to become the best teacher that I personally can be?

Subsequent newsletters brought many suggested responses, among them schemes for peer observation as well as workshops on Jungian Perspectives and Intervention Analysis. Most significant for this version of the story was Jon Roberts' (1986:10) contribution to Newsletter No. 4: *Action Research: an Introduction*, which concluded with another question:

I hope to re-think, and to change my practice. Isn't that teacher development?

By the time the TD SIG evolved its new organisation in 1990, this area of overlap between teacher development and teacher research was a central interest for many members.

The decision to organise a conference was a deliberate one, in the sense that we did want an event which would attract some attention. We felt that times had changed in the years of TD SIG's existence and that some successes had been achieved in establishing such concepts as self-development and empowerment on ELT's main agenda. It was time to give ourselves another kind of forum in which to meet, and it was time to see if such a relatively large-scale public experience could not only be successful in its own right, but might also add further momentum to the processes it was celebrating.

The establishment of the Research SIG in 1990 immediately suggested a collaborative venture. Together, we wanted to reclaim the difficult term 'research' to characterise a teacher's personal investigations, and we wanted to establish the personal outcomes of research as a valid point of focus. We also wanted to broaden the base of people who might be attracted to the conference. At Aston University, we, the editors, had a potential conference centre, and we taught on a master's course in which our individual options were Classroom Research and Teacher Development. Empowerment lies in our own hands.

The title of the conference came easily: Teachers Develop Teachers Research. No punctuation and the ambiguities come free. It was interesting to see how different people punctuated an interpretation into those four words when they wrote them. What we had not fully realised was just how varied a landscape the many available interpretations of 'development' and 'research' would produce when overlaid.

Nor, as we set out to organise this exploration of the cognitive and affective, did we have a clear idea of how much time would be invested in such mundane tasks as arranging for extra blankets and responding to dietary requirements. But that is, for the time being, merely a sidetrack.

What was clear to us at this stage was that the conference should have a dual function: we wanted to broaden our horizons and we wanted to share our experiences. These two functions gave an overall shape to the conference. In order to formalise the sharing, we asked contributors explicitly not to talk about research and development as topics, but to report on their actual experiences. In order to broaden our horizons, we invited three plenary speakers, to whom we now turn.

Three plenary speakers

We wanted to hear about human inquiry and personal development outside the world of teachers and learners. Shell is a serious multinational organisation, and it pays high fees to make tuition in Transcendental Meditation available to its top executives on a one-to-one basis. Yet many people in ELT seem to regard explicit approaches to personal development as an embarrassing affectation. What is the bigger picture? What is happening among doctors, accountants and other groups of workers?

We wanted to hear from an educationist from outside ELT who could speak authoritatively on the area of teachers' research into their own classrooms. Once again, the relatively closed nature of ELT has led some teachers to regard the idea of teacher research as the latest publishing gimmick, whipped up in the absence of a new method to sell. We wanted to hear about the progress of this approach in other areas of education where it has an established history. And then, to pull these ideas together in more specific ways, we wanted a speaker with experience of teacher research and development inside ELT who could give us a perspective on the contemporary scene.

We wanted all three speakers to take a broad, strategic view and to raise what seemed to them to be central issues. We also wanted them to speak of their own involvement and personal experiences, and perhaps to share some of their intuitions for the future. It is difficult to imagine how we could have been more fortunate in the people who accepted our invitations: Mel Myers, co-founder of the Individual and Organisational Development Agency; Bridget Somekh, co-ordinator of the Classroom Action Research Network; and David Nunan, asociate director of Australia's National Centre for English Language Teaching and Research.

The three plenary sessions were not arranged end-to-end as they are presented here, but to read them in this way is to re-emphasise the synergetic effect which the three statements had at the time.

Linking ELT with the wider field of education, and then with still broader areas of committed human endeavour, are common themes which each speaker illuminates from a slightly different perspective.

One such theme is that of awareness. Self-awareness is raised through reflection and questioning. Increased self-awareness and the sharing of questions leads to an enhanced awareness of others, be they students, colleagues or administrators. The world seems a less arbitrary place and one is empowered to seek more fulfilment in it. Myers describes approaches to self-exploration, Somekh writes on interpersonal and institutional aspects of change and Nunan provides data from teachers involved in the process.

The importance of data is another theme. The lived experience of the individual is seen as central. Myers describes approaches to self-organisation which help us analyse and understand this data. Somekh argues that the careful collection of this information, and the building of intersubjective perspectives on shared experience is the very stuff of authentic research in the humanities. Nunan addresses directly the status of such established terms as validity and reliability in the context of what he calls this 'inside out' approach.

It is almost time to let the plenary speakers speak for themselves. But just before they do, there is a brief welcoming address from Professor Nigel Reeves which contextualises a vision of quality in a world which demands quantity. The themes of awareness and the collection of experiential data, as well as the larger topics of teacher development and teacher research, all inform his statement:

> *If we take quality seriously, and as professionals this is not a matter in which we have choice, we have got to get closer to our learners, their needs, their learning styles, their motivation.*

Introductory address: classroom research in the quality versus quantity debate

Professor Nigel Reeves OBE

Aston University

◆

Ladies and Gentlemen,

It is my first, pleasant duty to welcome you all warmly to Aston University and to this important conference, which has been organised jointly by Aston's Language Studies Unit and IATEFL. Some of you have travelled half-way round the world to be here and we have delegates from some 22 countries. While it is obvious that the English weather could not justify this, I am confident that the insights we shall gain in the next three days will amply recompense your effort.

I said this conference was important not as an empty word of flattery, but to highlight its centrality in the current world-wide educational debate. The welfare of advanced and advancing societies depends crucially on education. Increasingly what counts in a competitive trading environment is a lead in the knowledge-intensive industries. Workforces at all levels have to be ever more literate and ever more numerate. Economics are almost certainly the driving force in this, but the concomitant intellectual and personal empowerment of the individual can make for enhanced self-realisation, and forms the essential basis for any informed, democratically active society.

Around the world, the learning of English illustrates this double benefit with great clarity: the economic and technological reasons for attaining proficiency in International English are so evident that they require no elaboration. But the ability to communicate in a second — or third — language brings with it cognitive and cultural benefits as perspectives are gained from which to view one's own language and culture, while winning access to new value systems which are historically related yet diverse and which traverse the world from Australia and New Zealand through Asia and Africa to Britain and the United States.

But as we embrace this vision of the benefits of education and of English teaching and learning, we find the objectives of our governmental paymasters expressed in starker terms: more people, children *and* adults, need better education for longer. The sheer quantity of those needing to and being required to learn English is expanding. The resources available for dealing with this expansion are, however, being reduced in relative terms.

This is not only because of the current world recession and the decline in governments' tax-take. It is because of demographic trends. In the advanced industrial countries, governments face the problem of ageing, long-lived populations that have to be supported by smaller young populations. So there is relatively less state money for the young and for education. In many less advanced societies, better medicine and better living conditions have led to a huge growth in the young population, and hence a similar reduction in available resources per capita.

At the same time governments are fearful that the standards of education will fall — hence the familiar call for quality despite quantity. Quality is not an easy term. Politicians use it in its technical and its everyday sense at the same time, because the consequent ambiguity is advantageous to them. In common parlance, quality means expensive, durable, bearing the hallmarks of craftsmanship. In educational/learning terms it means an education that is sound, individual, presented professionally and, probably by connotation, exclusive. But quality in the management sense which politicians also intend implies fitness for purpose, appropriacy to needs. In mass school, university and continuing education, those needs are increasingly diverse, as diverse as the learner (or in management terminology the 'customer') base. The consequence of all this is a growing emphasis on the requirement for the teacher to modify at the least, and in some cases to devise, the curriculum for the learners. This cannot be done with fitness for purpose without research into learners' needs and learning difficulties. Thus classroom research has to assume centre-stage. If we take quality seriously, and as professionals this is not a matter in which we have choice, we have to get closer to our learners, their needs, their learning styles, their motivation.

Governments want us to be more efficient — that is, for more learning to occur for less spend. *Our* aim is to be more effective. In language teaching and learning we cannot be effective without knowing our learners' needs, shaping our teaching to those needs and monitoring its impact. In this process, the simplistic distinction beloved of government between teaching and research becomes blurred. The profoundly affective and individualistic nature of language learning, together with its enmeshment in cognitive development, means that every effective teacher has to be a researcher with the classroom as the primary location where fieldwork occurs.

To do this research we need techniques. But fortunately we are not researching issues which are idiosyncratic, despite their attachment to human individuals. It is my hope that in the coming days we will share our personal experience of classroom research and, at the same time, learn new techniques and investigative approaches. That, I think, is the purpose of our conference and you will be the judge of its quality as facilitators and learners — or perhaps I should say, as suppliers and customers.

Thank you.

To boldly go …

Mel Myers
Individual and Organisational Development Agency

◆

Introduction

This is an invitation to live dangerously and to contemplate an exploration of inner space … the last frontier … but the one most immediately accessible to us … and the one whose exploration, though initially daunting (and liberally strewn with 'No Entry' and 'Here be Dragons' signs) will be personally revealing, rewarding and enabling to us as individuals, groups and people working within whole organisations.

The session will cover the way you interpret, make sense of, and act in the world — and to enable you to consider new and different possibilities for your own personal professional development within this context.

Two main sets of psychological principles and associated practical skills will be made accessible — in an interactive and participatory way — to give an overview of the concepts and to enable you to try out the ideas by planning and evaluating your own development through the Conference.

Why is an applied psychologist invited to address a conference whose members are concerned with the Teaching of English as a Foreign Language?

There are two main reasons. One is the overlap between my own areas of interest and experience as a psychologist with the title and theme of the conference, Teachers Develop Teachers Research. My interests and experience have covered ways in which psychological principles and skills can be made available to help individuals to learn. In particular, I have been involved in developing action research approaches which enable practitioner research to be driven by, and inform, practitioner needs; which encourage the use of everyday experience and situations as the raw material for such research; and which, above all, promote and inspire the vision of the practitioner as learner — whatever their level of seniority, whatever their experience and whatever their level of skill.

The second reason is to underline, as someone having relevant experience outside the TEFL field, firstly that the difficulties associated with meeting the two requirements (to research one's own practice in order to improve it, and to have some systematic form of continuing education) are by no means unique to this particular professional group and, secondly, to make reference to links and overlaps with the way in which other groups have responded to these two requirements.

My plan for this plenary session is to look at what is implied by continuing education for the individual and for the organisation in which she or he is involved. Following this, to overview one particular scheme and, after discussing some of the limitations of this scheme, to outline two action research approaches (informed by psychological principles and practice) which individuals can adopt to facilitate their own personal and professional development in a way which uses their everyday experiences and work — but which is not dependent on the organisation within which they are working.

Why continuing education?

Most professional groups have a process of training, similar to that depicted in Fig. 1, where a broadly standard, generic initial training is followed by practice in a range of possible situations.

Fig. 1

Once in practice, the individual needs to be involved in continuing education in order to be able to maintain and improve their level of competence and to ensure continuing job satisfaction. Through this, and in a world which may change rapidly and frequently in terms of the demands made on them, they will be able to stay up-to-date with new ideas, practice and information, and with the changing requirements of local and national legislation.

In terms of career progression, the individual may wish to acquire the experience which will lead to more responsibility, promotion or a move to a specific type or area of work (for instance, to do with facilitating the learning of others) and to do all or some of this in a planned, systematic and practicable way.

The organisation itself will need to consider continuing education as one of the ways it maintains and improves the ability to perform its functions, meet statutory or professional requirements, and plan its own development. (What sort of needs will there be in one, three, ten years' time — will it be best to train from within or recruit outside specialists?)

What happens in practice?

Once in the professional workplace, the volume of work to be undertaken, coupled with any lack of experience in time management and organising personal learning, may combine to fix (or embalm) the practitioner at a level of competence which can sometimes be barely beyond that attained by the end of initial training.

Further, in areas which have undergone rapid growth — as is the case with TEFL — practitioners can be under pressure to take on roles within the organisation (to do with management, links with other organisations or organisational development for instance) for which neither their initial training nor their previous work experience within the organisation has equipped them and where, again, there may be no systematic way of acquiring the necessary skills. This may obtain both for relatively new as well as for more experienced practitioners.

Practice varies over the different professional contexts. At one level, initial training may be the only systematic component in the process (in terms of content, timing, duration and predictable skills/knowledge outcomes) with the possibility of an entitlement to attend the occasional course or conference. At another level, as with Chartered Accountants and Lawyers for instance, continuing education is prescribed and is a requirement for those wishing to maintain their membership of the professional group.

At yet another level, approaches have been developed which attempt to provide for a more individualised continuing education programme, whilst recognising the need to reconcile the requirements of the individual with those of the team, department or organisation itself. Such approaches attempt to find ways of identifying and prioritising individual training and development needs and of allocating organisational time and funding in a way which is systematic and equitable.

A SPECIFIC APPROACH TO CONTINUING EDUCATION

The Planning Professional Development (PPD) scheme (Watts et al., 1988) originated in the context of a continuing professional development programme for educational psychologists (EPs) at Birmingham University. It is useful to refer to PPD firstly because it represents an attempt to reconcile — to harmonise — the needs of the individual with organisational needs. Secondly, it is a generic approach which, with appropriate changes in the checklist content, could be used by any professional group. In addition, I was involved in its development and also had the opportunity to observe its implementation in eleven West Midlands Authorities.

Broadly, PPD operates through the use of four components: a checklist, a personal planner, a collation instrument and an evaluation process.

The checklist consists of just over 200 items which cover the broad range of EPs' knowledge, experience and practice. Individual EPs complete the checklist by indicating, for any item, their current level of Awareness, Knowledge, Skill or Ability to Train Others and, at the same time, their desire to improve or consolidate their level for that item.

The completed checklist items are reduced to a list of about six items, prioritised, and a personal plan negotiated with the EP's line manager for one or two of these. All the personal plans can be collated so that an overview of targets is available for the whole team or service. The personal plans as well as the collated data can act as a basis for evaluating progress for the individual, the team or the organisation as a whole.

Some concerns

PPD was generally helpful, both for individuals and for their organisations, in getting a measure of the repertoire of skills, the areas in which there was a skill deficit and an idea of how many people could act as trainers. It was certainly an improvement on the somewhat ad hoc approach to professional development in use at the time.

There were, however, some concerns. Of these a proportion were to do with the way that the PPD process operated. They included: variability from LEA to LEA in entitlement, funding and the different number of people drawing from the same funding, concerns that all the work involved in completing the checklist may not result in any tangible benefits, that completing the checklist honestly might lead to one's identified training needs being perceived as lack of competence, that the price of supported continuing education might be one of loss of professional autonomy.

Other concerns were expressed which were qualitatively different and which are the point of departure for this session. In essence, these concerns were to do with being taught rather than being enabled to learn — with acting routinely rather than with awareness and critical self-review — and were expressed variously as:

> *Where's the psychology in what I did this week/month/term/ year?*

That is, what did I do that reflected the understanding which comes from my training rather than being an automatic response to the situation? And what did I do that was psychological (i.e. informed by psychology) and that was different to what any of my (non-psychologist) colleagues would have done?

> *How can I get personal enrichment at the level of principles and understanding rather than the mere accretion of skills and knowledge?*

In both this and the following item, people seemed to be saying that they wanted new knowledge and new skills to have an impact on them — to affect the way that they thought and perceived rather than just be another tick on the skills checklist.

> *I've been on any number of management courses, but still don't have any coherent set of principles and associated skills which I can transfer to any management situation.*

Some people felt that the framework within which they worked deadened the spirit which had led them to do that sort of work in the first place, leading to concerns for alienation or burn-out. At the same time, whilst recognising a need to confront rather than succumb to organisational pressures, people felt a lack of skill and understanding of interpersonal communications which would enable them to challenge in a systematic and rational way. They wanted a way of talking things through, with the people who they managed or with their line managers, which would not appear to be threatening and which would not put their jobs or promotion prospects in jeopardy, but which would lead to an improved situation.

SO, WHERE NEXT?

How can one have an approach to one's continuing education which complements and adds to the options which are typically available?

What seems to be needed is an approach which will enable individual practitioners to maintain their enthusiasm and motivation, to be able to negotiate positively with others and to be able to learn in such a way that what is learnt makes personal sense and leads to improved competence.

The two approaches, Self-organised Learning (S-OL), and Increasing Professional Effectiveness (IPE), which are described below, enable practitioners to become more active and independent learners — more able to define their own learning agendas and more able to exploit to this end both the formal opportunities for continuing education as well as the transactions of everyday working life. Increasing Professional Effectiveness, in particular, provides a very helpful approach to interpersonal communications and management issues.

Psychological background

Both approaches are based on psychological principles and have a good track record of application.The two approaches were developed independently, but have some interesting aspects in common. They both treat the individual as central, they both suggest that in order to be more effective learners we need to be aware of our learning processes and they both have techniques for preventing us from behaving in an automatic fashion.

The most important assumptions behind both approaches, from a practical point of view, are that we actively process and make personal sense of what's going on around us, that we decide what to do on the basis of this processing and that the processing and decision-making tend to be carried out without our conscious awareness.

Fig. 2

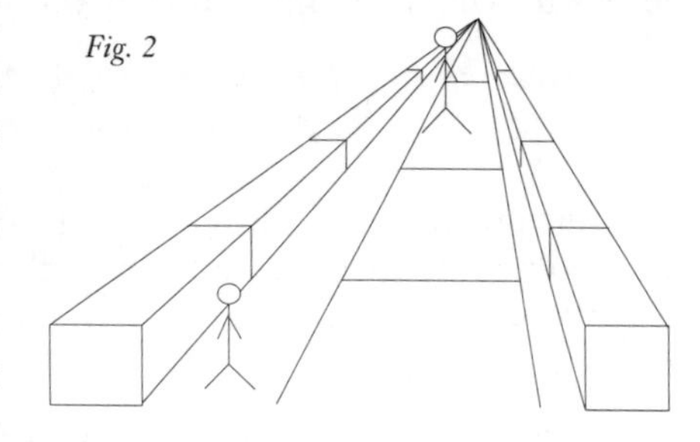

To get an idea of this unconscious, active processing at work, have a look at the drawing in Fig. 2. The two stick people are the same size, but one of them looks bigger. For many people the illusion is quite compelling — and persists even after they've confirmed for themselves that the two stick people or lines are, indeed, the same size.

If there were no processing going on, then we would see the stick people as the same size — indeed, in their image at the back of our eye (before it's processed by the brain) or on a camera film they are the same size. The fact that we 'see' them as different is strong evidence that some (internal) processing has taken place.

To get an idea of the richness and complexity of this processing, let us consider why the illusion (of a difference in size) occurs. An explanation given by Gregory (1966:131-63) is that we use a set of rules to enable us to interpret visual information. One such rule is that objects in the distance appear to be smaller than they really are. When we apply this rule, we (unconsciously) compensate for the size of distant objects by enlarging them in proportion to their apparent distance.

In the case of Fig. 2, the two stick people are actually the same distance from us but the receding railway lines suggest that one of them is further away than the other. We therefore compensate by seeing the 'distant' figure as larger and, as it's actually the same size as the 'nearer' stick person, we 'see' it as larger than the foreground stick person (because it would have to be larger than the foreground stick person to be so far away and still look so large!).

The reason for referring to visual illusions is because they provide a vivid illustration of active processing at work in our normal, everyday functioning (making sense of the world we see), and also indicate how sophisticated and complex this processing is, how rapidly it occurs and how inaccessible this processing is to us. We know that it must have happened, but we are not aware of it in action.

The suggestion behind S-OL and IPE is that much of our behaviour, especially with regard to our own learning and our interactions with others, is similarly governed by rules which are applied automatically and which are not, normally, accessible to us.

If we are not aware of what it is that's driving our behaviour, then it is difficult to change what we do (or the way that we do it) at anything other than the surface or cosmetic level. Thus, it is difficult to become a better teacher, researcher or learner. A personal history of unsuccessful attempts to change at this, cosmetic, level can lead us to feel despondent, and to resign ourselves to accepting that there is no way of improving the situation. One of the main intentions of S-OL and IPE is to enable us to become more aware and, hence, more in control of the processing which lies behind our behaviour.

Self-organised Learning (S-OL)

Self-organised Learning has been developed by Laurie Thomas and Sheila Harri-Augstein at the Centre for the Study of Human Learning at Brunel University (Harri-Augstein & Thomas, 1991). S-OL is a very powerful approach which has found major and successful applications in industry, commerce, government departments (in this and other countries) as well as in education. S-OL enables practitioners to use the work that they do — whether as teacher, student or manager — as a launch pad for improving that work.

The main mechanism used is that of enabling workers/practitioners to become researchers (action researchers) into their own learning processes related to the work that they do, in such a way that all activities can become transformed from daily routines into invitations to learn.

S-OL is itself based on the ideas of George Kelly who proposed a model of psychology (Kelly, 1955) in which each person made sense of their world by actively viewing or constructing it along a number of dimensions. The dimensions or constructs were seen as bipolar and as being peculiar to each individual. Thus, one might have a construct such as:

encouraging ——————————— *puts people down*

or

organised ——————————— *unclear*

Kelly further suggested that the constructs are organised hierarchically into a construct system, so that not only are the constructs themselves personal, but the actual way they are related gave rise to a uniquely individual way of understanding and predicting events.

To gain an idea of the personal nature of constructs, imagine a construct such as the one below:

and decide what word or phrase you would put at the other end. Try it out on your colleagues. You are likely to get many different responses such as unimaginative, conforming, cold, destructive, boring or organised. Kelly stressed that these responses are not right or wrong, they are not dictionary-defined opposites — they are an indication of how people view or make personal sense of their world.

The significance of personally constructed meaning becomes even clearer when one considers the way in which a hierarchical system can operate — as opposed to the individual constructs which make it up. In a system consisting of the same constructs, but arranged in different hierarchies, different outcomes would be predicted.

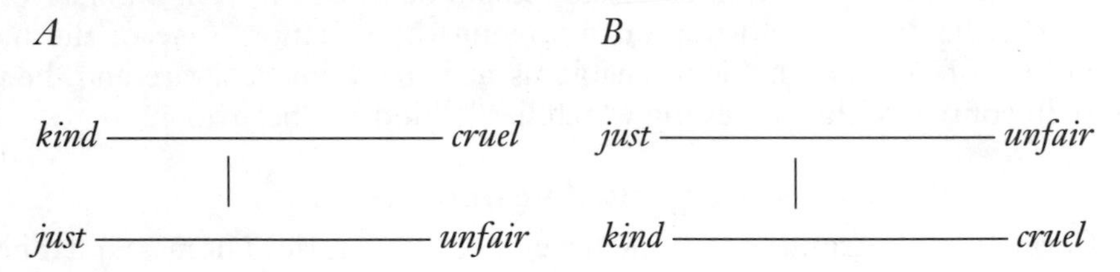

Thus, in system A, where the super-ordinate construct is kind-cruel, one might be unfair in order to be kind, whilst the super-ordinate construct in B (*just-unfair*) might enable one to be cruel in order to be just. An implication of personal construct psychology is that the same word, phrase or idea can have significantly different meanings for different people because they will all process the word or phrase via their (different) construct systems.

Kelly suggested that people use their construct systems in much the same way that scientists use hypotheses to try to describe, explain and predict the events that they are interested in. Good scientists would be constantly testing and trying to disconfirm their hypotheses or theories as the only way of improving their understanding.

However, not all of the people are all good scientists all of the time — it can be so much easier to go with the ideas and beliefs that we're comfortable with and to be guided by these and even to protect them (and hence ourselves) from rude disconfirmation ... and so 'count ourselves king of infinite space'. S-OL refers to hypotheses which are not challenged, and which may constrain our development, as 'myths of learning'. Examples of myths may include such thoughts or beliefs as:

- I can only learn with the radio on.
- As a manager I have to treat people firmly.

- Because the brain has a limited capacity new knowledge can only be stored at the expense of losing old knowledge.
- There is only one way to do this job.
- I am no good at languages.

To the extent that such myths are unchallenged and influence our behaviour, that behaviour can be described as robotic. Fig. 3 represents a robotic response to a challenge (for instance, wanting to be able to speak another language). The learner's behaviour is guided by their myths about learning and, in true self-fulfilling prophecy mode, the feedback from the outside world reinforces the myths — perhaps resulting in the learner only going to places where their own language is spoken or restricting foreign language speaking situations to those where a phrase-book can be safely used.

Notice that the learner's behaviour is not guided by their real purposes, nor does it call upon learning methods which have been successfully deployed in other situations, nor on a realistic set of expected outcomes. (This interactive trio of 'purposes', 'methods' and 'expected outcomes' is represented by the initials PMO.)

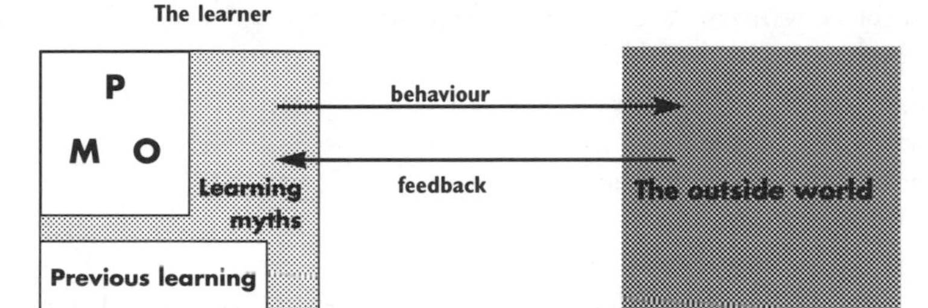

Fig. 3

Notice, too, that the learner has learnt (!) to discount previous learning and learning strategies, that the myths have taken over in a particularly disabling way. One of the main aims of S-OL is to enable people to become less automatic — to de-robotise — to challenge their myths — and to become increasingly aware of, and in control of, the way their construct system functions.

There are a number of ways in which one can access and describe construct systems (Bannister and Fransella, 1986), but in S-OL the main approach is through learning conversations held between the learner and a learning coach. In the initial learning conversation the learner is encouraged to describe something they wish to do in terms of their purpose (what they wish to do and why they wish to do it), their methods (how, and over what sort of time scale they will do it) and the outcomes they expect to result from their methods (the tangible results which they hope for).

The job of the learning coach is to help the learner to de-robotise by exploring their own learning processes. In subsequent conversations the learner and the coach review the progress made in terms of each of the components of the learning conversation — exploring whether the expected outcomes were achieved, the methods were appropriate, whether the purposes have changed or if additional or alternative purposes have come to light for which relevant methods and expected outcomes need to designed. Thus, in Fig. 4 the learner is more aware of their own learning purposes, and is beginning to use the results

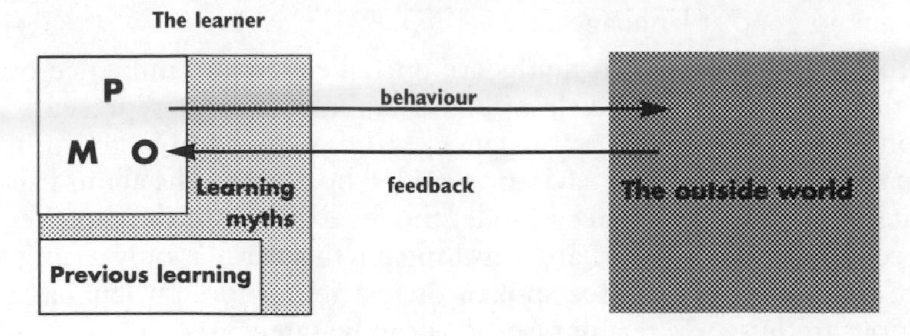

Fig. 4

in the real world as a way of giving themselves information as to what they need to do next (rather than as confirming that they can't do something).

The coach does not, necessarily, have to be a domain expert but facilitates learning by posing a certain type of question. The questions tend to be open-ended and to encourage the learner to identify any problems, difficulties or concerns they have with their learning:

- What do you really want to be able to do?
- What sort of difficulties are you encountering ?
- What strategies/methods are you using — are you happy that they are the most appropriate ones?
- How will you check out your progress?

and in particular to identify strategies from their own previous learning which could transfer to the present situation:

- Have you come across a problem like this before?
- Can you break this problem down into smaller pieces, or into stages?
- Let's talk about something else that you've already learnt to do, identify the strategies you used there and then see if you can use them in this situation.

During such a learning conversation, the learner might identify some previous learning — for instance learning to drive a car. They might recognise that, although they were taught some of the component skills (such as starting, gear changing, steering and reversing), they had to learn for themselves how to co-ordinate these skills and that they had to identify small goals along the road to mastery which they could practise and which were the basis for feedback. It may also have been the case that the small steps which were important to them were not always only the ones which the instructor saw as being important.

Whilst learning to drive may not, itself, have direct relevance for learning another language, useful learning strategies identified in one situation can be generalised and used to inform other learning. Thus the learner might try to develop some sort of map of the language they wish to learn, and an idea of the path they might take together with a way of practising and obtaining feedback.

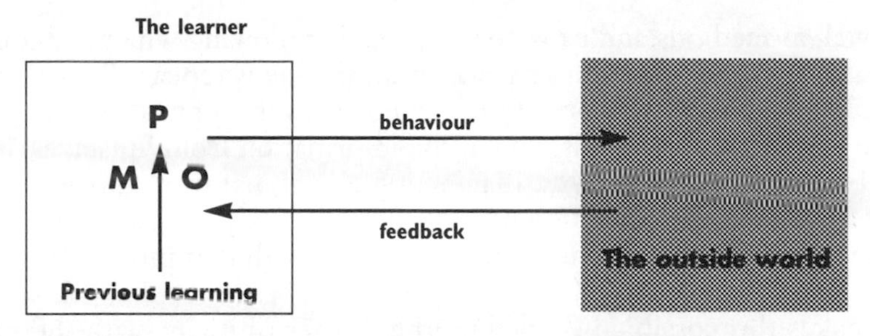

Fig. 5

Two key goals are achieved by this process: feedback is used to inform the learner's purpose, method and expected outcomes rather than reinforce any learning myths, and the learner is more able (as the myths are exorcised) to acknowledge and benefit from their previous learning and life experiences (as in Fig. 5).

At this stage the learner might usefully consult, in addition to their learning coach, a domain expert such as a language teacher or someone who already speaks that language. Because the learner has been able to specify personal learning needs, the domain expert will not function as a (didactic) teacher but, rather, as a learning resource because they will be responding to the learner's needs and any 'teaching' will be in the learner's terms. (Ultimately, the learner becomes de-robotised enough to act as their own learning coach.)

The approach leads to what is, essentially, an action research project focused on one's own learning behaviour and processes with the outcomes of any one stage informing the direction and focus of the next stage in an on-going and cyclical process. The outcomes in the real world can be recorded and used as feedback to be related to one's subjective experience and to further inform and challenge one's construct system. Indeed, in S-OL, the learner is encouraged to devise learning tools which can help them obtain objective measures of their performance against which they can compare their subjective perceptions of what was happening and, if there is any gap between the subjective and objective record, proceed so as to reduce the gap.

Thus our language learner might audio tape or video their use of the new language as a basis for further learning conversations in terms of whether they had achieved their expected outcomes, whether their methods were working, were appropriate or needed modifying and, most importantly, whether their original intentions or purposes, too, were realised, whether they were the same or whether they needed modifying or adding to. (Some helpful examples of learning tools and their use can be found in (Harri-Augstein, Smith & Thomas, 1982.)

This last step is important because the S-OL action research model outlined here has five phases: planning the action derived from the learning conversation, carrying out the proposed actions, logging the outcomes in terms of some form of objective record, identifying any gap or mismatch between the planned action and the actual outcomes and then, the crucial phase, feeding any mismatch information back to where it matters so that one can rethink one's purposes, as well as methods and expected outcomes (following which, of course, a further learning conversation takes place and the cycle is repeated).

The old adage that we learn from our mistakes is right — but only if we learn from our mistakes! That is, only if the information from 'mistakes' is used to engender radical change rather than acting as a signal to do the same thing again but with (superficial) differences — more quickly, more loudly, with a smile, with musical accompaniment, with firmness, with that indescribable je ne sais quoi ...

S-OL makes this possible by enabling the learner (initially, with the help of the learning coach) to use feedback to identify, be relaxed with and to welcome — even embrace — their problems as the nodes or springboards for new learning rather than using the feedback to confirm any learning myths — or allowing such myths to act so as to deny disconfirmatory feedback or even distort it.

Increasing Professional Effectiveness (IPE)

In the context of professional practice, an important aspect of one's own processes which one might wish to research is to do with interpersonal behaviour — the way one acts and interacts with others.

Increasing Professional Effectiveness (Argyris and Schon, 1974) has as its major focus the nature of the interactions which individuals experience within their organisations — with colleagues and clients, with their line managers and with those whom they manage. In particular, IPE focuses on those interactions — conversations, discussions, formal meetings and conferences — which are in some way unsatisfactory and which you wish could have had a different outcome or which you anticipate without pleasure.

Throughout the working day and week, we experience a myriad of such interactions many of whose outcomes are unsatisfactory in the sense that they can leave us feeling frustrated, angry, baffled, guilty, hurt or embarrassed. The interactions themselves and their content are not necessarily of great moment and might involve scenarios such as the following — together with possible personal outcomes described in brackets immediately after each scenario:

> *X's secretary would neither let me speak to X, nor give me any indication of X's whereabouts or availability — and took some persuading to leave a message for X to contact me ... and I didn't want to do that anyway, because it might look as if I was trying to put X under pressure to do something when, in fact, I felt that it was my responsibility to make the running.*

(the phone call couldn't have lasted more than two or three minutes but I felt angry and frustrated at the end of the interaction and embarrassed with the negative and incorrect impression that X might receive of me);

> *Y called yet another of those team meetings that went on for ever, and then asked me how I thought it had gone — I said that I thought some interesting points had come out of the meeting and just wondered if there was some way of us being able to contribute more usefully and, perhaps, of finishing a little bit earlier. Y thanked me and reassured me that all of our contributions were useful.*

(I wanted to tell Y that these meetings are a debilitating waste of time — you have to go because it's required — you daren't leave early in case an item comes up which puts your bit of the empire at risk if you're not there to defend it — there's no real communication — and you suspect your job (or at least your prospect of promotion) is at risk if you make negative comments about them — they leave me feeling anxious, frustrated and a bit depressed and I would like to see them happening in a different, more structured and more useful format … but I just don't know how to say this without appearing critical to Y);

> *Z told me that W had let one of the students borrow my personal copy of the new coursebook and, on seeing my response, recounted similar episodes involving W.*

(the coursebook is crucial to my planning for next term — I don't know who's got it — and W had absolutely no right to lend my book without my agreement. This has happened before, and I just don't know how to stop it without unpleasantness. On top of that, Z has used the opportunity to try and involve me in talk about W in W's absence. I feel angry about W's behaviour, baffled about what to do and uneasy about my (passive) collusion in gossip about W).

When people discuss this sort of interaction, some general features tend to emerge. Typically, the interactions (or, rather, the problematic sections within an interaction) are quite brief — a few seconds, usually no more than a minute. The content of the interaction seems to be trivial — so much so that the person recounting can feel embarrassed at giving time and attention to what others might see as trifling.

Our finding is that despite the speed and apparent insignificance of the interactions, their cumulative effect can be to leave people with a growing burden of anger and frustration and a feeling of being powerless to affect their outcomes.

Argyris suggests that the way we behave towards others is governed by what he calls our theory of action. This is a set of rules, of whose existence and power (as with our construct system) we are usually unaware, which act to direct our own actions and lead us to predict the actions and responses of others. The rules lead to a highly polished, automatic behaviour and, because of this and because we're not usually aware of our rules, they are difficult to access and hence difficult to modify and we are left with the option, again, of trying out superficial modifications at the cosmetic level.

If you ask people to describe how and why they interact with others, they tend to respond in terms of their espoused theory of action. This describes the way they fondly believe they are, but their actions in real life usually differ from those that would be predicted from their espoused theory. This is not, necessarily, because they are devious but because they really believe that they act as they really believe they act!

The bad news about our interactions which go wrong is that we are at least partly responsible. The good news is that if we are responsible, then by changing what drives our behaviour we will be in a position to affect the outcomes in a positive way. As a first step towards effective behaviour change we can try to identify which set of rules we are operating under. Whilst it's difficult to look at the rules directly, we can look for their effect in our interactions — in particular, we can look at what we say, the way that we say it, why we say it and what we were thinking during the interaction.

Argyris' research suggests that most people have a theory of action which he has dubbed Model One. This is a set of rules whose primary purpose is to keep you in control, to frame all interactions as win-lose situations and to make sure that you win (or at least that you don't lose).

Associated with Model One is a set of strategies that people tend to use to enable them to stay in control or to put/keep the other person at a disadvantage. These include:

Asking a question without explaining why you're asking or giving the background to the question. For instance:

> If someone asks you whether you're busy that evening, you're at a disadvantage because you don't know why they're asking, and neither do you know what will happen if you say that you are free. Are they going to invite you to the theatre? Or are they going to ask you to babysit whilst they go to the theatre?

(A clear example of this genre can be seen in, 'Can I ask you a personal question?' You don't know what they're going to ask you and the word 'personal' sounds worrying, and usually — by the time you've thought through your response — they've already asked the question.)

Similarly, one can *suggest a course of action without enquiring whether the other person has the time, wants to do it or understands your suggestion*. Examples might include:

> 'I've arranged for you both to meet the new students in half an hour', or, 'Just give me a quick run down on the main arguments for and against teaching in the target language as opposed to mother-tongue teaching', or, 'Have a look at my holiday snaps'.

(This can leave the other person feeling aggrieved because they might feel they lack a polite or reasonable way out and have very little option but to go along with the suggested action.)

Acting on the basis of assumptions without first checking them out is a further example of Model One strategy at work. In almost any situation we make assumptions — come to conclusions — about the other person, and we are so used to this happening that we are not, perhaps, fully aware of the extent to which our actions are guided by them.

> Take an everyday example; imagine that you are five minutes into a meeting that you had arranged with someone and that that person keeps looking at their watch. What do you find yourself thinking — what assumptions do you make — what conclusions do you come to?
>
> Perhaps you assume that the person is under some sort of time pressure? That they would like to finish the appointment as soon as possible? That

looking at their watch is their way of signalling this to you? That they are aware that they keep looking at their watch?

What do you do, as a result of your assumptions? Perhaps you think you need to let them know that you've seen the signals — but feel that it would be indelicate or embarrassing to mention them directly — and you decide to say something like, 'I can see that you're busy, would you like to finish the appointment a bit early?'

All of this happens very quickly, and is guided by our assumptions. But the aspect of this Model One strategy which makes it powerful derives from the private confirmation (rather than public or up-front testing) of our assumptions. Notice what may happen when the other person replies.

If they indicate that they would be happy to arrange another meeting, this is immediate confirmation of our assumptions (they *were* under pressure, they *did* want to finish the appointment). On the other hand, if they say that they are happy to complete the meeting as arranged this, too, can act to confirm our assumptions (they *were* under pressure, they *did* want to finish the appointment, and my question has let them know that I saw the signals *and* my sarcastic tone has shamed them into a more proper behaviour). Heads they lose, tails I win — and my assumptions are left intact.

Privately testing assumptions in this way has direct parallels with maintaining learning myths and leads to the same, automatic, robotic behaviour. The use of Model One strategies leads to the sort of outcomes described above (in brackets after each scenario) which are difficult to avoid or to change precisely because they are maintained by the Model One rules. A way out of the 'doomed interactions' syndrome is offered by Model Two in which you are encouraged to pursue two main processes: double-loop learning and seeing yourself and the other person as part of a single interactive system.

Double-loop learning is similar to de-robotising in the sense that one gives oneself feedback *and* ensures that the feedback influences what is driving one's behaviour rather than it acting at a cosmetic level. The ongoing monitoring and feedback to yourself will be about the type of strategies you are using during the interaction:

- giving sufficient background;
- checking that the other person understands/wants to talk/has the time to talk;
- identifying your assumptions;
- checking them with the other person so that they can be disconfirmed.

So, under Model Two, the comment to the person who keeps looking at their watch might take the form,

1	'I can't help noticing that you keep looking at your watch,	(some background — lets the other person know why you're saying what you are saying)

2	and I wonder if this means that you're under some time pressure.	(an assumption identified and made explicit for the other person to comment on and confirm or disconfirm, whilst …
3	If you are, we can rearrange this meeting for a time that's more convenient for you — if that would be helpful.'	inviting the other person into a joint problem-solving process with uncertain outcomes)

Rounds 1 and 2 make double-loop learning possible for three reasons. Firstly, because an assumption has been made clear to the other person (as well as to the speaker), secondly because the other person can comment directly on the speaker's assumption and, thirdly, the other person's comment about the assumption will (because it is the assumption which is behind the speaker's behaviour) enable the speaker to modify their behaviour at source — they will be able to modify that which is driving their behaviour.

This leads on to the second process — that of enabling both participants to see themselves as part of a single, interactive system. The speaker — by being up-front about their assumptions, by checking out, by responding to what is said — invites the other person to share in discussing a problem or a perception, rather than encourage win/lose attitudes. The speaker will, in this way, be able to affect the *process* of the interaction (although the *outcomes* will be unpredictable) and, rather than feel powerless in the situation, be able to optimise the likelihood of positive outcomes for both participants.

The example given, of someone looking at their watch, is of course only used for illustrative purposes. The action research process outlined can be used in any interaction — just recall your own response when your students look bored or puzzled. Do you respond? Or do you first hear your own assumption (that they are bored or puzzled) and then check it out with the students? In fact, this seems to be a useful guideline; when you feel an assumption coming on, first identify it and then check it out. Just don't let yourself be driven by it!

To sum up this outline of IPE, the essential difference between the two Models is to do with intention and associated process. In Model One, the intention is to have control and to win (and for the other person to lose). The interaction is characterised by having outcomes which are reasonably certain and by the speaker having a content purpose only ('I'm going to let the other person know that I've seen them looking at their watch, that I know that it is a signal, that I know what the signal means, and that I'm angry that it's happened.'). In particular, the speaker is driven by assumptions which are not made public and which can not, therefore, be commented on or modified.

In Model Two, the intention is to have dialogue. The speaker is happy to share and request information and feedback relevant to the interaction and to trade certainty of outcome for the benefits of a shared, and jointly steered, conversational process.The isomorphism with action research comes about primarily because, in a real-life situation characterised by uncertainty, the direction and focus of the research (conversation) is affected by the response to enquiry (questions, checking-out, requests for dis/confirmation rather than by the certainties of the researcher).

Both S-OL and IPE have been outlined as a way of enabling any practitioner to reflect on — to research — their own behaviour in their own situation and, through boldly exploring inner space, to consider new and different possibilities for their own personal, professional development.

Quality in educational research — the contribution of classroom teachers

Bridget Somekh
University of East Anglia

◆

Introduction

In the Oscar-winning animated film, Creature Comforts, by Aardman (1989), the voices of human beings, captured in interview, speak from the mouths of animal puppets. The subject is life in the zoo, the comfort and well-being of the animals, and the animals' likes, dislikes, frustrations and needs. The impassive faces and postures of the puppets come suddenly to life through a series of movements, expressions and gestures which are immediately recognisable as human. As we watch the film we are looking at ourselves speaking English in a variety of regional and national accents. It is funny, it is delightful, it is fascinating. The everyday realism of the voices and gestures of the puppets emphasise the common humanity of the figures, while the latex forms strip away clothes and appearances which are important elements in the triggers of snobbery and xenophobia. The figures are talking not only about a zoo but about life itself; they have become ourselves, expressing our own experience as we live now, today, in Britain, whatever our birth-place or origin.

The Aardman film is a metaphor for my theme. To understand important things about our everyday world we have to shift perspectives. Experience can be a negative force trapping us into pre-determined responses. For example, it may take the un-English rhythms of a Brazilian accent to place sufficient emphasis on key necessities of life such as 'meat', and 'space', but only when the voice is lifted out of its everyday context by a puppet form are we able to hear it with sufficient clarity to shift our views. In this paper I want to suggest the need for a new perspective on research and the processes of educational change. Although I cannot reproduce the magic of the Aardman film, it may be that my voice as an outsider in the world of TEFL will bring some shifts of emphases to the subject and enable you to challenge the accepted wisdom of your experience. My subject is quality in educational research and, in particular, the contribution of classroom teachers.

=

The action research tradition in British education since around 1970

Action research, as an approach to integrating theory generation with practice, has a long tradition. John Elliott traces it back to Aristotle.

> *Long ago Aristotle outlined in his Ethics a form of practical philosophy or moral science which involved systematic reflection by social practitioners on the best means for realizing practical values in action. Aristotle called this form of reflection 'practical deliberation'.*
>
> (Elliott, 1988)

In Britain, during the last twenty years, action research has had a strong influence on pre-service and in-service teacher education and some influence on established educational research. Since the focus of this paper is on quality in research I want to concentrate in particular on the latter. During the life of the Schools' Council, as a result of the work of Lawrence Stenhouse, teacher action research became an important component of curriculum development. Through his work on the Humanities Curriculum Project, Stenhouse came to the conclusion that traditional forms of curriculum research and development were not working. He realised that, to be effective, curriculum reform had to overcome the problem of the gap which regularly opened up between curriculum specifications and classroom practice. Stenhouse's theory of the 'process curriculum' saw curriculum not as a set of knowledge objectives, but as the exercise of students' cognitive processes. These cognitive processes resulted from students' and teachers' interactions with a selection of ideas and materials. Thus, the curriculum needed to be specified in terms of classroom tasks and interactions with ideas and materials; and these specifications needed to be developed by means of co-research with teachers, and tested and continually refined by teachers in the classroom, both during the development stage and in the years to come (Stenhouse, 1975).

During the last ten years of Stenhouse's life, and for a while after his death in 1982, teachers in Britain played an increasingly important role in curriculum research and development. Recent British government initiatives in curriculum and assessment have reverted to a much simpler model of curriculum and pedagogy — in which knowledge is specified as content organised in subjects, to be 'delivered' to learners by teachers using a set of teaching 'skills'. This radical change will, ironically, enable us to test out Stenhouse's belief that such an approach is doomed to failure, although the momentum of teachers' increasing ownership of curriculum development during two decades may prove too strong an influence within the education system to be completely reversed.

The impact of action research on curriculum development and research more generally, during the past twenty years, has been sustained by a network of informal and formal contacts between teacher-researchers in schools, support personnel in local education authorities, and teacher-researchers in higher education. The Classroom Action Research Network[1] has played an important part in promoting and maintaining these contacts both in Britain and internationally. CARN was founded by John Elliott in 1976 with funding from the Ford Foundation to follow up the work of the Ford Teaching Project. Since that time it has grown from a small group of teachers in East Anglia to a large national and international network. CARN stands for a united education profession, drawing its members from all types of schools, colleges, education authorities and higher education institutions, including those engaged in TEFL — and, more recently, from institutions engaged in educating other professionals such as nurses, police officers and social workers. Through its conferences and publications CARN has given teacher-researchers a forum for publication for the past two decades, and from 1993 this will be strengthened by the launch, in association with CARN, of the international journal, *Educational Action Research*. The focus of EAR is broad, conceiving of action research as a methodology appropriate to a broad range of research questions in a wide variety of social situations. Its policy is developing along the following lines:

> Educational Action Research *will publish accounts of a range of action research and related studies, in education and across the professions, with the aim of making their outcomes widely available and exemplifying the variety of possible styles of reporting ... Two kinds of paper are particularly welcome: (1) accounts of action research and development studies; and (2) contributions to the debate on the theory and practice of action research and associated methodologies. Readability and honest engagement with problematic issues will be among the criteria against which contributions will be judged. The journal can be construed as carrying out — through its contributors and reviewers — action research on the characteristics of effective reporting and the Editors will, therefore, welcome exploratory forms of presentation.*
>
> (EAR, 1993)

Notes on action research methodology ... about its importance

Action research is a research methodology, not simply a means of supporting professional development. The value of action research in enabling teachers and other professionals to become reflective practitioners in Schön's terms (1983), or 'self-monitoring' in the terms of the Ford T project (Elliott, 1976), has tended to distract serious attention from its importance as a research methodology. I see two reasons why it is important to remedy this misunderstanding: the first strategic and political, the second epistemological.

First, if action research is not recognised as a research methodology, the knowledge generated from action research is neither taken seriously nor disseminated widely and effectively. If it is seen merely as an outcome of a professional development process, this knowledge becomes devalued into something which concerns only the individual who carried out the action research — local, private and unimportant. In this way, the operation of power in the social system works to neutralise the voice and influence of practitioners and promote the hegemony of traditional academic researchers.

Second, it would appear that traditional forms of research place limitations on the kinds of knowledge which can be generated. They deal well only with stable situations where it is possible to deal in relative certainties. While this is clearly a serious limitation on any research into social situations (which are inherently unstable), it renders research into innovations at best pointless and at worst dangerous. If we take the case of information technology, during its initial introduction to schools, it was simply impossible to find examples of good practice which were worth the time and effort to research. Many traditional studies were carried out in classrooms where teachers had little or no knowledge of how to integrate information technology as an effective learning tool, and attempts to produce generalisable knowledge from this research can only be seen as unwarranted. Traditional research into innovation can only tell you how the innovation is failing; it cannot find examples of practice which are worth researching because they do not yet exist. As a result, in addition to being time-wasting, the outcomes of such research are unsound and may have a retrograde effect on development. Action research, which incorporates an intention to integrate change and development within the research process, is the only viable methodology for carrying out meaningful research into innovations.

... about its nature

There is not the space here to discuss the nature of action research methodology in any depth. My views should be read in relation to detailed accounts, such as Elliott (1991), Carr and Kemmis (1983), Winter (1989) and Altrichter et al. (1993), from most of which they differ to some extent (even when I am a joint author!). Inherently, I believe action research to be a flexible methodology, not merely in terms of being eclectic in research methods, but more fundamentally in needing to adapt to the social and political situation in which it is employed. In broad terms it is a methodology which includes the following features:

- the research is focused on a social situation;
- in the situation participants collaborate with each other and with outsiders to decide upon a research focus and collect and analyse data;
- the process of data collection and analysis leads to the construction of theories and knowledge;
- the theories and knowledge are tested by feeding them back into changes in practice;
- to evaluate these changes, further data is collected and analysed, leading to refinement of the theories and knowledge, which are in their turn tested in practice, and so on and so forth ...;
- at some point, through publication, these theories and knowledge are opened up to wider scrutiny and made available for others to use as applicable to their own situation. This interrupts the cyclical process of research and action, but is useful in bringing the research to a point of resolution, if only temporarily.

The chameleon-like quality of action research means that it varies considerably according to the social and political context in which action researchers find themselves and their personal and professional biographies. Because of its integral relationship with practice, action research loses its force if it does not adapt in this way: it becomes powerless to effect action. It also loses its integrity if it fails to meet the needs of participants embedded in a particular culture: arguments about this or that approach not being 'real action research' fail to recognise that the attempt to establish detailed specifications of 'what counts as action research' is a form of cultural imperialism.

Action research is inclusive rather than exclusive, participatory, valuing and empowering of individuals within systems. These core values remain firm amid a methodology which adapts in their pursuit.

... about what distinguishes it from self-organised learning

It is interesting to reflect on what differentiates action research from the self-organised learning and learning contracts which Mel Myers describes in this volume. The differences stem mainly from action research being a form of research in addition to being a means of supporting change, but it is useful to be specific, particularly as this may serve to fill out the more theoretical discussion of action research methodology in the section above. So, here are four practical points which are characteristic of much action research:

- There is a deliberate stage of data collection. This enables participants to reflect on the situation after the event, in a concentrated way, with some kind of record or 'memory jog' which prevents them from being locked into one set of perceptions and one set of memories.
- Use is made of the process of triangulation which places one piece of data against another, and then a third, so that differences in perceptions are revealed and made available for reflection.
- There is collaboration with a partner — sometimes called a facilitator or critical friend — who is a co-researcher, although likely to be concerned more with his or her own role and intentions in the situation. This is, as much as possible, an equal relationship in which each adds to the perspective of the other. Among other things, it provides support if and when the action research process reveals mismatches between intentions and outcomes and consequent loss of self-esteem for either partner.
- There is honest debate and problem-sharing, in a situation of trust, promoted by a written ethical code setting out the conditions under which data may be released for publication and how it may be used. This ensures that any inequality in status between the research partners is not used consciously or unconsciously to manipulate the weaker partner.

QUALITY IN EDUCATIONAL RESEARCH

Quality in educational research resides in its ability to explore, resonate with, explicate and improve practice. Insofar as it has the ability to do this well, action research is high quality educational research. It may be hard to justify, at all, forms of educational research which have no impact on practice, although it can be argued that some research will have a long-term rather than a short-term impact.

I began by saying that action research has had a strong influence on work in teacher professional development and teacher training, but only some influence on educational research. This separation between professional development and research is rooted in the traditional separation between theory and practice. On the whole, in Britain, the more abstract and theoretical your work, the higher your status in the academic hierarchy; and the more useful and applicable to practice, the lower your status in the academic hierarchy. For example, physicists who are commonly engaged in analysis and abstraction are perceived to have a higher status than engineers and materials scientists who are commonly engaged in development and production. In modern language teaching in universities in recent years, there has been a move towards much greater emphasis on teaching students to speak the language and less upon the study of literature, and it is no surprise to find that this change has been strongly resisted by some of those who wish to maintain modern languages as a high-status academic subject.

There are grave dangers in separating educational theory from practice. O'Hanlon (1992) gives an example of how teachers on an in-service BEd course used theories of language development to develop a set of expectations of the role played by adults in children's language learning. They then set up 5-10 minute discussions with children, tape-recorded them, and analysed the talk to see to what extent the practice demonstrated the theories. They found that there was an almost total mismatch between what the theories predicted and their own practice recorded in the data.

What appears to have happened is that these teachers were using a special kind of language — the language of school — in which factors other than reciprocal communication of ideas were predominant. They were using language to gain control (preventing the child from finishing/asking unexpected questions); they were using language to focus attention on what *they* thought was important rather than what the child thought was important. The research from which the theories were originally developed may have used non-teachers who did not have these established patterns of language use when talking to children. It may never have occurred to the researchers that the language of teachers is strongly influenced by the classroom context and that this enculturation may continue even when teachers and children meet in informal settings. Disembodied from a real context, these theories of language development were of little value to the teachers and possibly even damaging, in that they may have lulled them into complacency. However, as O'Hanlon describes, they were useful as the focus for the teachers' action research into their role in supporting children's language development.

When research is undertaken separately from practice, there are always problems to be overcome in transferring the knowledge into practice as a separate second step. In materials science research, for example, samples produced on a small scale, in a particular piece of equipment, have to be mass-produced at the production stage. The need to produce larger quantities, at an economic cost, will mean developing specialist equipment and adapting the manufacturing process (N.B. no account of work of this kind is available because of the need to maintain commercial secrecy). When the research is concerned with people and their behaviour, rather than materials produced in a vacuum chamber, the problem is on a much larger scale.

In the case of traditional educational research, there are often serious difficulties in translating the knowledge generated by research into practice, at a later stage. Sometimes this is the result of the kinds of question which were asked in the first place — some questions may not be seen by teachers to be of practical importance, so they will see no point in applying the research findings to practice (this, for example, might explain Bennett and Desforges' (1984) account of how teachers failed to put into practice the knowledge generated by professional researchers, despite being given specialist training). Another factor is that the knowledge from traditional research is presented in a reified form which does not invite teachers to engage with it intellectually, but is simply presented as a 'given'. One could argue that the more carefully the knowledge generated from traditional research is validated and given the status of generalisations, the more passively it constructs the teacher-as-learner who is supposed to apply it in practice. As Desforges points out elsewhere (1989), learning needs to be stimulated by *'challenging pupils' schemas, setting problems and investigations, posing questions and engaging in critical, socratic conversation'*. There is no reason to suppose that teachers' learning needs are substantially different from those of students.

Since quality in educational research resides in its ability to explore, resonate with, explicate and improve practice, I would argue that all educational research must have at least an action research component to achieve quality.

QUALITY OF IMPACT: THE STATUS AND AVAILABILITY OF EDUCATIONAL KNOWLEDGE

Impact upon practice is the first marker of quality in educational research, but the value of this impact is, of course, grounded in the knowledge the research generates. The nature of the impact is important; it is possible to change for the worse, if the knowledge is not trustworthy. In addition, research needs to be grounded in what is already known.

- We need to question the status of the knowledge generated and how it can be used.
- We need to ask whether the knowledge was already available and could have been acquired in any other way.

These are questions often put to action researchers by those whose ideology sometimes makes them ill-prepared to listen carefully to the answers. They are important questions which need to be addressed.

The status of the knowledge generated from action research is no different from the status of any other knowledge. Knowledge is not something which exists to be discovered, or something which can be acquired by one individual and then packaged and passed on to others. Knowledge is:

- more than information: consisting of concepts and mental schemas which construct meaning from information;
- context-bound: particular to a situation and dependent upon that context for its construction;
- personally-constructed: individual to the knower, and dependent upon his or her prior knowledge;
- socially-constructed: shaped by the social context in which the knower lives and learns, and dependent upon the ideologies of social and political groups in that context;
- provisional: specific to here and now and hypothetical in the long term;
- ambiguous: made up of meaning constructed on the basis of rich, diverse

evidence and therefore capable of other constructions;
- generative: thought-provoking in being open to creative reconstruction.

There is not space here to set out in detail the methods which can be used in action research to cross check and scrutinise the trustworthiness of the knowledge and theories which it generates. Two methods have already been mentioned: the procedure of triangulation, by which data from different sources is compared and cross-checked and the process of testing theories in practice, through implementing actions based upon them and collecting further data to evaluate the effects. Ultimately the rigour of action research lies not so much in any particular method as in the reflexivity which is deeply rooted in action research methodology: a belief that interpretations, theories and meanings must be subjected to a continuous process of questioning and scrutiny, in which the researcher's attention shifts back and forth between interpretation and evidence — exploring, hypothesising, checking and reformulating.

The knowledge generated by action research is put into use as an integral part of the action research process, but is also available through publication (often, but not necessarily, in written form) to be used by others. It is knowledge of the particular, rather than generalised knowledge, and, although it can be reported in many different ways, it lends itself particularly well to a form of case study reporting which selects and interprets significant details and events. Ginzburg (1990) traces the importance of this tradition of research and analysis for detectives, psychoanalysts and art historians (e.g. in identifying fake paintings by examining details such as finger nails and ear lobes). He argues for a similar approach to the interpretation of historical events, recognising the importance of 'the taste for tell-tale detail', 'discarded information', and 'marginal data'. Elliott, in his writing as well as in oral presentations, often tells a significant story as the basis for illuminative interpretation. When such stories are grounded in action research they serve something of the function of parables. Rather than setting out to prove the correctness of any one interpretation, they invite the interpretation of the listener or reader. This form of reporting, which is sometimes dismissed by traditional researchers as 'anecdotal' does not claim spurious generalisability for knowledge and invites a constructive rather than a passive response from the learner. By this means teachers publish their knowledge and theories to other teachers in a form which can easily be used to explore their own practice. Knowledge which claims this kind of status and is reported in this form can make a profound impact upon practice.

The quality of educational research must also be judged in relation to the previous availability of the knowledge it generates. Although there may be value from a professional development point of view in re-inventing the wheel, it is a waste of resources as a form of research. I have outlined, at length, the problem which exists in enabling the knowledge generated by traditional research to have an impact upon practice, but this does not mean that such problems cannot and should not be overcome. O'Hanlon's work (1992, op. cit.) gives an example of how existing theories can be used to focus action research into practice. This is similar to the way in which Stenhouse envisaged that curriculum specifications, developed by teams of teachers and professional developers, would be tested and modified by other teachers. In both cases, theories are not received passively, but instead are used as the starting point for reflection and action. I see the widespread failure of action research to engage with existing theory as a feature of the way in which it has been marginalised into becoming predominantly a form of teacher professional development. Ultimately, such an attitude is self-defeating, because the knowledge produced by action research itself becomes part of existing theory, and others need to read about it (or hear about it) and engage with it, if it is to have any impact beyond the context of the original action research study. The problems experienced by full-time practitioners in finding time to engage in research are, of course, increased by the need to explore existing theory through reading; and, to ensure that action research meets the criterion of quality research, it is particularly helpful if partnerships include full time researchers/facilitators as well as practitioner-researchers.

IMPACT UPON PRACTICE: THE PROBLEM OF CHANGE FOR INDIVIDUAL PROFESSIONALS

The impact of research knowledge upon practice is rooted in the ability of individual professionals to change *what they do* and *how they think*. The problems in using traditional research knowledge to change practice result from two human characteristics:

- the capacity to routinise action;
- the strong ties between an individual's actions and his or her values and beliefs.

Routinised action is what enables me to drive for long periods without any great consciousness of the road. This makes the car an excellent place for thinking, but it has drawbacks — like the day I found I had driven forty miles in the wrong direction because I was so busy thinking about what I would say when I arrived at the meeting! In classrooms, action is not only routinised by the teacher, it is a routinised interaction of teacher and students. For example, something like this may have become an unconscious routine:

- the teacher asks questions and individual students answer (in alternation);
- the teacher repeats the student's answer, signalling whether it is 'right' or 'wrong', before asking the next question;
- the teacher expects answers to be given as one word or a short phrase and the students give their answers as one word or a short phrase;
- the teacher calls on students by name and the students wait to be called on by name (a variation of this is when students signal to the teacher that they want to be called on by raising their hand);
- the teacher does not allow a pause to last for more than three seconds after asking a question before calling on another student by name, and students who do not wish to answer questions (whether or not they know the answer) pause so that the question is directed to another student.

(For an analysis of this kind of routinised pattern of behaviour, see Altrichter et al., 1993, Chapter 6.)

Routinising action makes it possible for teachers to handle the complexity of the classroom; they can be planning the opening remarks of the lesson while taking the register, or thinking about setting homework while listening and responding to a student's answer. Routine is very useful in practical terms, and has the added benefit that it gives all those who participate in routinised action a sense of security, because they know what to expect. But it makes it very difficult to change our behaviour. This is the 'robot-like' aspect of human action that Mel Myers discusses in his paper.

Now look at the second factor: the link between action and values and beliefs. In a profound sense we are what we do and say. Every action and every utterance expresses something of what we stand for. Our movements, the expression on our faces, the words we use, all give other people strong clues about our fundamental beliefs. When we believe in what we are doing we can summon up energy to put much more effort into it. When we don't, our actions are likely to be uncertain, and appear half-hearted, and we are unlikely to feel good about them. The value conflict which results also builds up stress. Arguably, many teachers in Britain are currently trying to leave the profession because they find that in teaching a national curriculum specified in terms of content, and spending a relatively large proportion of their time in operating the assessment procedures, their actions are in conflict with their educational values.

People's self-images are strongly bound up with their values and beliefs, and their attachment to them is highly emotional. When those values and beliefs are held in common with others, the group develops a shared way of thinking and a shared discourse. And the more this system of values and beliefs becomes detached from personal experience, the more it becomes an ideology in which individual items are accepted as part of a 'job lot' — the whole set represents loyalty to a particular social and cultural group. Mere words, spoken or on a page, cannot change people if they present a challenge to such a monolithic belief system.

Two factors complicate matters even further. One is that the routinisation of action is actually tied into these personal values and beliefs. The routines have been developed in practice. When we first became teachers we had to learn how to manage a classroom. Our methods of questioning students were partly based on imitation, partly on experimentation. We did what we believed would be effective in achieving our aims, until the methods were internalised and we could go through the procedures without conscious thought. They have become bound up in our self-image and feelings of professional confidence and security. In that sense these routinised actions have the status of rituals, which create meaning for us and are integral to our professional self-image and feelings of control over what we do.

The second is that the values and beliefs we hold are only partly conscious and explicit. Our explanations of what we think we do and say, and why, rarely tally exactly with what an observer sees who observes what we actually do and say. Much of what we do and say is guided by either half-known (what Elliott calls 'tacit') or sub-conscious values and beliefs. However hard we try to act upon newly appropriated, conscious ideals, we may be unable to break the mould of routinised, ritualised actions, which have their roots in these tacit and subconscious theories, hopes and fears.

The power of action research, as a means of bringing about change and development, is that it investigates, and makes an impact upon, these two areas which are so critical in laying the foundations for action. By collecting evidence in our own classrooms (or for me, recently, in collecting evidence about the way in which I was interacting with others in the project I was co-ordinating) we can begin to explore the actuality of what we do and say and what happens in response. Because we are investigating situations in which we ourselves are participants, we have the best possible opportunity of gaining access to the values and beliefs which underpin what we do and say. Through a process of reflection, we can make numerous cross-references between the data we have collected about events and actions (our own and our students'), on the one hand, and our theories and beliefs, on the other hand. Through this process we come to understand our tacit and sub-conscious theories and beliefs and are able to develop and change our explicit value system. It is this change in our value system which makes changes in our practice possible.

In addition, because action research is a collaborative process, which involves the other participants in the situation, it also makes an impact on their theories and beliefs. In interviewing students to find out their perceptions of classroom interactions (or in interviewing those involved in the project I am co-ordinating) I am sensitising them to the questions I am asking. Not only do I gain insights from their answers to my questions, they also gain insights to my thinking from the questions I am asking. Through this a form of debate arises naturally which begins to involve all the participants in the situation as researchers, rather than merely as informants. This is what makes it possible to make changes to the routinised interactions upon which, not only I, but all the other participants, rely for security and some sense of control — and of which they too may have previously been largely unconscious.

IMPACT UPON INSTITUTIONS: THE PROBLEM OF CHANGE IN SYSTEMS

If quality in educational research resides in its impact upon practice, the scope of that impact becomes a further determinant of quality. I have said enough to persuade you (if your values and beliefs permit) that the impact of action research on the practice of individuals is potentially considerable. Likewise, I have said enough to suggest how easily this impact spreads to all those directly involved in the research situation. But can it go further? To what extent can action research have an impact on the institution within which the individual action researcher is framed — or the wider political and social institutions within which that institution is framed?

Of course, to have such an impact on institutions, action research methodology needs to adapt to suit an institutional frame, in exactly the same way that it always needs to adapt to a particular context. There is only space to sketch out here the broad outline of how this can operate in practice (for a more detailed treatment see Somekh, 1990, and 1992). This should not be taken to indicate that I am unaware of the potential problems. Marxist analysis teaches us that systems have the ability to render individuals powerless, through the tendency for existing power structures to reproduce themselves and maintain the status quo. According to post-Marxist critical theory it is only when individuals become critical (aware of the bureaucratic and administrative structures in which they are trapped) that they are emancipated from their inherent powerlessness. In suggesting that action research may be a means of influencing institutional development, however, I am adopting a theoretical perspective which is much nearer to Giddens' social theory. He rejects such a simplified analysis of the relationship between individual agents and social institutions. Building on the work of Lukes (1974) and Goffman (1959), he sees individual agents as able to exert influence through a range of subtle behaviours. In addition to the naive operation of power, Giddens sees social theory as a potent force by which, as individuals, we can influence and shape our destiny.

To have an impact on institutional development, individuals at different levels in the formal and informal power hierarchies need to carry out action research collaboratively. Although this is clearly much easier to establish in democratic institutions, the problems in establishing some form of collaborative action research in a more hierarchical institution need to be balanced against the difficulties in bringing about development and change by any other means. The management of development is an innovation in itself and may only be achievable by those in power engaging in action research into their management practices. In addition, although action research will undoubtedly encourage movement towards more democratic management practices, its focus on effective development will almost certainly encourage evolution rather than revolution. Action research does not enforce democracy. If the way the institution changes is through a top-down approach there is no reason why that cannot be recognised and built upon. Top-down does not have to mean that individuals are repressed. Patriarchies and matriarchies can often look after the interests of individuals better than democracies where the weakest tend to get pushed to the wall.

My experience of this kind of collaborative action research into institutional development has so far been limited, but my work to date suggests that it is effective in making an impact upon practice. I am necessarily tentative, but I judge that such forms of action research would always need to involve individuals at different levels in the formal and informal power hierarchies of the institution. In other ways, the adaptation of action research to an institutional context might take many forms. However, in order to examine and explicate both individual values and beliefs and group ideologies, it would be likely to focus upon ways of:

- identifying and exploring the different theories and beliefs which motivate individuals;
- explaining differences in purposes by communicating the theories and beliefs of individuals to each other;
- communicating information effectively to all individuals;
- clarifying points of conflict and investigating possible ways forward;
- developing strategies for collaborative action;
- developing strategies to support all those involved;
- developing shared values and purposes.

Just as in any other form of action research, the collection and interpretation of data, undertaken collaboratively (perhaps in partnerships or small groups), within the framework of an agreed ethical code, will help to ensure that participants focus their joint attention upon actual examples of practice rather than speaking from their disparate experience of half-remembered events. Such action research will depend upon the sensitivity of a very senior manager, who will certainly need to carry out action research into this difficult facilitator's role, as well as supporting other members of the group in their own action research activities. However, 'democratic' the institution, the dilemmas of this leadership role are likely to include balancing the need for the freedom of individuals against the necessity of organising and co-ordinating a large-scale group in undertaking collaborative activity.

Notes

1 Further information about CARN is available from the CARN secretary, Centre for Applied Research in Education, School of Education, University of East Anglia, Norwich NR4 7TJ

Action research in language education

David Nunan
Macquarie University

♦

Introduction

In this paper, I hope to provide a rationale for the use of action research in second and foreign language education. Questions addressed in the paper include:

What is action research in language education?
Is action research 'real' research?
What are some of the problems confronted by teachers doing action research?
What are some of the solutions to these problems?
What are the views of the teachers on the action research process?

The paper will be illustrated with data from a longitudinal action research project.

Action research: description and rationale

Until comparatively recently, the focus of concern in much of the writing on second and foreign language education was at the level of method. Methodological prescriptions were generally argued logico-deductively, and prescriptions for practice were generally devoid of data. This tended to reinforce the gap between theory, research and practice, a gap which, according to van Lier, is due in part to the obstacles which prevent teachers from doing research:

> *Those of us who work in teacher education know that one of the most difficult things to balance in a course is the tension between theoretical and practical aspects of the profession. ... Theory and practice are not perceived as integral parts of a teacher's practical professional life. ... This situation is the result of communication gaps caused by an increasingly opaque research technocracy, restrictive practices in educational institutions and bureaucracies (e.g. not validating research time, or not granting sabbaticals to teachers for professional renovation), and overburdening teachers who cannot conceive of ways of theorising and researching that come out of daily work and facilitate that daily work.*
>
> (van Lier 1992:3)

Despite the difficulties referred to by van Lier, there is some evidence that the picture is beginning to change. The change has been prompted in part by a growing sensitivity on the part of many researchers to the complexities of the teacher's task. Practitioners, on their part, seem to have grown tired of the swings and roundabouts of pedagogic fashion, and are looking for evidence before embracing the latest trend to appear in the educational market place. This is not to suggest that a revolution has taken place, however.

> *While position papers, and logico-deductive argumentation have not disappeared from the scene (and I am not suggesting for a moment that they should), they are counterbalanced by empirical approaches to inquiry. I believe that these days, when confronted by pedagogical questions and problems, researchers and teachers are more likely than was the case ten or fifteen years ago, to seek relevant data, either through their own research, or through the research of others. Research activity has increased to the point where those who favour logico-deductive solutions to pedagogic problems are beginning to argue that there is too much research.*
>
> (Nunan, 1992a)

An important concept underpinning action research (AR) is that of reflective practice. In his excellent book on reflective teaching, Wallace (1991) argues that reflective teaching provides a way of developing professional competence by integrating two sources of knowledge, received knowledge and experiential knowledge, with practice. Wallace's conception is captured in the following figure:

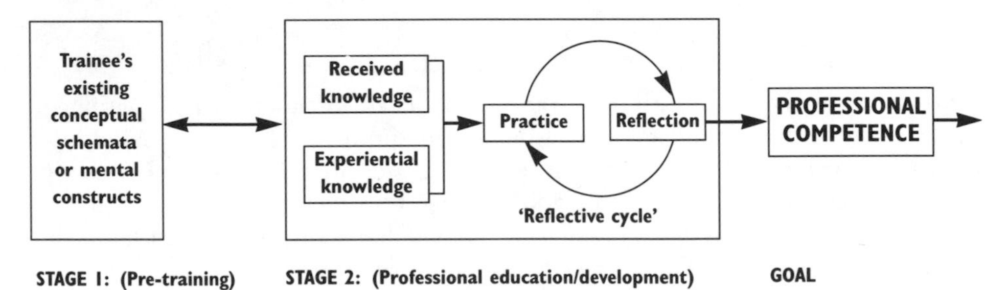

Fig. 1: Reflective practice model of professional education/development
(Source: M Wallace, 1991. *Training Foreign Language Teachers: A reflective approach.* Cambridge University Press.)

He links this with action research, arguing that:

'action research' can be attractive for two reasons:
1 It can have a specific and immediate outcome which can be directly related to practice in the teacher's own context.
2 The 'findings' of such research might be primarily specific, i.e. it is not claimed that they are necessarily of general application, and therefore the methods might be more free-ranging than those of conventional research.
... 'Research' of this kind is simply an extension of the normal reflective practice of

many teachers, but it is slightly more rigorous and might conceivably lead to more effective outcomes.

(Wallace 1991:56-7)

As we can see from the selected extracts presented above, action research is justified on the grounds that it is a valuable professional development tool. It represents what I would call an 'inside out' approach to professional development. It represents a departure from the 'outside in' approach (i.e. one in which an outside 'expert' brings the 'good news' to the practitioner in the form of a one-off workshop or seminar). In contrast, the inside out approach begins with the concerns and interests of practitioners, placing them at the centre of the inquiry process. In addition to being centred in the needs and interest of practitioners, and in actively involving them in the their own professional development, the inside out approach, as realised through action research, is longitudinal in that practitioners are involved in medium to long-term inquiry.

I believe that the benefits to professional development are justification enough for the development of an action research agenda. However, I believe that a further rationale for the development of such an agenda comes from the research process itself, and I shall deal with this in section three of my paper. First, however, I should like to look at the steps involved in the action research process.

STEPS IN THE RESEARCH PROCESS

The action research process is generally initiated by the identification by the practitioner of something which they find puzzling or problematic. This puzzle or problem may, in fact, have emerged from a period of observation and reflection. The second step is the collection of baseline data through a preliminary investigation which is designed to identify what is currently happening in the classroom without trying to change anything. Based on a review of the data yielded by the preliminary investigation, an hypothesis is formed. The next step is the development of some form of intervention or change to existing practice, along with a way of evaluating the effects of this change. The final step is reporting on the outcomes of the interaction, and, if necessary, planning further interventions. Two examples of the action research cycle are presented in Tables 1 and 2.

Table 1: The Action Research Cycle: An ESL Example

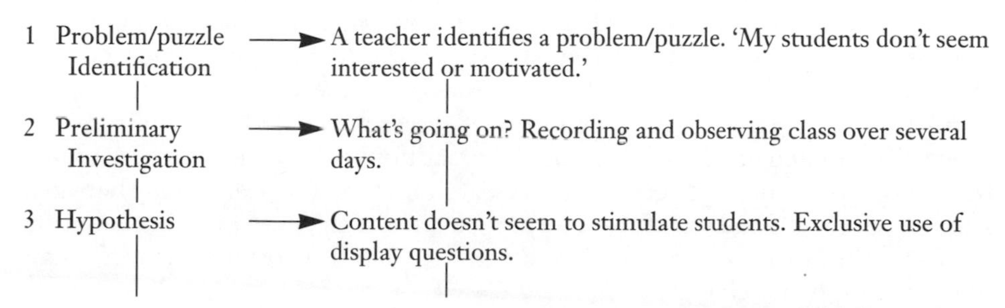

1 Problem/puzzle Identification	→	A teacher identifies a problem/puzzle. 'My students don't seem interested or motivated.'
2 Preliminary Investigation	→	What's going on? Recording and observing class over several days.
3 Hypothesis	→	Content doesn't seem to stimulate students. Exclusive use of display questions.

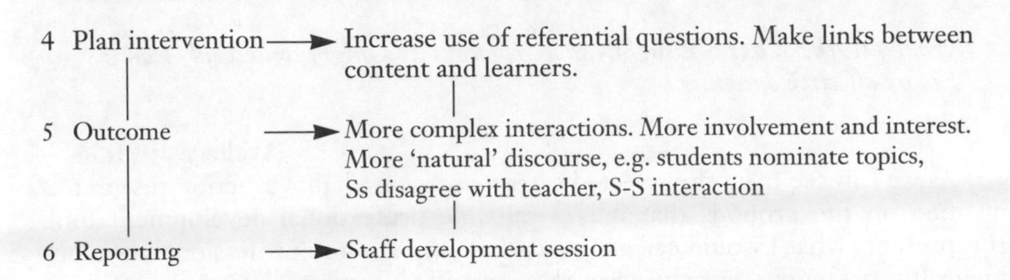

4 Plan intervention	Increase use of referential questions. Make links between content and learners.
5 Outcome	More complex interactions. More involvement and interest. More 'natural' discourse, e.g. students nominate topics, Ss disagree with teacher, S-S interaction
6 Reporting	Staff development session

Table 2: The Action Research Cycle: A Foreign Language Example

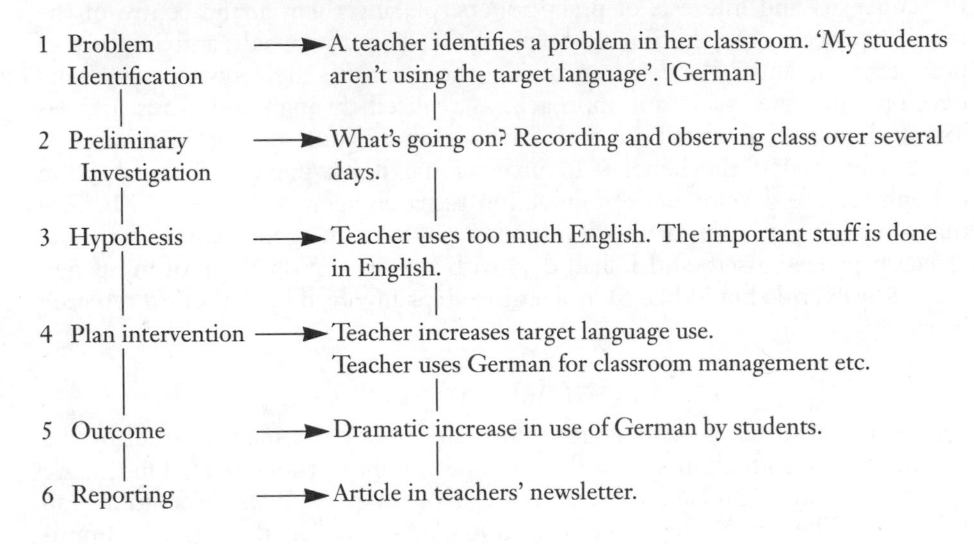

1 Problem Identification	A teacher identifies a problem in her classroom. 'My students aren't using the target language'. [German]
2 Preliminary Investigation	What's going on? Recording and observing class over several days.
3 Hypothesis	Teacher uses too much English. The important stuff is done in English.
4 Plan intervention	Teacher increases target language use. Teacher uses German for classroom management etc.
5 Outcome	Dramatic increase in use of German by students.
6 Reporting	Article in teachers' newsletter.

ACTION RESEARCH AND 'REAL' RESEARCH

In the first part of this paper, I argued that action research can be justified on professional development grounds. However, I believe that AR can also be justified on research grounds. In fact, I believe that there is something essentially patronising in the view that, while AR might be good for professional development, it hardly counts as research. Let us, to use a currently fashionable term, 'deconstruct' this view. First of all, what do we mean by 'research'? What is the function of research?

Elsewhere, I have defined research as *'a systematic process of inquiry consisting of three elements or components: (1) a question, problem, or hypothesis, (2) data, (3) analysis and interpretation of data'* (Nunan, 1992a:3). Action research incorporates these three elements and therefore qualifies as 'real' research. For me the salient distinction between AR and other forms of research is that in AR the research process is initiated and carried out by the practitioner. As far as I am concerned, the opposition is not between action research and 'real' research, but between good research and bad research. A further characteristic, perhaps differentiating AR from other forms of practitioner research, is that it incorporates an element of intervention and change.

Fundamental to any discussion of research is a consideration of the researcher's conception of notions such as 'truth', 'objectivity', and the status of knowledge. I recently attempted to deal with the tensions of objective and subjective knowledge by suggesting that they represent two alternative ways of looking at the world:

> *Two alternative conceptions of the nature of research provide a point of tension within the book. The first view is that external truths exist 'out there' somewhere. According to this view, the function of research is to uncover these truths. The second view is that truth is a negotiable commodity contingent upon the historical context within which phenomena are observed and interpreted. Further '[research] standards are subject to change in the light of practice [which] would seem to indicate that the search for a substantive universal, ahistorical methodology is futile.' (Chalmers 1990:21) … This second, context-bound attitude to research entails a rather different role for the classroom practitioner than the first. If knowledge is tentative and contingent upon context, rather than absolute, then I believe that practitioners, rather than being consumers of other people's research, should adopt a research orientation to their own classrooms. There is evidence that the teacher-researcher movement is alive and well and gathering strength. However, if the momentum which has gathered is not to falter, and if the teacher-researcher movement is not to become yet another fad, then significant numbers of teachers, graduate students, and others will need skills in planning, implementing and evaluating research.*
>
> (Nunan, 1992a)

There are those who would argue that my definition of research as a systematic process of inquiry involving formulating a question, collecting relevant data, and analysing and interpreting that data is inadequate, that in order to count as research, the process should also meet the twin strictures of reliability and validity. Key questions for establishing the reliability and validity of research are set out in Table 3.

Table 3: Questions for establishing the reliability and validity of a study

Type	Key Question
Internal reliability	Would an independent researcher, on re-analysing the data, come to the same conclusion?
External reliability	Would an independent researcher, on replicating the study, come to the same conclusion?
Internal validity	Is the research design such that we can confidently claim that the outcomes are a result of the experimental treatment?
External validity	Is the research design such that we can generalise beyond the subjects under investigation to a wider population?

(Source: D. Nunan, 1992. *Research Methods in Language Learning.* Cambridge University Press.)

While I would argue that any research needs to be reliable, the issue of validity is more problematic. If one is not trying to establish a relationship between variables, but (for example) to describe and interpret phenomena in context, does the imperative to demonstrate that one has safeguarded one's research from threats to internal validity remain? By the same token, if one is not trying to argue from samples to populations, then it would not be unreasonable to assert that external validity is irrelevant. I would argue that as most AR is not concerned with arguing from samples to populations, external validity is not at issue. (For an excellent discussion of issues to do with reliability and validity in qualitative research, see Le Compte and Goetz, 1982.).

It is popularly assumed that the purpose of research is to test theories. For example, *'That communicative language teaching is more effective than audiolingualism.'* Allwright and Bailey have pointed out that there are problems with this proposition. In the first place, some theories are untestable (for example, Krashen's attestations on 'subconscious' acquisition). Secondly, classrooms are too complex for us to control all the variables in the manner prescribed by experimental research. They propose an alternative purpose for research, namely to try and understand and deal with immediate practical problems facing teachers and learners (Allwright and Bailey, 1991). If we accept this alternative purpose, we are drawn immediately into embracing AR, because it makes no sense for an outsider to arbitrate on the practical problems facing teachers and learners. This does not mean that outsiders, such as university-based researchers, have no role to play in practitioner-based research. However, the role is one of collaboration and advice rather than direction and control.

PROBLEMS AND SOLUTIONS IN DOING ACTION RESEARCH

I would now like to reassure those who might feel that I am looking at teacher research through rose-coloured glasses. It is certainly not the case that everything is rosy in the AR garden. The principal problems identified by teachers with whom I have worked in a number of different contexts include the following:

- Lack of time
- Lack of expertise
- Lack of ongoing support
- Fear of being revealed as an incompetent teacher
- Fear of producing a public account of their research for a wider (unknown) audience

We have experimented with a number of solutions to the problems. I believe that the chances for an action research agenda to succeed will be maximised under the following conditions:

- There is someone 'on the ground' to 'own' the project.
- One or more individuals with training in research methods are available 'on tap' to provide assistance and support to teachers.
- Teachers are given paid release time from face-to-face teaching during the course of their action research.

- Collaborative focus teams are established so that teachers involved in similar areas of inquiry can support one another.
- Teachers are given adequate training in methods and techniques for identifying issues, collecting data, analysing and interpreting data, and presenting the outcomes of their research.

In order to facilitate the process, colleagues and I have developed an in-service programme (see Burton and Mickan, this volume) . This programme was initially devised for the LIPT project (Languages Inservice Project for Teachers) in South Australia, and has been further modified and refined in Sydney, where a project has been established bringing together mainstream teachers, ESL teachers, and teachers of LOTE (Languages Other than English — a term which is preferred to Foreign Language Teachers as most non-English languages are widely used within the Australian community, and the term 'foreign' is therefore a misnomer). In Table 4, I have provided a summary of the professional development programme as it currently exists.

Table 4: The inservice programme in outline

SESSION 1 An introduction to classroom observation and research

a A series of reflective activities designed to get teachers thinking about their own teaching style.
b Reflecting on the teaching of others: teachers examine and critique extracts from a range of classrooms identifying those aspects of the extracts they liked and disliked.
c Identification of ideological beliefs and attitudes underlying critiques.

Between session task: Teachers record and reflect on their own teaching.

SESSION 2 An introduction to action research

a Teachers report back on the between session task.
b Introduction to issues and methods in action research.
c Introduction to the action research process.

Between session task: Teachers develop a draft action plan.

SESSION 3 Focus groups and action plans

a Formation of focus groups and appointment of facilitators.
b Sharing of draft action plans.
c Refining questions.

Between session task: Baseline observation, focus group meetings, preliminary data collection.

SESSION 4 Analysing data

a Participants develop ways of analysing and making sense of their data.

Between session task: Ongoing data collection and analysis, focus group meetings.

SESSION 5 Writing up

a Participants receive input on presenting their research.
b Development of draft reporting outlines.

Between session task: Production of draft reports.

SESSION 6 Refining reports
Participants receive feedback on and discussion of their reports.

SESSION 7 Evaluation
Participants evaluate the LIPT process and provide feedback on how their involvement changed them.

EVALUATING ACTION RESEARCH

From what has already been said, it is clear that action research is difficult, messy, problematic, and, in some cases, inconclusive. It consumes a great deal of time, and often strains the goodwill of the teachers involved, as well as those with whom they work. However, evaluative data from teachers themselves suggests that teachers who have been involved in action research are overwhelmingly in favour of it. For example, Mickan, who collected data on the reaction of outside teachers to his LIPT project writes:

> *Teachers have welcomed the articles from LIPT. They have found them particularly useful and relevant because they depict the complex circumstances of classroom life in an honest and direct way. They have found them a rich source of ideas and valuable for informing their own practice. The warts and all descriptions (including failures and successes), the research techniques used, the analysis of results and the contextual detail are all elements which readers relate to and understand. As such they possess a validity which derives from the detailed narration of classroom ecology. The experiential reports give other practitioners models and ideas for their own practice. They also suggest topics and procedures for classroom investigations in different contexts.*
>
> (Mickan, 1991)

An evaluation by Lewis (1992) is also favourable. She reports on a study conducted with a group of teachers of French immersion programmes in British Columbia. The focus of her research was the effect on the professional practice of the teachers of engaging in AR. She drew the following conclusions from her research.

1. Through the process of systematically implementing their own choice of action project based on the needs of the students in particular, each teacher learned more about their own theories, or frames for teaching, and modified these frames to a certain extent.
2. The frames for teaching of the participants in this study are related to the bigger questions of second language education and education in general. Practice cannot be understood thoroughly without appreciating how educational theory is expressed within teachers' frames and neither can theory be useful without recognising that what counts is how theory becomes expressed within practice.
3. The 'teacher as researcher' or 'reflection in action' approach to teacher education can be a very powerful way of facilitating change in curriculum.

In evaluating the last of the LIPT projects, we asked teachers to complete the following statements:

Action research is ....

Action research is carried out in order to ....

We also asked them to respond to the following:

1 What are the most significant things you have learned in carrying out your classroom research?
2 What questions/issues have your classroom research raised for you?
3 What further areas/ideas are you interested in pursuing?

Sample responses to the first of these probes on the most significant outcomes for the participants are set out in Appendix 2. It can be seen that these are overwhelmingly favourable, the participants choosing to focus either on the substantive content outcomes *('By collecting and analyzing data on my children, I found that they were more highly motivated than I had given them credit for.')*, learning process outcomes *('The active involvement of the children in the learning process facilitates learning.' 'I discovered that kids know how to learn — the project taught me to listen to them.')*, or reflections on the research process itself *('In working through the action research process, I discovered which methods of data collection are most suited to my research question — next time I will be better prepared as I will be more aware of what I am looking for, and will be better able to match my questions and data.')*. The enthusiastic validation of learner-centred approaches to instruction, even though this was not a primary aim of most research, is also worth noting.

Finally, participants were asked to complete a checklist to indicate how their teaching had changed as a result of their involvement in the project. Results are set out below. It can be seen from the survey that, if self-reports are to be believed, the experience was, for most teachers, an overwhelmingly positive one.

Table 5: How has your teaching changed? Complete the following:
Since I have been doing action research, I find that when I teach I now ...

		More	About the same	Less
1	tend to be directive	1	14	10
2	try to use a greater variety of behaviours	16	6	0
3	praise students	15	10	0
4	criticise students	0	11	13
5	am aware of students' feelings	18	6	0
6	give directions	4	16	5
7	am conscious of my non-verbal communication	11	14	0
8	use the target language in class	19	6	0
9	am conscious of non-verbal cues of students	12	12	0
10	try to incorporate student ideas into my teaching	20	5	0
11	spend more class time talking myself	1	9	15
12	try to get my students working in groups	15	18	0
13	try to get divergent, open-ended student responses	14	10	0
14	distinguish between enthusiasm and lack of order	9	15	0
15	try to get students to participate	18	7	0

CONCLUSION

In this paper, I have argued that the adoption of an action research orientation can be justified in professional development terms and research terms. Despite the bureaucratic difficulties and obstacles which are placed in the way of teachers, the elitism of a certain cadre of researchers (some of whom were once classroom teachers themselves!), and the suspicion which is sometimes directed at academics who are trying to promote a closer relationship between theory, research, and practice, there is evidence that things are beginning to change. I can offer no more fitting conclusion to this paper than the following extract from the work of two of the profession's foremost advocates of the development of harmony between theory, research and practice, who have striven in their own teaching, writing and research, to enhance the status of both practitioner and researcher within language education.

> *Slowly, the profession as a whole is realising that, no matter how much intellectual energy is put into the invention of new methods (or of new approaches to syllabus design, and so on), what really matters is what happens when teachers and learners get together in the classroom. ... This shift in emphasis from concentrating on planning decisions ... to concentrating on looking at what actually happens in the classroom, has led researchers to have much greater respect for classroom teaching. The more we look, the more we find, and the more we realise how complex the teacher's job is. And teachers, in their turn, faced at last with researchers who have at least some idea of the enormous complexity of everyday classroom life, are beginning to be more receptive to the whole research enterprise. ... Being a good classroom teacher means being alive to what goes on in the classroom, alive to the problems of sorting out what matters, moment by moment, from what does not. And that is what classroom research is all about: gaining a better understanding of what good teachers (and learners) do instinctively as a matter of course, so that ultimately all can benefit.*

(Allwright and Bailey, 1991)

Appendix 1

THE LIPT PROJECT: SOME FOCUS GROUP AND RESEARCH TITLES

1 LITERACY AND LOTE

Big books and the German classroom
Journal writing in action
Making big books
Tell me more …
Developing writing skills
A literature-based program
It's too hard!
Writing what I want to in German
Language arts and LOTE

2 DEVELOPING LEARNING STRATEGIES

Cross-age tutoring in German
'No stop-start' learning centres and language Learning
Cross-age tutoring in Pitjantjatjara
Learning together
Learning contracts and LOTE
Cross-age tutoring in Greek
Learning centres rule OK?
Learning how to learn

3 LOTE TOPICS

Back to the drawing black board
Two heads are better than one … or are they?
'Reading in German? Not a problem!'
Assessing primary French
What's that word again?
Towards a positive classroom
Making a game
He can't hear you nodding Sophie
Mistakes are for learning
Beginning at the beginning or immersion of tadpoles
Extending a primary German program
Dai, Forza Giochiamo! Let's play!
Speak!
Learning through games
Let's play games
In French, please
Immersion — or in at the deep end
Using more Indonesian in the classroom
When I speak German I feel great!
Motivation and language learning
Heaps more French??
Who's speaking German?
Using an activities-based approach

Appendix 2

What are the most significant things you have learned in carrying out your classroom research?

- The active involvement of the children in the learning process facilitates learning.
- Children have different learning preferences and teachers need to allow for this in their instructional practices.
- Children find it difficult to express feelings and opinions on paper.
- It is easy to 'spoon feed' children, but this leads to ineffective learning.
- Teaching problems only go away if they are recognized and tackled.
- The most important outcome for me was that I learned how to do action research. To benefit, I therefore have to do it again!
- Working with the children together (e.g. finding their thoughts/feelings and acting on them).
- In working through the action research process, I discovered which methods of data collection are most suited to my research question — next time I will be better prepared as I will be more aware of what I am looking for, and will be better able to match my questions and data.

- The process removed my tunnel vision to teaching.
- It helped me to making links with other teachers of Mandarin, as well as parents and the community.
- The process dramatically enhanced my rapport with students.
- I found that by careful, step-by-step direction of students, I was able to give them tools to manage their own learning.
- By collecting and analyzing data on my children, I found that they were more highly motivated than I had given them credit for.
- The most important outcome for me was that I discovered the children enjoy (and respond well) to being consulted about their learning and being given some say in what they learn.
- There was a negative outcome for me — I've learned not to expect children to have completed tasks or to value something just because they're important to me.
- I found that Year 7 learners still need lots of structure and guidance, even when independent skills are encouraged.
- I was disappointed. I expected too much in my initial project — book flood! Only book trickle is possible in such a short time.
- The most important discovery for me was that my students need more time and opportunities to work in groups as they need to learn to work on their own without teacher directed lessons all the time.
- The need for informed input in this process — one needs to read etc., recent research and thinking in order to maximize value of one's own research, and move beyond one's own 'blinkered' vision.
- The positive benefit of concentrating on one particular area because the attitude/approach of openness and inquiry carries over into one's teaching in general.
- I have learned that students with a very limited knowledge of the target language are prepared to try to write more than I expected, and that in future I should try to foster this willingness in my classes.
- Contrary to my expectations, I found that the children were keen to be part of a 'project'. This led to increased motivation (maybe Hawthorne Effect?).
- I have learned that one needs to undertake classroom research. One needs to intervene — observation alone isn't a good enough indicator of how much children are learning.
- In my research, I delved into how my lessons were arranged and the effectiveness (or not) of my teaching. I looked closely at my learning strategies. It allowed me to construct a unit that was designed for junior primary students' needs and interests and my research allowed my to construct strategies accordingly.
- I discovered that kids know how to learn — the project taught me to listen to them.

Acknowledgement

Grateful acknowledgment is made to the British Council for financial support. Fig. 1 (p 40), 'Reflective practice model of professional educational development' from *Training Foreign Language Teachers: A Reflective Approach* (M. Wallace, 1991) is reproduced by kind permission of Cambridge University Press.

TDTR: Conference as catalyst

Julian Edge & Keith Richards

Aston University

◆

Part 2

The coherence of the three plenary sessions considered as a whole was a matter of design, implicit in the idea of the conference; the rest was a mixture of planning and accident.

We had a clear picture of what we wanted and a determination to stick to it, but — ironically perhaps — we failed to take into account the process of development which would eventually shape the conference and this collection. The lessons we learnt seem relevant to the conference theme.

As our plans for the conference moved from conception to realisation, we were forced to come to terms with the fact that our picture of reality was only one of many. Wrapped up in our idea of the conference, we came to inhabit the reality of its published expression, including its timetable of deadlines and decisions. But the real timetable of events dictated a long silence, with most of the proposals arriving a week either side of the final date, and by then our questions had more to do with the existence of the conference than with its shape.

This, however, made us receptive to new ideas and allowed us to rethink our own position. Eventually we had more proposals than we could accommodate and a selection had to be made — but we were different people then, and ownership of the conference was already shared.

Our second encounter with other realities was in the interpretation of the conference theme. Until the first proposals arrived we had seen the conference only from our own perspective, as 'ideal' participants who 'understood' the deliberately ambiguous title and were sensitive to the force of 'personal discoveries and outcomes'. The arrival of the written papers was where the world started to leak in. We saw potential participants as falling into two groups:

- The first group identified this as an academic conference with all the requirements implicit in that. Its members, whose professional concerns lay in the overlap between research and development, responded to the conference title and offered papers conforming to accepted academic norms.
- The second group saw the conference as an invitation to take up the issue of personal outcomes, irrespective of whether their work fell into the category of 'academic' research. Their voices were inevitably personal, their relationship to academic norms sometimes unconventional.

The arrangement of this collection reflects this division, or rather, our interpretation of responses to the title. Our development was towards a recognition of how much we had taken for granted, and in the light of this it would be foolish to pretend that our selection of papers for this collection is in any way sanctioned by special insight. We fought space as best we could and lost more than we had ever anticipated. The imperfections of this collection lie in our omissions.

The papers in the first group focus on the process of development in professional rather than personal terms. The authors are involved in the process as catalysts or observers; we learn nothing of them as 'inhabitants' in the process. However, this loss is offset by gains in terms of perspective: the application of appropriate tools and techniques in professional development is brought into sharp relief and the developmental process itself is carefully observed. The arrangement moves from a predominant concern with the former to a focus on the latter, but the link between the two is never lost.

Rees' paper offers a natural point of departure because of its concern with observation. Its importance lies in its consistently practical orientation. Observation is fundamental to understanding and understanding underlies development, yet it is a sad fact that many of the observation instruments available require trained observers and are impractical for the classroom teacher. Rees emphasises the *personal* element in instrument design and presents a simple but sensitive model which teachers can easily adapt. His paper offers an example and a challenge to academics and teachers.

Observation features in the action research described in Belleli's paper, but her use of the repertory grid as an analytical instrument is particularly interesting. Her paper provides a link between the ideas explored by Myers and their application to a specific aspect of teachers' work. Her claim that personal construct theory should be '*an integral component of teacher education programmes*' is one that deserves serious consideration. (For ease of reference, the editors have included a brief note on personal construct theory at the end of the article.)

'Experiment' is, for some, a dirty word, but as Nunan says, there is really only good research and bad research. Vanermen's paper is important because it provides an example of how 'traditional' research *can* be undertaken by the practising teacher and applied directly to a teaching situation. This is something we must not lose sight of.

It raises the question of the relationship between description and intervention, which is where Peck comes in. He explores the relationship between accurate description and practical experimentation, drawing our attention to a nexus of fundamental importance in action research. His paper is concerned with foreign language teaching in general and provides a useful reminder of something which we thought was important when we discussed the idea of the conference: the wider world of teaching and the transferability of insights.

Van Thielen's paper focuses on the process of induction into that wider world and may have important insights to offer to teachers in the English educational system loaded with new responsibilities crudely transferred from teacher training institutions by central government. The paper explores the role of the mentor in helping new teachers adapt to their professional environment. It offers a revealing analysis of the process of response and adjustment which is central to any successful induction programme.

Ellis offers a useful pendant to Van Thielen's picture. She is concerned with re-training teachers using a project-based approach. The reflective orientation here raises interesting and important points. Is a problem orientation in action research potentially threatening, and if so do we need to rethink the standard formulation of it? At the very least we need to take seriously Allwright's suggestion (in his paper in this collection) that we use 'puzzle' rather than 'problem'. To what extent, if at all, can we protect ourselves against 'bombshells'? What is the relationship between reflective practice and risk-taking?

These questions are not asked rhetorically. However, as Burton and Mickan point out in their paper, while the idea of classroom research has sold well, practice has often been left behind on the shelf. Their contribution to this collection is threefold. They show that large-scale classroom research projects with a strong interpersonal element are possible *and* productive. They also show that collaboration between the academic-researcher and the teacher-researcher is natural and mutually enriching. Finally, they point to the importance of finding a voice. This voice — or distinctive aspects of it — will be heard in the second group of papers in this collection.

Segmenting classroom activities for research purposes

Alun Rees

Essex University

◆

Engaging in classroom research offers one route to personal professional development. Such research can take many forms. This paper describes an observation scheme designed for the systematic observation of EFL classrooms, based on a conceptualisation of teaching events in a form familiar to teachers. The 'segment', a naturalistic unit designed to capture this aspect, is defined. This acknowledges the multi-dimensionality of classroom events by enabling the observer to code four major aspects simultaneously: Topic focus, Teacher activity, Learner activity and Class grouping. The resulting observation device — the 'Rees Observation Template' (ROT) — may be readily adapted by researchers, trainers or teachers for their own use.

Research and classroom complexity

The very word research can daunt practising teachers for a variety of understandable reasons (see Rees, 1992). But personal research offers a route to awareness of the routinised and often unconscious behaviours of which much teaching is composed. Routine is essential for a sense of security, otherwise chaos rules. But routine can mask aspects of reflex behaviour which the teacher might not approve of were they actually reflected upon. Research can encourage a personal de-robotising process by forcing into consciousness not only those aspects of our teaching which we endorse, but also those which we may not consider conducive to student learning. Lest we forget, the ultimate aim of all classroom research should be to improve learning.

However, there are as many ways to consider classrooms as there are classrooms. Furthermore, classrooms and the language used in them operate on many levels at once. Attempts to unravel this surprising complexity have ranged from the statistical quantification of teacher/learner verbal and non-verbal behaviours, to ethnographic analysis modelled on the techniques of anthropology. There is no right or wrong in this matter, for in the final analysis, the approach each researcher adopts depends on personal preference and interest.

How then should the tyro researcher proceed? The normal initial move is the prudent one of familiarisation with some of the existing instruments developed in the brief history of systematic classroom observation. Fortunately, the task is facilitated by the wide-ranging schemes described in anthologies such as those by Simon and Boyer (1970), Galton (1978) and Allwright (1988b). This avenue offers the advantage of avoiding rediscovery of the wheel. However, the bewildering array of devices with which the reader is faced can be demoralising for the faint-hearted, and often difficult to grasp.

Why difficult to grasp? Part of the answer lies in the apt words of de Bono (1969:30), even though he did not have classroom observation in mind when he wrote them:

> *... Matters are often made more and more complex by the ability of man to play elaborate games that feed on themselves to create bewildering structures of immense intricacy, which obscure rather than reveal. The only thing that these structures do reveal is that man has the ability and compulsion to play such conceptual games.*

A glance at the above-mentioned anthologies will swiftly reveal that the complexities of classroom happenings are all too frequently reflected in the impenetrable intricacy of the instruments devised to disentangle them.

And matters are made yet more complex by the lack of universal conformity among learners, teachers, classrooms, methodologies and educational goals. This renders it extremely unlikely that an observation instrument designed for one context will readily adapt to another without modification.

The problem of wholesale borrowing is aggravated further by the fact that published accounts of instruments are constrained by space considerations and can rarely be explicit enough to encompass the multifarious problems that crop up in coding real-life classrooms. Neat published accounts of research tend to conceal the complexity, uncertainties and rough edges of the activity.

However, there is a more fundamental principle at work here. Trying to operate a ready-made instrument demonstrates that the categories do not echo some shared reality 'out there', but are the product of the compiler's personal construct — an individual conceptual framework of the world which affects the interpretation of classroom events. In essence this is acknowledged by Long, Adams, McClean and Castaños (1976:152) who admit that: '*As for objectivity, like all systems for analysing classroom interaction, our categories are subjective, and classification of language into them intuitive.*'

To compensate for this phenomenon, instrument compilers are obliged to formulate comprehensive ground-rules which define mutually exclusive categories which can be applied without question by other researchers. But it should be clear from the foregoing that these can never be explicit enough. Viewing classrooms through other people's spectacles tends to produce a blurred and uncomfortable perspective, and we inevitably feel compelled to regrind the lenses to obtain a more personally familiar picture. Hence, cries for a respite in instrument production to allow for consolidation will remain unheeded. There will always be new classroom observation instruments, or rumours of them.

IN SEARCH OF AN INSTRUMENT

In constructing a research package to survey the teaching of English at secondary school in Catalonia (Spain), a core systematic data-gathering device was required for the task. Lacking intensive personal training or experience in the techniques and subtleties of ethnography, there was no viable alternative but to carry out the central part of the survey with a prepared checklist. The possibility of an analysis based on transcription, following a model such as that formulated by Sinclair and Coulthard (1975) was also ruled out — with some 20 hours needed to transcribe the verbal interaction of just one lively lesson, and that merely in readiness for embarking on subsequent analysis, this would have precluded the wider sampling the survey demanded.

How was the task to be tackled? In another context, de Bono (1969:7) again strikes at the heart of the matter which the apprentice researcher is forced to consider in answering this question:

> *The difficulty lies in deciding at what level of organization it is best to explore the functioning of a system. If the level is too detailed and the units are too small, then the over-all function of the system may not be disclosed at all. On the other hand, if the level is too high, one may only be able to describe the system in broad functional terms that are of no practical use whatsoever.*

The question of the basic research unit is indeed a crucial one, and will remain a bone of contention among researchers. Timely warnings are offered by Dunkin and Biddle (1974:77):

> *Since classroom events have a rhythm of their own, their boundaries may or may not correspond with the arbitrary time boundaries we are forcing upon them.*

and by Biddle (1967:342):

> *Since analytic units reflect the sophisticated concerns of the investigator rather than those of the participant, their use entails the risk of moving away from phenomenal reality and the problems of having to translate results into some convenient form usable by educators.*

Although the classroom may be operating physically as a series of discrete events, the learner, teacher and observer naturally infer a continuity and consistency among them. Yet the imposing of a not well-understood, artificial boundary with an arbitrary tempo upon this holistic psychological reality, threatens to mask if not destroy it. Here is an example of broad, naturalistic episodes occurring in class-time:

1. 9.05-9.08 Teacher greets class, followed by general hubbub as she sorts out her papers and sets up the tape-recorder.
2. 9.08-9.11 Teacher asks a learner to collect completed homework, counts the pieces returned, identifies defaulters, then listens to and queries their excuses.
3. 9.11-9.20 Teacher returns marked homework from the previous day. Deals with general points first, using the blackboard to illustrate, before commenting on individual efforts as she returns them.
4. 9.20-9.22 Teacher outlines the procedure for the next part of the lesson (various tasks connected with listening to a tape-recording).
5. 9.22- etc., etc.

The question now arises: Can a research instrument be devised which preserves such units? The answer may lie in the adoption of the 'segment' as the basic unit of analysis.

THE SEGMENT

The segment may be described as an episode occuring in real time. The concept is derived from American studies in ecological psychology, principally the work of Barker (1968) and Gump (1974). The essence of the ecological approach lies not in the study of a particular environment or a person's behaviour in isolation, but in the recognition of their inter-relationship. The temporal units identified by Gump were defined by a taxonomy of subsettings occurring simultaneously:

1 general academic or other concerns (topic);
2 the role played by the teacher;
3 the size of the working groups and the extent of interdependence among pupils in their work;
4 the nature of the pupil activity;
5 the extent to which the pupils' work is self or externally paced.

This concept was adopted by Mitchell, Parkinson and Johnstone (1981) in the construction of a somewhat ingenious observation scheme designed to examine the teaching of first-year French in secondary schools in Central Scotland. They defined the segment as a stretch of lesson discourse, having a particular topic, and involving the participants in a distinctive configuration of roles, linguistic and organisational. An arbitrary minimum length of 30 seconds was specified per segment, with no upper limit being set. Five dimensions of the segment were recognised:

1	topic of discourse	(11 subcategories)
2	language activity	(8)
3	teacher mode of involvement	(7)
4	pupil mode of involvement	(6)
5	class organisation	(7)

THE 'ROT' INSTRUMENT

The personal attempt to transport this instrument to the Catalonian context quickly led to drastic modifications in its structure. Seventeen variations were devised to cope with the new situation, each tried out and then rejected. The eighteenth version, the 'Rees Observation Template' (ROT), appears on the following pages. This is the 'exasperated version'; there can never be a final one, for each trial inevitably tempts the user to tinker with it.

The instrument is presented here through a coded checklist of a genuine lesson which consisted largely of a debate conducted in English by the learners. The categories are then elucidated line by line for the reader, and a sample segment selected for explanation. It will be noted that the scheme basically consists of four dimensions operating simultaneously:

TOPIC FOCUS (what the interaction is mainly concerned with)
TEACHER ACTIVITY (the teacher's role)

LEARNER ACTIVITY (the ways in which the learners participate)
CLASS GROUPING (how the learners are grouped)

When there is a change of sub-category on any one of these dimensions, and this new configuration is sustained for 30 seconds or more, then a new segment is considered to have begun. Only on the LEARNER dimension can several subcategories operate at the same time, for example, during a dictation learners will be listening, writing and reading. But any major switch of activity here will also signal a new segment, e.g. if the learners stop writing and just listen for 30 or more seconds to an explanation by the teacher.

In operating ROT, a single channel tape-recording is made of each lesson, and this is played back so that individual segments can be identified, timed with a stopwatch, and coded on the checklist. To code comfortably in real-time would require a reduction in the number of subcategories. The analysis is aided by reference to a running description of key points which were written down by the researcher during the observation of the lesson.

Explanation of the ROT checklist

Title: The term Template is designed as a reminder that the instrument is a flexible model, not a cast-iron product.

Identification: The serial number of the observation, name of the teacher, and level of the class.

Segment: Segments numbered continuously from left to right across the grid. Each vertical column contains all the coded components of any one segment. There were twelve separate segments in this particular lesson.

Counter: The counter setting on the tape-recorder at the start of each segment, beginning at 000 (entered vertically). For example, the counter is set at 199 for segment 2 (Fig. 1).

Ragbag: Reserved as a reminder of various items of interest to the observer, not catered for by the main ROT instrument (and often operating below the 30-second limit), e.g. use of the blackboard, a dialogue, dictation, extraneous interruptions, strong grammatical focus, a game, chaos, reference to home work, a joke/anecdote, music, use of the OHP, spelling, a song, translation, vocabulary emphasis, video work, etc. They are coded in shorthand form.

Language: Indicates the prevailing language employed in each segment, E for English and M for the Mother-tongue. E= (2 minus signs) would signify the predominance of English, but with 2 samples of Mother-tongue use.

TOPIC: This dimension distinguishes areas of discourse dealing with the main purpose of the lesson from those merely ensuring that it is being carried out.

No: 39 Name: A. Nonima Level: 4th Year

	Segment	1	2	3	4	5	6	7	8	9	10	11	12	13	14	15	16	17	18	19	20	21	22	23	24	25
Counter		0																								
		0	1	2	2	3	3	3	6	6	8	8	9													
		0	9	4	6	1	4	7	7	9	3	6	6													
		0	9	2	2	5	9	1	9	4	2	1	5													
Ragbag		Bb								Vc			Hk													
Language (–)		E⁻	E	E	E	E	E	E	E	E	E	E	E													
TOPIC	manag./routine		✓	✓		✓					✓		✓													
	study: intro.	✓																								
	study: subst.				✓		✓	✓	✓	✓		✓														
	real life																									
exper.	*teacher* (•)								•																	
	learner ↓				•		•	•	•	•		•	•													
	immediate ↓			•									•													
	local ↓				•		•	•		•			•													
	gen. knowl.		•		•		•	•	•	•	•	•														
TEACH.	lecture			✓		✓	✓		✓		✓		✓													
	lecture/inter.																									
	conducting	✓			✓			✓		✓		✓														
	monitoring																									
LEARNERS	listening	✓	✓	✓	✓	✓	✓	✓	✓	✓	✓	✓	✓													
speak	form pract.	✓																								
	comm. pract.																									
	real. comm.				✓			✓		✓		✓														
read	read –											✓														
	read+																									
	read + teach																									
	read aloud																									
write	write –	✓																								
	write semi –							✓																		
	write free																									
GROUP	class	✓	✓	✓	✓	✓	✓	✓	✓	✓	✓	✓	✓													
	individual																									
	pair/group																									
Time (mins. in decimals)		0	0	0	0	0	0	1	0	0	0	0	0													
		5	1	0	1	1	0	2	0	6	1	5	1													
		7	4	6	8	1	8	7	7	7	5	5	6													
		8	2	8	7	5	3	7	2	0	0	2	5													
	Segment	1	2	3	4	5	6	7	8	9	10	11	12	13	14	15	16	17	18	19	20	21	22	23	24	25

ETHOS: Communicative ✓ Traditional/Communicative ___ Traditional ___

Fig. 1: Rees observation template

Subcategories:

management/ routine: Almost exclusively conducted by the teacher, and concerned with moving the class forward by organising the learners/ materials/environment in readiness for, or to sustain, the learning task.

study/ introduce: A teacher-conducted setting-the-scene prelude to an immediately following segment.

study/ substance: Discourse not overtly concerned with the learning and its management but containing a substantial non-pedagogical element, and hence a lack of formal linguistic constraint.

Experiential: A subcategory of the TOPIC focus which captures some selected areas of content at 'subsegmental' level which serve to allow the learners a degree of personal or familiar involvement in the discourse, e.g. teacher or learners talk about selves, there is reference to the immediate or local environment, or to general knowledge. As the purpose here is to record whether these features arise at all, their presence is noted but once in each segment no matter how many times they occur (one-zero time sampling).

TEACHER: Records the degree and nature of teacher intervention in the lesson.

Subcategories:

lecture: Teacher monologue, largely uninterrupted by any meaningful overt interaction with the learners.

lecture/ interaction: The teacher is imparting information, interspersed with contrived or spontaneously generated teacher/learner verbal exchanges, most commonly through the solicit/response mechanism.

conducting: The teacher actively officiates and leads a sustained episode of learner rehearsal/manipulation to ensure practice/mastery of the material taught. The predominant sequence will be solicit/response/reaction, and the teacher's contribution typically oral.

monitoring/ helping: Embraces periods when the learners are being super vised as they privately tackle an assigned task without their attention being constantly focused on the teacher.

LEARNERS: The only major dimension on which subcategories may co-occur.

Listening: Attending to any auditory language source. This category can only record when aural output is available to be listened to by most of the learners, and not if anyone is *actually* paying attention.

Speaking: Embraces periods where the learners are performing individually, rather than at the same time. Essentially focused on the current professional concern with communicativeness.

Subcategories:

practice of form:	Speaking where the focus is overtly pedagogical, and concentrated on language form rather than function.
practice of communication:	Pre-communicative oral practice, where there is some shift of communication focus from form towards meaning.
realistic communication:	Learner speech exemplifying natural language use or closely approaching it, within the pedagogical constraints imposed by the classroom (not, incidentally, a necessary consequence of *authenticity* of topic).

Reading: Attending to any written language or other graphic code, including printed text, blackboard writing and the pupils' own manuscript. Only recorded if most learners are engaged in it in corporate fashion. Reading, like speech, is recorded on an accuracy/fluency spectrum.

Subcategories:

reading -	All restricted silent reading from words to individual sentences.
reading +	Silent reading beyond sentence level, where reading fluency skills are being exercised with connected text for information/ content, as when tackling a reading comprehension passage. It is not designed to record a teaching context where substantial periods of uninterrupted silent reading prevails.
reading + teacher:	The learners follow a text silently as the teacher reads aloud from it.
reading aloud:	Normally, a reading-round-the class type activity where one reader reads at a time, with the rest of the class in listening mode. A 'Ch(orus)' code may be used to indicate choral reading aloud.

Writing: Purposeful imitative or creative graphic text, not casual note-taking. This item again focuses on communicative concerns.

Subcategories:

write-	Minimal, constrained, imitative, non-creative writing.
write semi-	Semi-constrained writing at sentence level or above without slavish adherence to a pre-specified model e.g. writing answers to a reading comprehension passage.
write free	Writing beyond the sentence level with little or no imposed syntactical demands.

GROUPING	Records seating arrangements and learner groupings.
Subcategories:	
class:	The class is functioning as a single unit controlled by the teacher or teacher-substitute.
individual:	Teacher independent. Pupils are set to work alone as individuals, without sanctioned co-operation, and the task set is identical for all. Typically an episode where all the learners are assigned the same exercise which they complete individually at their desks within a set time limit.
pair/group:	Teacher independent. The interaction takes place between pairs or groups of learners, with no ongoing input from a central public source such as the teacher. All pairs/groups have been allocated the same task.
Time:	Each segment is timed to the nearest second (minimum length: 30 seconds), written vertically down the column. Seconds are converted to decimals to facilitate statistical analysis.
Segment:	The number of each segment appears at the top and bottom of the coding grid for ease of reference.
ETHOS	This footnote stands outside the ROT system proper, and represents merely a global, impressionistic assessment of the 'communicativeness' of each complete lesson on a broad tripartite scale ranging from Communicative to Traditional.

Segment Nº 9 in detail

As further illustration, segment Nº 9 on the checklist is delineated below:

Counter:	Commenced at tape-recorder counter setting 694 (and ended at 832).
Ragbag:	Some vocabulary (Vc) explanation occurred in the course of this segment.
Language:	Conducted entirely in English (E).
Topic:	Concerned with the main study part of the lesson.
Experiential:	Personal reference made to the teacher, and also to the local environment, at least once in each case.
Teacher:	The teacher was overtly conducting the proceedings.
Learners:	The learners were listening, and engaged in realistic oral communication.
Group:	The class was functioning as a single unit (not in pairs/groups).
Time:	This particular segment of the lesson lasted 6.7 minutes (just under 6 3/4 minutes).

Remarks

1 It has already been emphasised that space-restrictions tend to hamper a workable description of any published scheme for classroom observation. This paper is no exception. However, a supplementary two-page account appears in Rees (1988) and a two-volume comprehensive study of its development in Rees (1989).

2 The instrument was not designed to record, for example, a self-access session where learners spend a prolonged period in silent reading of texts of their choosing; nor would it capture learners working on different tasks in pairs. This is because these possibilities did not feature in pilot observations and were therefore correctly assumed not to be widespread among the research population. All researchers are obliged to select by donning blinkers of one kind or another.

The problem of topic

To provide additional clarification of the model, a flow-chart (Fig. 2) is included, indicating the kind of decisions required when classifying a particular episode, in this case on the Topic dimension.

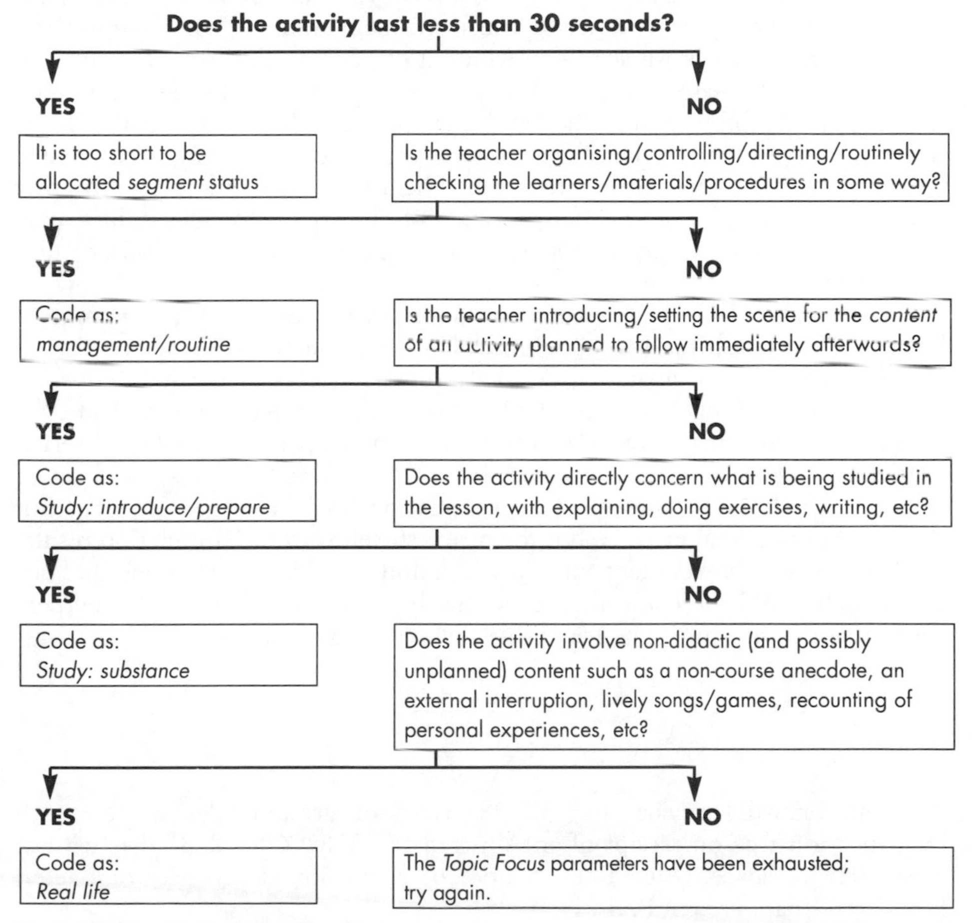

Fig. 2: Flow-chart for Topic Focus identification

That common sense, whatever it may be, cannot always come to our rescue, even when dealing with a naturalistic unit, is evidenced by discourse topic which is, surprisingly perhaps, very difficult to characterise for research purposes. Other researchers have experienced this. For example, Gardner (1984:112-13) summarises the topic predicament as follows:

> *With regard to discourse topic, there have been a number of attempts at defining topic, none of them entirely satisfactory … Some of these definitions appeal to logical systems, but in the final analysis one is forced to identify topic intuitively … Van Dijk (1977:132) says on this point: "terms like 'topic', 'theme' or 'being about' are intuitively applied to longer stretches of discourse and conversations".*

This explains why the subcategorisation of the topic dimension in the ROT system may seem somewhat gross at first sight; but it is at least workable!

CONCLUDING REMARKS

Criteria guiding the construction of ROT included relative ease and unobtrusiveness of use, a limited number of categories, replicability and, as we have seen, a conceptualisation of classroom events in a form familiar to teachers. The remit of this paper has been to describe the instrument, rather than to report the results of the broad-brush survey in which it played a central role. However, it should be mentioned that it served its purpose well, and performed very satisfactorily in reliability trials. The 'study: introduce' subcategory on the Topic dimension highlighted a particularly interesting feature of classroom discourse which is not often singled out in research. The use of ROT seems to confirm that its basic concepts do identify a stable unit of classroom discourse which may serve as the basis of a high-inference, multiple-category, systematic observation instrument.

The teacher, trainer or researcher who decides to overhaul the instrument in the dry-dock of his or her study in readiness for a personal voyage of discovery, is more likely to encounter, not new lands, but leaks that require constant caulking when relaunching it on the turbulent seas of the classroom. And even when such a voyage is under way, the farther one journeys in teacher observation, the more one realises how far there is yet to go. Perhaps the facet of research which contributes most to personal professional development is not the chimera of a final product, but the process itself with the stimulation resulting from personal investment, and the revelation of hidden shoals along the way. For some it will lead to a healthy cynicism, but few will not marvel at the perception, ingenuity and diligence of those who have gone before.

Note

The author will provide the full 28 pages of ground-rules for category identification free on receipt of an Amstrad PCW 8256/8512, 3" disc with at least 102k of space. (Alun Rees, School of Education, University of Exeter, Heavitree Road, Exeter, EX1 2LU)

How we teach and why: the implementation of an action research model for in-service training

Lily Belleli

Oranim University

◆

This study investigates the extent to which teachers' reflection on their teaching affects their perception of what happens in their classrooms. The research was based on the deployment of an Action Research model of counselling with a group of seven in-service teachers, once a week, for a period of six months. The effects of the reflection-contact period were investigated through the use of a Curriculum Perception Instrument based on Kelly's Personal Construct Theory. The instrument identifies the constructs underlying teachers' practice before and after the contact period. A semi-structured interview was also applied as a measure for changes in teaching behaviour. Findings reveal interesting differences in teachers' perceptions of their teaching and of curriculum materials before and after the contact period.

Theoretical background

The main objective of the in-service project was to help teachers understand and identify their approaches to teaching and teaching materials. The project also aimed at developing teachers' ability to revise and adapt curriculum materials to the needs of diverse student populations as they shared experiences with other colleagues in team work (Ebbutt & Elliot, 1985).

The underlying assumption was that instructional improvement is brought about through getting teachers to reflect on their own teaching (Easen, 1985; Fullan, 1982). Within this context, reflection comprised two levels:

> Analysis of Understanding: a teacher's capacity to identify and become aware of the implicit theories guiding his/her practice is a matter of analysis. Bringing to a conscious level the structures operative in one's teaching is a way of discovering one's implicit theories. Implicit theories can also be revealed by investigating the criteria by which teachers select, adopt and interpret curriculum materials available to them. These criteria reveal the constructs or theories inherent in teachers' practices, which in turn determine their professional activities in the planning and implementation of lessons (Brumfit and Rossner, 1982).

Monitoring of performance: performance monitoring entails the revision and reformulation of assumptions in the light of practice, as well as the adjustment and development of curriculum materials as a result of these reformulations.

KELLY'S THEORY OF PERSONAL CONSTRUCTS

The main instrument developed for evaluation in the project, the Curriculum Perception Instrument, has its theoretical underpinning in Personal Construct Theory (Kelly, 1955, Myers, this volume, and see Editors' Note at end of this paper). According to Kelly, people strive to make sense of new experiences by developing a set of personal constructs.

Constructs cluster in a system that represents an individual's knowledge and view of the world. The system's boundaries are defined as a result of one's interaction with the environment. Consequently, no two systems are the same, although they may be similar when people inhabit similar internal, as well as external, worlds (Bannister, 1970). This conceptual framework provides a tool for investigating the unique processes of development of individual teachers and groups of teachers.

Teachers spend much of their time interpreting and transforming materials into lesson plans. This would mean, in Kelly's terms, using personal constructs in order to make sense of their teaching environment. Since constructs differ from individual to individual, every teacher will make predictions and construe activities from curriculum materials in his/her unique manner.

THE RESEARCH

I conducted regular counselling sessions (once a week for two hours, over a period of six months) with a team of seven in-service teachers, from four different schools in a deprived neighbourhood in the Sharon area in Israel.

The team systematically engaged in analysing practice by reporting on their work to one another and by evaluating and developing curriculum materials. As a tutor, my role was to facilitate the interaction among the members of the team and help them clarify their own thinking. The point of departure was the problems of teachers as defined by the teachers themselves. Thus, counselling sessions were devoted to discovering the pertinent practical personal knowledge that the teachers possessed to help solve pedagogical problems. This knowledge was applied by the team to working out methods and preparing materials suitable to the special needs of their classes.

The theoretical framework for the design of the project followed an 'action-research' cycle based in the model of action-research described by Kemmis and McTaggart (1982). In practice, the cycle of activities included:

1 identifying the main idea or statement of the situation one wishes to change or improve;
2 deciding on a form of action — describing the facts of the situation and the context in which the action takes place;
3 constructing a general plan of the actions to be undertaken;

4 monitoring the process of implementation and its effects on action;
5 observing the effects of action; and
6 revising the general plan through reflection on the effects of action as a basis for future planning and subsequent action.

The study was designed to assess changes in the teachers' behaviour and in their conceptualisations of teaching while they were taking part in the sessions as well as after they had completed the training.

I will describe changes in the relationships among the members of the group and in teaching behaviours that could be observed during the sessions. In addition, I will report on significant changes in how teachers construed curriculum materials after the six-month period. In this connection I attempted to answer the following questions:

1 How did teachers' constructs develop in the course of the contact period?
2 Could any prevalent constructs, common to all teachers, be identified after a six-month contact period?
3 To what extent did changes in teachers' constructs reveal patterns of teaching behaviour?

PROCEDURES

The first session was devoted to open discussion of various pedagogical issues in order to release tension and create a non-threatening atmosphere in which teachers would experience the benefits of sharing experiences with each other. My role as a co-ordinator at this point was to provide the team with a basic framework within which they would organise their thoughts, share insights and consequently arrive at a definition of the problem they wished to explore and try to solve.

During the six month contact period the group completed four cycles, each with a planning, action, observation and reflection phase. Some of the problems that were analysed through the four cycles were:

1 weak learners in mixed ability groups (the need for a more structured rationale and methodology);
2 discrepancies between stated aims and classroom experience (teachers reported on different tasks they had devised that seemed suitable in terms of content, gradation and clarity, yet the results in class were not satisfactory);
3 teaching or testing (by investigating different questions that teachers had posed during their lessons, the balance between teaching and testing activities was discussed).

The most interesting feature that characterised the four cycles completed by the group was the way in which plans changed and developed in the light of observation and reflection. In relation to materials development, there was a drastic shift from devising specific tasks for specific levels to devising frameworks suitable for weaker or stronger learners in general. In terms of group work, there was a change in the perception of collaborative team work, from a view of team work as a product facilitator (i.e. in order to produce materials) to a view of collaborative team work as a process facilitator (i.e. in order to help reflect on and analyse practice).

Throughout the six-month period, teachers engaged in continuous, concrete and precise talk about teaching practice. Thus, they built up a register of professional language which they could share during the workshops. They planned, designed, and evaluated teaching materials together. Workshops were characterised by a climate of interaction, collegiality and exchange of ideas. Teachers experienced a sense of meaningfulness and practicality relatively early in the process, because they tried the materials in their classrooms and reported their findings, impressions and insights to the group.

They were constantly encouraged to analyse discrepancies between stated aim and classroom experience as a basis for the further development of curriculum materials. It is important to point out that the adaptation and development of material for their own schools constituted the basis for experiencing the meaning and practicality of the project among team members. Furthermore, it generated the need for collective 'reflection on practice'.

FACTORS AFFECTING IMPLEMENTATION

Fullan (1982) identifies major factors influencing the implementation of any kind of educational change, several of which are of salient importance to the implementation of the project reported on here. We must view proposed changes in terms of: need, relevance, clarity, complexity, quality and practicality. Our project focused on the identification of special pedagogical problems perceived as 'priority needs' by the team. The relevance of change to a solution was thoroughly discussed during the 'reflection' and 'developing action' phases and much time was devoted to clarifying the problem(s) and identifying 'goals and means'. The project was implemented in an incremental manner and teachers were not expected from the beginning to interact in a collaborative manner. Gradually, as a result of recognising the benefits of team work, collaboration developed. Materials development was used as a starting point and as a springboard to reflection on practice. Materials prepared by the team were relevant to their teaching at that particular time and workshops enabled participants to spend time on preparation. This collaboration was a major feature of the project.

Three factors, according to Fullan, relate to the social conditions: the history of innovative attempts in the district, the adoption process, staff development and participation. Participating teachers had had no previous experience with implementation attempts and some of them were sceptical at the beginning about the purposes of the project and the potential for implementing change. The project was taken very seriously by principals and teachers and there was full collaboration. However, participation in decisions during the implementation and 'planning ahead' phase was solely a team process; other members of the school staff were not involved in decision-making of any kind.

One of the members of the team, a veteran teacher, was responsible for providing constant support to two members of the team who were inexperienced. This was provided in the form of regular meetings during and after school sessions. The purpose of these meetings was to discuss practical classroom problems. All team members took equal part in decisions concerning project operations and modifications, regardless of the extent of their teaching experience.

A major drawback was the fact that there was almost no possibility for paired observation, due to the constraints of the schools' scheduling. Most of the teachers taught on the same days, at the same hours. It was therefore very difficult to release them on a permanent basis for paired or group observation in addition to the two hour workshop.

INSTRUMENTS

In order to monitor the project the team relied on several techniques. Observation sheets with criteria devised by the group were used as tools for observing lessons. Field notes and protocols were kept by members of the team during the workshop sessions. In addition, observations, interpretations, reactions and feelings were noted in a diary kept throughout the six-month contact period.

The main instrument used for the evaluation of the project was a curriculum item repertory grid (CIR) (Ben-Peretz and Katz, 1980). This is an extension of the 'role repertory grid' used in psychology, and is based on the methodology of triadic sorting (Bannister and Mair, 1968:54). Triadic sorting methodology (see Editors' Note on page 74) requires respondents to relate to random triads from a set of items, and to decide for each triad, which of the three items differs from the other two, according to a self-generated criterion. By establishing the criteria for comparing and contrasting items, the subject is expressing a personal interpretation of the materials in question as a dichotomous construct.

The instrument (CIR) consisted of a set of fifteen curriculum items, selected from a set of available EFL materials. Items judged to represent diversity of form and content were included. The items included paragraphs, illustrations, unit headings and exercise types extracted from units of a textbook.

Every participant received a copy of the fifteen items numbered from one to fifteen and a grid form to be completed during the investigation. Teachers were asked to take random triads and establish a self-generated criterion by which one of the items differed from the other two. The criterion and the number of the item which 'differed' were then indicated on the grid form. The procedure was repeated ten times with the same fifteen items. When respondents were asked to take random triads, it was possible for the same item to be reviewed more than once; nevertheless, every time the item reappeared, it would be in a different environment/context. Hence, it would generate new possibilities for establishing constructs. The constructs generated by participants were then classified by investigators. The investigator and two teachers who were not taking part in the procedure classified the constructs generated under superordinate categories. Inter-rater reliability here was above 70%.

THE SEMI-STRUCTURED INTERVIEW

To evaluate the long-range effects of the contact-period upon teachers' constructs, a semi-structured interview was carried out four months after the end of the contact period. It was agreed by investigators that teachers' attitudes in regard to collaborative team work and the particular framework developed for the project would be explored in as informal a manner as possible. Instead of asking predetermined questions, we opted for free discussion. Points for discussion were extracted from the CIR findings. The interview was tried out with two typical respondents, commented on, and revised in the light of such comments.

Seven participants were interviewed on an individual basis. Each interview lasted for about three quarters of an hour. The interview was carried out by a trained teacher colleague who had not met the participants before. She met the teachers in their own schools. The interviewer aimed at creating a balance between friendliness and objectivity. At no point was there any attempt to guide the participants or to bias the direction of their responses. On the contrary, the interviewer repeatedly questioned the relevance and validity of the project. The transcribed interviews were double-checked by two readers and areas of disagreement were analysed and discussed.

FINDINGS — REPERTORY GRID

Examination of the criteria and their distribution among the superordinate categories disclosed interesting predominant constructs in relation to curriculum materials among all seven respondents.

At the beginning of the project the category of highest frequency was: text, task-type, content and format of materials. The category of next highest frequency was: pupils' tasks specified by materials. The category of lowest frequency was: the methodology advocated by materials.

At that point, teachers were concerned mostly with the 'form' and 'content' of materials used for teaching in terms of language, exercise-type, topics, grammatical points and skills. Little emphasis was given to differences in the way in which 'items' could be presented or practised in the classroom (i.e. methodology implied by materials).

In the category, 'pupils' tasks specified by materials', teachers were mainly concerned with the type of task the pupil is required to perform rather than with the extent to which the task takes the learner's needs/lacks or desires into consideration. Here, again the emphasis was on the 'requirement' of the task, in terms of 'content' rather than on the learner's capacity to perform a particular task.

Participants' personal construct systems indicated a high degree of similarity in their relation to curriculum materials. The predominant categories occurring in all seven grids emphasised the 'What?' rather than the 'How?' implicit in the items. At the end of the project, however, the two categories of highest frequency were ability level implied by the materials (71%) and methodology advocated by materials (50%) — format of materials occurred in only two grids.

FINDINGS — INTERVIEW

Most of the constructs disclosed by the CIR were also elicited in the interview. They were evident in teachers' accounts of the different activities they had tried in their classrooms. Teachers referred to the aims they had set as well as the procedures used. Moreover, constructs relating to 'methodology' and 'students' knowledge' which were not manifested in a number of grids were elicited in the interview.

It was not possible to identify patterns of teacher behaviour in terms of teacher/pupil interaction. However, most of the participants expressed concern for the degree of student involvement (and the implication for classroom organisation) as advocated by the activity they were describing.

In the interviews, teachers also described classroom practices. Those cited included:

1 eliciting information from students (through brainstorming for example) as a way of introducing material or as a follow-up activity;
2 introducing new language material through known concepts;
3 adapting activities involving the production of language to activities involving the recognition of language in weak classes;
4 using tasks that require non-linguistic response in weak classes;
5 grading tasks and the amount of teachers' input/students' output according to the level of the class;
6 integrating the four language skills through a common topic and different types of classroom management for different types of activities (pair and group work used for information gap activities).

Most of the interviewees showed concern for students in terms of the world knowledge they bring to the English lesson. The interview revealed how a number of teachers used this concept of 'student world knowledge' in the planning and implementation of their lessons.

Generally positive attitudes to the project's framework were disclosed by the interview. Teachers raised a number of points in relation to the project. They felt that a useful amount of time was spent on defining the problem, developing action, monitoring, and revising the plan. They also felt that feedback sessions after monitoring the materials in the classroom were productive. Feedback sessions provided the teachers with the opportunity of seeing how the same topic could be realised through different teaching styles. Teachers mentioned that there was a constant pooling of ideas and the workshops provided the teachers with a forum for discussing day-to-day problems.

They felt that the interaction among them was productive and that decisions made in the workshops were their responsibility. Contact with teachers from different schools was felt to be an encouraging experience. Interviewees were, however, quite honest in pointing out the weaknesses they were aware of. They recognised that personal biases caused certain innovations to fail at the level of procedure. Moreover, they felt that there was a need for a tutor to guide the group. However, they all stressed that the tutor should be an outsider and not a member of the group.

CONCLUSIONS

From analysis of the findings it was possible to draw several conclusions:

1 Teachers learned adaptability by recognising the possibilities of developing different teaching strategies for the same activity item. The criteria they developed did not specify exactly how to go about an activity, but rather

revealed a general awareness of the existence of different teaching strategies applicable to a single item.

2 A major common concern amongst the seven participants after the contact period was the extent to which an activity demanded the use of recognition or production skills among students. Here again, constructs revealed teachers' awareness of the possibilities of modifying an 'activity' so as to cater to different ability levels.
3 Criteria related to 'content of materials' put little emphasis on the skills, vocabulary, or grammatical points inherent to an item. Rather, teachers' criteria stressed the students' world knowledge and production/recognition skills implicit in the content.
4 An interesting discovery was the finding that constructs suggested by all seven participants were predominantly complex and it was possible to extract many 'categories' from a single criterion. Teachers tried to interrelate form, content, teaching strategies and cognitive demands in one criterion.

In comparing the findings at the end of the project with those obtained at the beginning, we found that teachers came to show more concern for the ability level implied by a specific task. Criteria that considered the difficulty of the item (in relation to a student's age and/or the complexity of material) were seen from a different perspective. The emphasis was on the 'ability level' of the activity and on whether the task involved the recognition or production of language. There was less emphasis on the categories of 'content of materials' and 'text type'.

In their concern with the demands of pupils' tasks, teachers emphasised not the task's content/or format, but rather the field of knowledge incorporated as well as the ability level it subsumed.

Teachers' overall focus was on the teacher and his/her ability to manipulate different teaching strategies. Wherever a concern for the student was manifested, it was usually through constructs which related to the interaction between 'student's ability level' and 'teaching strategy'.

It is possible to evaluate the effectiveness of the action-research model in terms of the definition of ineffective in-service training as provided by Hopkins (1986). He claimed that most current in-service work is ineffective because it is frequently based on single shot workshops involving large or undifferentiated groups of teachers, providing limited time for teachers to learn, and enabling little evaluation or practical follow-up support. Furthermore it is not usually linked to a particular classroom or school problem (1986:268). In evaluating the project described here according to these points, it is possible to say that:

- workshops were held on a regular basis;
- teachers participated as planners, decision-makers, and evaluators of in-service activities relevant to their immediate practice;
- teachers had the opportunity to apply and assess specific techniques in their classroom;
- teachers interacted, shared ideas, and provided assistance to each other during and after the workshops.

In Hopkins' account of the problems to be resolved in school-focused in-service, he mentions the danger of *'becoming unnecessarily limited to immediate problems and attached only to the teaching role'* (1986:56). He therefore urges institutions adopting INSET (in-service training) models to focus on a *'balanced approach'*, i.e., a balance of action and reflection, which provides teachers with the opportunity to *'conceptualise more complex approaches to teaching'* as well as *'to observe specific practices and practice specific techniques'* (1986:54).

This balance of 'action and reflection' was a major factor taken into consideration in the design and implementation of our project. The cyclical nature of the model provided teachers with the opportunity to reflect 'in' and 'on' action. Nevertheless, since the programme concentrated on identifying and solving specific immediate problems as defined by the group, 'reflection in action' occurred mainly on the level of analysis of specific practices rather than on the level of conceptualising broader aspects of teaching/learning.

Despite the fact that the project could be defined as 'effective' in Hopkins' terms, it would seem appropriate to evaluate its 'degree of effectiveness' as far as the project's overall objectives were concerned. The programme was effective in terms of the extent to which it increased self-confidence, reduced anxiety and developed an awareness of individual differences and a tolerance of others. Teachers also developed an ability to transfer concepts, principles and skills from one medium to another and to bring intuitive practice to a conscious level.

However, the programme was far less effective in fostering an awareness of processes and perceptions of how learners at various levels of development respond. Although the CIR and interview findings point to an increase in teachers' concerns with the 'ability level implied by the task' and 'methodology implied by materials', the increase was manifested only on the level of skills and application. The shift from intuitive action to conscious action was not apparent on the level of understanding students' learning strategies. This might have been achieved through the adoption of a different focus. A framework that would focus on systematic individual student observation could provide insights into students' construct systems and their patterns and behaviour. We did not account for this dimension in a fully systematic manner mainly because teachers could not engage in paired or group observation beyond the two-hour workshop.

Personal constructs and the in-service framework

The impact of the framework upon teachers' constructs can also be evaluated by comparing the way in which the four cycles of action research developed and the way in which teacher construct systems developed. Collaborative work, mutual reinforcement and support had strong implications beyond the surface level of experiencing a new model of interaction.

Positive attitudes and predispositions are crucial for the development of cognitive skills (Stern, 1983). Hence, teachers' ability to apprehend their teaching and curriculum materials in a more divergent and complex manner (as reflected through their personal constructs) bore a direct relationship to the particular framework of collaborative team work developed. By sharing insights, learning about others' behaviour and supporting one another, teachers' motivation and self-confidence were enhanced. This led to the development of a greater capacity for diversification of their approaches to teaching.

If constructs are dynamic and influenced by past and present experience (Kelly, 1955), then it is anticipated that teachers' future practice will, as a result of reflection, be more thoughtful and therefore appropriate and productive. In the four cycles of action research the teachers' constructs were characterised by a shift from 'What?' (i.e. what was done in the classroom) to an emphasis on 'How?' and 'Why?' (i.e. the rationale behind action). In much the same manner, constructs developed from a focus on the content and format of the item (i.e. What?) to the methodology implied by the task (i.e. How?).

Thus, in terms of the project's overall outcome, the development of teachers' interpretative abilities was more important than the development of materials.

From this study, I conclude that it is possible to draw on personal construct theory not only as a diagnostic tool but also as an integral component of teacher education programmes. A methodology based on personal constructs would encourage teachers to analyse their patterns of construing in relation to different curriculum materials during the course of the programme (and not only at its termination). This process might further sensitise them to learners' perceptions of curriculum material and to perceptions of how these are similar/different to their own perceptions.

EDITORS' NOTE ON PERSONAL CONTRUCT THEORY

Each individual can be seen as perceiving the world in terms of important elements and relations among those elements. This individual set of 'personal constructs' is the basis on which we each build our lives.

'Triadic sorting' is an investigative technique for exploring such constructs. We can best explain it in terms of doing it. Choose a topic. Let it be discipline problems. On separate pieces of paper, write down several important issues within this topic. Some of them might be: SOCIAL BACKGROUND, DRUG ABUSE, MOTIVATION, STUDENT-STUDENT RELATIONS, OUTDATED SCHOOL POLICIES, INSENSITIVE TEACHING. Some of these items might never have occurred to you, but that is part of the point: different issues will be important to different individuals at different times.

Turn your pieces of paper face down and select three at random. Let us take SOCIAL BACKGROUND, STUDENT-STUDENT RELATIONS and INSENSITIVE TEACHING as examples. Divide these three into a pair, which have something in common, and the odd one. Now say what the pair have in common, and/or what makes the third one different from the other two. These two descriptions of similarity and difference make up two poles of a 'construct'.

To continue our example above, one person might say that SOCIAL BACKGROUND and INSENSITIVE TEACHING belong together because these are external influences on the group, while STUDENT-STUDENT RELATIONS are internal to the group. So, this construct has the two poles of EXTERNAL TO GROUP and INTERNAL TO GROUP. Your construct may well be different.

Having established this construct, we can now go back to the other elements we listed and place them along the continuum between the two poles.

What about drug abuse? Is that more like the first pole or the second? As well as placing our other elements on a scale between the poles of this construct, we can select another three items at random and make explicit another of our constructs. Once again, we can place the other elements somewhere between the poles of this construct.

As we continue in this fashion, we build up an intermeshing grid of our personal constructs. This is the 'repertory grid', or 'repgrid'. These techniques are extremely powerful in helping a person become more aware of thoughts and feelings about issues under investigation. In the hands of a sensitive investigator, the accompanying talk and clarification can be even more illuminating.

Implementing CALL in advanced EFL-vocabulary learning

Urbaan Vanermen

ILT-Language Centre, Leuven University

◆

While students were working with a Comprehension-Training Package (CTP) programme in small groups it was noticed that most of them preferred the same lexical exercises. Some action research was done on the hows and whys. It became clear that gap-exercises should be presented to the learners in different ways depending on whether they are intended to be test exercises or vocabulary-acquisition exercises.

CTP AND EFL VOCABULARY LEARNING

During the past three academic years (1989-92) about 850 undergraduates from the Faculty of Social Sciences of Leuven University (Belgium) worked on the first version of the in-house experimental CALL programme CTP, which stands for Comprehension-Training Package for Dutch-speaking Learners of English (Vanermen, 1991). CTP is intended for adolescent and adult ESL/EFL learners with a history of a minimum input of 300 hours (or 1500 headwords) and some idea of reading strategies.

In April 1989 (Vanermen, 1991) and in May 1992 the students expressed their appreciation of CTP through anonymous questionnaires. About twenty percent of the CTP users, i.e. 165 students, volunteered to answer the questionnaires. The findings resulting from that inquiry were presented at the Third International NELLE Conference in Prague, 28-30 August 1992. We know for sure now that CTP users prefer the more cognitive, more demanding and more contextualised lexical exercises which hinge on databases.

Most of those exercises are lexico-graded in the sense that their level of difficulty is set by the initial lexicological analysis of the ad hoc text by means of the LET Vocabulary-list (Engels et al., 1981). All lexical exercises are contextual exercises in the sense that they refer semantically to the text in question or that they are generated by linking appropriate databases to the vocabulary/topical items of the text. The main CTP databases at present are:

1 false friends/pitfalls in context;
2 odd-one-out lexical strings;
3 inseparable and invariable collocations/'collocmatics' (inappropriate collocations generated by language learners because of L1 interference or transfer; Vanermen, 1985);

4 guided translation sentences on the use of separable and variable collocations/collocmatics or lexical phrases.

The two main reasons why the bulk of CTP users like to do the contextualised lexical exercises are: a) it is an interesting way of learning relevant new vocabulary; b) contextual alternatives are supplied in the exercise on separables and variables in guided translation sentences.

VOCABULARY ACQUISITION AND RETENTION WITHIN GAP-FILLING EXERCISES

Through observation, the impression was gained that when practising new vocabulary via the lexico-graded gap-filling exercise, the students either remembered the word right away from the previously read text or after receiving a few letters as a hint, or they could not recall the word at all. Is this really the case? Regarding the retention of the newly learnt vocabulary, a related question was posed by the teachers: 'Which words are best retained and why?'

On top of this, it became apparent that students working in groups of two or three around the computer mastered the exercises more efficiently and with better results than those working alone. Can this be the case?

In seeking answers to these questions, a decision was taken to conduct some research in co-operation with my colleague Caroline Greenman during January and February of 1991.

The experiment

The participants were 168 first year Social Science students with a history of an average input of four years of EFL spread over two hours per week. During their first university term, about two months prior to this research, they received an introduction to reading strategies as described, for example, by Grellet (1981).

The students were divided into three groups (A, B and C) of about 30 people who worked individually on the test described below, and 25 mini-groups (1-25) of about three students who performed the same task in groups.

An editorial of about 1400 words was taken from the British journal *The Economist* ('When cities smile again' 16 January 1988). The chosen text deals with the general subject of reviving inner cities which fits into the sphere of reference for students of Social Science.

The lexical complexity of the article is slightly above the level of the students in question, but didactically within the quantitative outsiders' criteria of the LET Vocabulary-list, with 44 'outsiders' in 495 different word-forms (=9%). The LET list names the 2000 most frequent headwords (their morphological clusters and their semantically-related derivatives) of contemporary English that should be known at the end of EFL secondary education in Belgium/Western Europe. The headwords with a lower frequency than the rankword 2000 are called 'outsiders'.

Sixteen of those outsiders were the object of study in the test, as well as four other words, two of which belonged respectively to levels two and three of the four ranges of five hundred items of the LET list. All twenty items were spread over the text. According to a clustered frequency classification of the

COBUILD-corpus vocabulary (1987) these word-forms occur in contemporary English less than 1/10,000, i.e. less than 2000 times in 20 million words. Ten of the selected word-forms occur in principal or key sentences and the remaining ten in sentences adding no significant information to the text, all of them evenly spread over the editorial. Each group of ten studied word-forms contained five items of very low frequency, i.e. occurring less than 100 times in 20 million words.

Each student received a photocopy of the original text from *The Economist* with an explanation and/or translation of all the 'outsiders' in the text. They were given fourteen minutes, i.e. one minute per 100 words, in order to read and understand the text. To arrive at a well-balanced reading of the text they were told after five and ten minutes that they should by then have covered respectively 500 and 1000 words of the editorial. In no case were the test sample told that a vocabulary test would follow.

After this reading session the test-subjects had to put aside the photocopied text and the lexical support sheets, and an explanation of the following task was given:

- Another photocopy of the original text was given in which the omitted words were indicated by a number with a blank (for group A) and a broken line, with one dash per omitted letter, for groups B and C and mini-groups 1-25. Those working in mini-groups received one answer sheet per group.
- One minute was allocated for recalling and filling in each word. After 15, 30 and 45 seconds respectively, the first, second and third letter of the word in question was written on the blackboard. Giving a fourth letter or more proved pointless as about 20% of the most frequently used English words and of the target words only comprise four letters (or fewer).

(Naturally, the test sample were all asked to indicate whether they had recalled the word in less than fifteen seconds or with the help of one, two or three hints.)

Percentage of hints used in the incidence of correctly filled in words in the reconstruction exercise

Number of hints	0	1	2	3
Among individual workers	31%	16%	18%	35%
Among mini-group workers	42%	17%	16%	25%

The advantage of common effort is apparent in recalling the words in question without any hints. Perhaps only a detail, but nevertheless worthy of comment, is the fact that group A, who were required to fill the missing word in a blank space, scored lower than the other two groups (B and C) of individual workers and also lower than 23 of the 25 mini-groups.

A month later, representative groups (group B and ten of the 25 mini-groups, because they were closest to the average band in the reconstruction exercise) were tested on vocabulary retention. These two groups consisted of 32 and 29 students respectively, all of them working individually this time. The twenty omitted words from the reconstruction exercise were omitted in twenty new ad hoc sentences in which the word was used with the same meaning as in the first text (i.e. *The Economist* editorial). The words that were to be filled in had been replaced by a dotted line, with one dot per omitted letter.

The help provided to half of the above-mentioned retention test groups was the definitions (in English) to which the students had had access in the first reading of the editorial a month before. However, the collocations and idioms in which some of the twenty word-forms in question had been embedded were left out. The other half was provided with the definitions as well as the translations (in their mother tongue, i.e. Dutch) of the word-forms. This time the test sample were given twenty minutes to fill in the omitted words. After 10 minutes they were reminded that half of the total time had elapsed.

Results of the Reconstruction Exercise and the Retention Test

Words *(following order of appearance in text)*	COBUILD cluster frequency *(out of 20 million)*	Former individual workers	Former mini-group workers
1 destitution	44	22% - 9%	44% - 0
2 crumbling	186	22% - 6%	52% - 0
3 jowl	20	38% - 78%	60% - 45%
4 dollops	6	13% - 6%	28% - 0
5 flight**	1335	80% - 68%	88% - 59%
6 rout	28	19% - 0	52% - 0
7 decaying	308	13% - 9%	36% - 0
8 civic**	115	44% - 59%	76% - 27%
9 instil	23	7% - 0	4% - 0
10 dereliction	64	35% - 0	44% - 0
11 sites***	1371	54% - 3%	88% - 14%
12 allocate	207	22% - 0	68% - 0
13 devolving	40	6% - 0	12% - 0
14 woolly	58	32% - 18%	36% - 6%
15 wean	116	15% - 0	20% - 0
16 foster	568	73% - 53%	96% - 14%
17 corporate***	221	17% - 6%	32% - 3%
18 upgrade	13	24% - 0	56% - 3%
19 altruism	53	70% - 41%	100% - 21%
20 shrewd	187	15% - 6%	20% - 3%
General average:		31% - 18%	51% - 10%

NOTES

1 Percentages indicate how many students gave the right answers in the reconstruction exercise (% to the left) and in the retention test (% to the right).

2 The underlined words appear in the principal sentences. The words marked with an asterisk belong to range 2 (**) or 3 (***) of the LET list.

While evaluating the data we observed — to our great relief — that the retrieval percentage was very similar in all three maxi-groups (A, B and C) and in all twenty-five mini-groups for both reconstruction and retention tests. However, what immediately catches the eye is the fact that the former individual workers achieved a better result in the retention test compared to the former mini-group workers who were now working on their own.

When we asked for an explanation of the rather disappointing scores of the retention test all subjects, by way of comforting us, said that they had not yet got down to 'learning/mastering' the offered text/new vocabulary because they had been cramming for Statistics and Economics exams that were to be taken a couple of weeks after the retention test. When we tried to convince them that 'learning/mastering' a foreign language should preferably be a gradual process so as to be effective over a whole year (or a lifetime), they all agreed and endorsed the idea of administering in the future a mid-year exam/test to enable two-way continuous assessment to function.

Conclusions

Within the limited length of this article the in-depth analysis — the hows and the whys — of the research material at hand cannot be offered, but the following conclusions can be drawn from the available data.

The test sample read the selected editorial more in terms of the content than in terms of word usage. Therefore it is important that those words, collocations and collocmatics should especially be practised in the learning situation in contexts that cover as many semantic fields as possible while introducing varied principal meanings and concepts. In terms of absolute frequency we envisage using neither the high frequency words nor the very low frequency words because the latter will normally be learnt/acquired naturally in a collocational, conceptual, and preferably contextual setting. Therefore *'learning materials must be designed to illustrate how new lexical items operate within the common core vocabulary or how specialist lexis serves to define particular frames of reference'* (Wardell, 1991:35).

In that respect, it is necessary that an Extended English Teaching Vocabulary-list or Lexical Ladder (Vanermen, 1990:7) be developed. It should contain sufficient ranges — preferably 7 to 9 — of didactically selected and graded clusters so that the words and collocations with an average absolute frequency can be suitably built into level-ranged lexical exercises which can be generated by or done on computer.

With this in mind, we draw attention to the need for the development and installation of EGP/ESP databases with not only 'grammatical and lexical collocations' (Benson et al., 1986:ix) but also 'lexical phrases' (Nattinger and DeCarrico, 1989:118).

When a semantic field has been covered via texts, presentations, audio and video sources, intermediate or advanced students can be tested through gap-filling lexical exercises. Here it is sufficient to provide the first letter of the missing word of each main component of the collocation/lexical phrase that has to be filled in or just to give blanks of uniform length.

However, if the student is meant to do vocabulary acquisition exercises, we recommend the provision of either an alphabetic list of the missing words or collocations above the exercise, or the first two letters (three with word-forms containing more than six letters) of the missing word or of the collocation components, because such clues appear to be a significant aid to the short-term memory and retention process. With very long, suffixed words, the additional provision of the last letter of the headword or etymon and even the first letter of the suffix itself may offer a sensible aid to the learning process, for example: 'al . . c . . . ' for allocate, and 'des . . . . t . . . ' or 'des . . . uti . . ' for destitution.

We regard carefully selected translation aid as valuable in such cases where the students only have a (very) few hours a week in which to focus on the target language and where all the students share the same mother tongue. Providing fairly advanced learners with another one or two translations from other — preferably international — languages they may have been studying and thus drawing more widely on their etymo-morphologically-related and intellectual resources may be considered because (language) learning is a holistic activity par excellence in our 'global village'. In that respect the statement *'For the native speaker of English, the most common form of vocabulary building is guessing from context and/or word formation.'* (Kruse, 1987:312) could to some degree be extended to encompass most fairly advanced learners of international (and also classical) languages.

The answers to the 1989 and 1992 questionnaires in connection with CTP showed that 75% of students preferred working in groups of two or three to working on their own because then they 'got more out of it'.

The results of the mini-groups in the reconstruction exercise were indeed better (more correct answers and fewer hints necessary) especially with words with a low or below average frequency. It looks as if teamwork enhances the opportunity of recalling those (contextual) word-forms in the (very) short term. But the results of the retention test suggest that more of an individual effort is needed to fix newly learnt vocabulary in the brain. So the acquaintance phase can quite enjoyably take place in teams but the fixing process is likely to be a more personal matter, especially if the number of teaching periods is limited.

That is one of the reasons why — from 1991 onwards — our fairly advanced EFL students are advised to make — individually and according to their own needs and pace — their three Ps: their Personal Learning Dictionaries, their Personal (Remedial) Pronouncing Dictionaries and their Personal (Remedial) Grammars, on which we hope to report some time in the future.

What emerges as important is the associative bond between the world beyond the classroom ('factual information') and the introduction and exercising of new semantic data, as well as the use of inferencing techniques: *'This is because the attempt to infer brings the unknown word into contact with an active searching and thinking process, involving consideration of possible meaning dimensions of the word (its denotation, field of application, syntactic behavior, connotations, etc.)'* (Honeyfield, 1987:319). Or as Nation (1990:119) puts it: *'Although vocabulary knowledge plays a large part in readability studies, it is partly a reflection of other factors like background knowledge and previous reading experience.'*

Repetition and contrast remain important learning aids in the process of vocabulary acquisition. The same goes for the collocationally/idiomatically embedded presentation of new vocabulary and concepts in both sensible and relevant contexts because:

> *... the EFL student cannot begin to read with full comprehension until he has been taught to conquer the unknown word (or collocation, for that matter) by using contextual aids. By this, I mean both the formation of the word itself and the environment in which it is found.*
>
> (Kruse, 1987:313)

This is especially true at the intermediate and advanced level where the boundary between EGP and ESP has to fade away.

General conclusion

Intermediate and advanced EFL-learners can indeed benefit from CALL programmes to enhance their vocabulary acquisition. To that end the provided exercises and tasks should be sufficiently challenging and sophisticated, which will very often mean that they are lexico-graded and contextualised, and therefore linked to appropriate databases.

The relationship between classroom process analysis and interventionist strategies in foreign language teaching

Antony Peck

York University

◆

The aim of classroom process research is to make language teaching more effective. Fundamental, descriptive research makes possible precise accounts of different teachers' methods. Differences in classroom practice provide scope for experimentation. A teacher in a comprehensive school made principled changes to her usual way of conducting oral practice. The link between descriptive research and interventionist experimentation is made; changes in the teacher's method are described; and the outcomes of the experimentation are examined.

THE NEED FOR RESEARCH

It is a basic thesis of this paper that there is a need for fundamental, descriptive research in foreign language teaching and learning. For twenty years, teachers and researchers have urged that more attention should be paid to basic research in order to make foreign language teaching more effective (Allwright, 1973; Stern, 1983; Brumfit and Mitchell, 1989). It is, above all, studies of classroom teaching process which are required, in order to discover how language teachers actually teach, as opposed to how they say they teach, or how they may be advised to teach by trainers, advisers, or by National Curriculum documentation.

DIFFICULTIES IN UNDERSTANDING LANGUAGE TEACHING

Two main difficulties prevent the full understanding of language teaching from being widely disseminated. Teachers work in isolation behind closed doors, and very few people, even in the same institution, have more than a hazy idea of what goes on behind them. The knowledge which teachers themselves have about what they do, and how they teach, is largely instinctive and automatic, since in the pressure of teaching large numbers of students each day, the opportunities for detailed planning or careful reflection are very few. Nevertheless, teachers have a vast store of accumulated observations of what happens in classrooms as the result of their teaching procedures. This awareness is often '*based on implicit models of what knowledge is and how it is learnt*' (Barnes, in Russell and Munby, 1992:20).

BENEFITS OF EXPERIMENTING WITH METHODS

If knowledge about processes of language teaching can be made precise and explicit, a number of benefits can be expected to ensue. Teachers who become aware of their own techniques of teaching, as a result of research, may become sensitised to the relative effectiveness of different aspects of their own methodology. Those who become aware of how other teachers attempt to attain similar objectives and deal with similar challenges may see opportunities for varying their teaching method in an attempt to achieve greater effectiveness in their own classrooms. This involves an ability on the part of the practitioner to study how colleagues in other classrooms go about their business, and a willingness to make principled changes to their own practice, and to observe what changes, if any, occur in the performance of their students.

In other words, a potentially direct link is proposed between descriptive research and changes, one hopes improvements, in effectiveness. This may be summarised as in Fig. 1.

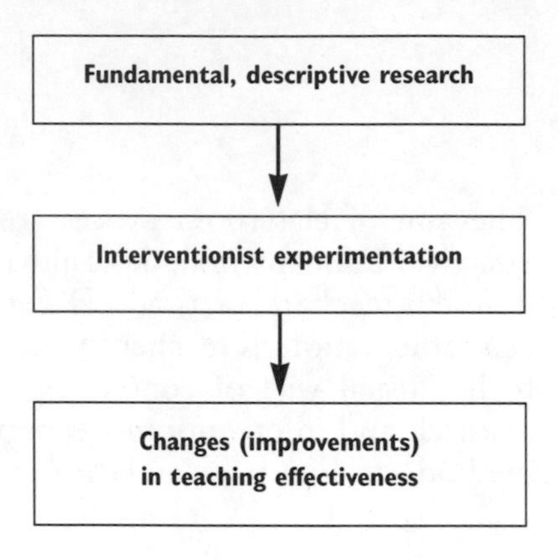

Fig. 1

CASE STUDY

Case Study is the research method chosen to provide the information on which the experiment described here was based. A case study approach to the observation of language lessons makes it possible to study the special and unique features of a teaching situation, or the method used by a given teacher, and to describe this, without prejudice, in the most explicit and vivid terms possible. A case study approach '*gathers evidence systematically in a "scientific" way … and is concerned essentially with the interaction of factors and events. Sometimes it is only by taking a practical instance that we can obtain the full picture of this interaction*' (Nisbet and Watt, 1978). The product of many observations of foreign language teaching, in the UK and abroad, was a taxonomy of the techniques used by language teachers to stimulate oral practice amongst their students by means of questioning. Each of the observations was verified with the teacher at the end of the lesson, in order to establish its validity.

The research questions

Observations of teachers conducting oral practice showed that there were many, discrete techniques available, but that no teacher, during the observed lessons, used them all. This led to the formation of the following research questions:

> Can a foreign language teacher change or add to his/her repertoire of teaching techniques? If so, will observable results ensue?

These questions are derived from proposals for experimentation in the conduct of oral practice resulting from my own earlier observations of foreign language teaching (Peck, 1988).

Background to the experiment

Mary teaches French at a Welsh-medium, bi-lingual comprehensive school. She agreed to take part in an interventionist experiment as part of her teaching of pupils aged 13-14 (see Peck et al., 1990).

The first part of the experiment consisted of an attempt to describe as precisely as possible her existing method of conducting oral practice. Since language teaching goes in cycles consisting of several lessons, it was seen to be necessary to focus on one small segment in order not to overload her with work. Accordingly, it was agreed that one lesson each week would be designated a 'research lesson'. Part of this lesson, though not necessarily all of it, would feature a substantial amount of oral practice, consisting of question-and-answer. The class was well aware that this lesson had something special about it, and it quickly became known as the 'York lesson'.

During the first half of the Autumn Term, some seven weeks, the class was taught in the normal way, except for the provisions described above. Mary kept notes about how she had conducted the oral practice during the designated lesson, but did not attempt any experimentation. It is, of course, possible, even likely, that she prepared these lessons with special care during this time, but no experiments were undertaken. Indeed, it was not until the half-term break that experimentation was discussed. The purpose of concealing until this time the subsequent progress of the research project was to throw into the highest profile any changes which she might make to her method, when she was invited to intervene in her normal process of teaching.

The old method

During the first half of the term, Mary kept track of how she used questions and answers, and prepared an inventory of her techniques. Here it is.

1 Questions categorised by type of answer required

a Mary frequently asked questions where pupils had to reply on their own behalf; that is to say, she did not know in advance what the answer would be. These questions related to a GCSE topic, not a point of grammar. Pupils consequently used different grammatical areas in each answer. Here are some examples:

Comment est-ce que tu arrives à l'école?
Qu'est-ce que tu manges à midi?
Quelle matière est-ce que tu préfères? Pourquoi?

Questions like this might account for about two-thirds of Mary's normal oral work.

b Another type of question she often used was designed to make pupils practise a particular feature of the language, e.g. a specific verb, such as 'finir', with its typical conjugational forms. Here are some examples:

A quelle heure est-ce que tu finis tes devoirs?
A quelle heure est-ce qu'il finit ses devoirs?
A quelle heure est-ce que nous finissons à l'école?

Or: Est-ce que la biologie est plus intéressante que la physique?
Est-ce que les maths sont plus difficiles que les sciences?

Or: Est-ce que Swansea est plus grande que La Rochelle?
Est-ce que la Seine est plus longue que la Tamise?
Est-ce que Paris est plus grande que Londres?

These sorts of questions would typically take up about a third of Mary's oral teaching time.

c Some of her questions were intended to check if pupils had understood a text. She put them verbally in Welsh, and pupils responded verbally in Welsh. Here are some examples:

In what class is Marc?
What day is it today?
What is his first lesson?

The above sets of questions could come from a textbook, or could be invented by the teacher. The differences between them tell us something about the syllabus this class was learning, but nothing at all about Mary's method of using question-and-answer. For that, we must look deeper.

2 Questioning described by method

a Mary invariably framed her questions so that pupils were required to respond, using a complete sentence. This was most often achieved by asking a question beginning with an interrogative:

e.g. A quelle heure …?
Comment …?
Qu'est-ce que …?

Just occasionally, she used the form: 'Est-ce que …?' but her intention, on those occasions, was that pupils should respond, using a specific grammar point in a full sentence. She would not accept 'oui' or 'non', by itself.

b She normally used each question once only. That is to say, she addressed the first question to one pupil, the second to another pupil, the third to another, and so on.

c Sometimes, she would get the pupils to ask each other questions. Here are some examples, showing how she did this.
How do you ask:

Is there a bank nearby?

What do I do to change money?
Do you accept travellers' cheques?

Nevertheless, it is true to say that Mary normally put all the questions herself.

The interventionist strategy (didactic elements)

At half term, the means of intervening in Mary's normal teaching method was discussed. An analysis of questioning techniques, derived from extensive observations of foreign language lessons in the UK and overseas, was presented for Mary's consideration. There was no obligation on her to use all the techniques, and in fact she only used about half of them. The choice was left entirely to her, to choose those which she felt accorded with her own established teaching style. The analysis was presented in the categories described below.

Questions categorised by type of answer required.

a Formal

Short, abbreviated, but acceptable answers:
e.g. What's your name? John.

Complete sentences, demonstrating a command of the structure to be learned and used:
e.g. What's your name? My name is John.

b Functional

Questions designed to elicit a grammatically-based answer. The answers to such questions would be known to the teacher in advance:
e.g. Are you cleaning your teeth now? No, I'm not.
Do you clean your teeth in the morning? Yes, I do.
Are you washing your face now? No, I'm not.
Do you wash your face in the morning? Yes, I do.

Questions designed to elicit a communicative answer. The answers to such questions would not be known in advance to the teachers:
e.g. How do you come to school?
What do you have to eat at midday?
Which subject do you prefer? Why?

Communicative questions, such as those described above, can themselves be sub-divided into discrete types. These also were presented to Mary as possible variations.

i Opinion questions. For such questions it would be understood that there was no right answer, and students would be encouraged to express an opinion.
ii Inference questions. For these, only part of the information required for the answer would be available, and students would have to speculate in order to respond; or ask elucidating questions.

iii Personal questions. A single question of this type could theoretically produce as many right answers as there are students present.

iv Group questions. For questions of this sort, students would need to collaborate in pairs or groups in order to provide an answer.

v Research questions. Questions like this would require students to go to a source of information, and possibly make notes, in order to be able to respond.

c Level of difficulty

It was put to Mary that the answers to her questions might also vary according to their difficulty. Thus, some questions might be answered accurately and fluently, while others might be answered, if at all, haltingly and with mistakes.

d Raising the level of difficulty

i First, ask a question beginning with a verb, and which, consequently, can be answered: 'yes', or 'no', e.g. Is it raining?

ii Second, ask questions containing an alternative. This allows the students to hear the answer within the question, and reduces the answering task to choosing and pronouncing, e.g. Is it raining, or snowing?

iii Third, ask questions beginning with an interrogative, thus requiring the student to produce an answer without any help, e.g. What's the weather like?

The interventionist strategy (pedagogical elements)

e Type of interaction

i The teacher asks the questions.

ii Students ask each other the questions.

iii Students ask the teacher questions.

iv The teacher puts the same question to a number of students in turn.

v The teacher uses a set of two or three questions, alternating them in random sequence in rapid succession with a number of students.

vi The teacher tells student A to ask student B a question, e.g. Ask Peter what time it is.

vii The teacher tells student A to ask a question, but leaves him/her to choose who should answer it, e.g. Now you ask a question, Ann.

viii The teacher has the students form a chain, e.g. A asks B a question, B asks C the same question, C asks D, and so on.

f Varying the method

Mary was invited to use a number of the above techniques, provided she felt they were appropriate to her personal style, and the needs and temperament of her class. It was also suggested that some linguistic problems could be satisfactorily dealt with by one type of questioning, whereas another might benefit from questioning of several different varieties. It was also pointed out that it might sometimes be appropriate to react to each student answer, while at other times a number of answers might be given before she, the teacher, gave any reaction.

If either of the above aspects of experimentation were used, it would be advisable to proceed systematically, if noticeable results were to be observed.

The experimental phase of the project

No pressure was put on Mary to expand her questioning techniques in all directions simultaneously. In the event, she made two major changes, one pedagogical, and the other related to content. She adopted the chain as a standard procedure for maximising the number of questions which were asked and answered in a given space of time, and she encouraged her students to prepare sets of general, personal questions and to put these to other students in the class in the form of interviews. It was impossible to record other, more subtle changes in her teaching, or to detect whether she used her habitual techniques more confidently, purposefully or systematically as a consequence of having reflected carefully about this aspect of her work. Of far greater importance for other teachers who may undertake similar interventionist experiments is the assistance that Mary had in detecting changes in her students as she made changes in her teaching.

The period of experimentation lasted about ten weeks, from late October to mid February. Each week, Mary sent back to York her evaluation of the effects of her teaching, described in a number of precise ways. These evaluations were returned immediately after the lessons, so that trends and movements only became apparent subsequently.

Analysis of questioning by polarity scale

One cannot be precise about language teaching methods and their effects; however, extreme statements are likely to attract from observers general agreement or disagreement. Accordingly, Mary was provided with a number of statements, arranged in extreme opposites, and invited to describe the experimental part of her lesson as tending towards one or the other extreme. These polarities are given below.

1 By answer type

a	Teacher allows short, abbreviated answers.	Teacher requires full, complete sentences.
b	Teacher uses questions to elicit grammatical structures, exclusively.	Teacher uses questions requiring the communicative use of the language, exclusively.

2 By method of use

c	Teacher asks all the questions.	Students ask all the questions.
d	Teacher achieves full coverage of the class; each student participates.	Many or most students do not participate in the lesson.

e	Teacher uses one question at a time, thoroughly, before continuing to the next.	Teacher uses each question once only.
f	Teacher uses one technique of questioning only.	Teacher uses great technical variety.
g	Teacher's use of questions is systematic and thorough, gradually increasing the cognitive and linguistic demands on the students.	Teacher's use of questions is random and unsystematic.

3 By the observable effects of questioning

h	Teacher uses very difficult questions exclusively; students' answers exhibit many errors and hesitations.	Teacher uses very easy questions exclusively; students' answers are fluent and accurate.
i	Lesson goes at a fast pace; teacher obtains many student responses.	Lesson goes at a very slow pace; teacher obtains very few student responses.

Descriptors of oral practice

The above polarity scales were combined in a number of ways, shown below, partly because the process of language teaching is so complex that it would be unrealistic to extract any given discrete feature for examination, and partly in order to emphasise the inter-relatedness of all on-going processes in a lesson. It would be tempting to argue that these descriptors also show cause and effect, but here the researcher must be wary, since cause and effect, while not being excluded, cannot be proved. Of greater importance is that the same descriptor, if applied a number of times in succession, can show changes of process taking place, enabling teachers not only to reflect on their teaching with a degree of precision, but also to plan the course of future teaching with some accuracy.

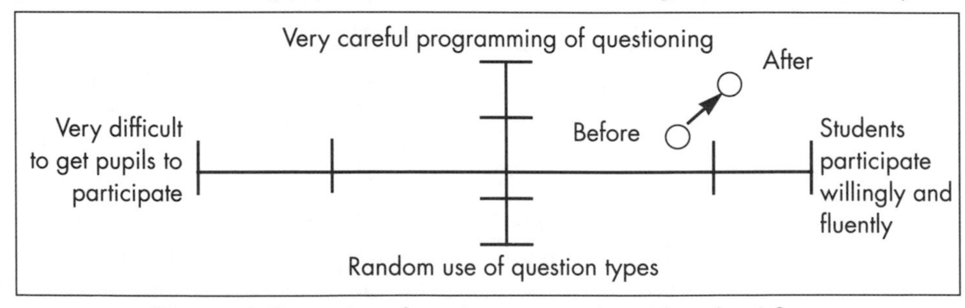

Diagram 1: Comparison of question-programming with students' fluency and willingness to participate

Result 1

The vertical axis is a measure of the care with which Mary constructed a battery of questioning techniques. It is, of course, subjective and global. The direction of the arrow is upwards, and this indicates that, in her opinion, as she became familiar with the various techniques of using questions, she deployed them increasingly systematically, bringing several to bear in each lesson in a principled sequence.

The horizontal axis enables pupils' willingness to participate and their fluency to be described. Since the direction of the arrow is from left to right, this shows that pupils' participation became more willing and fluent as the experiment progressed.

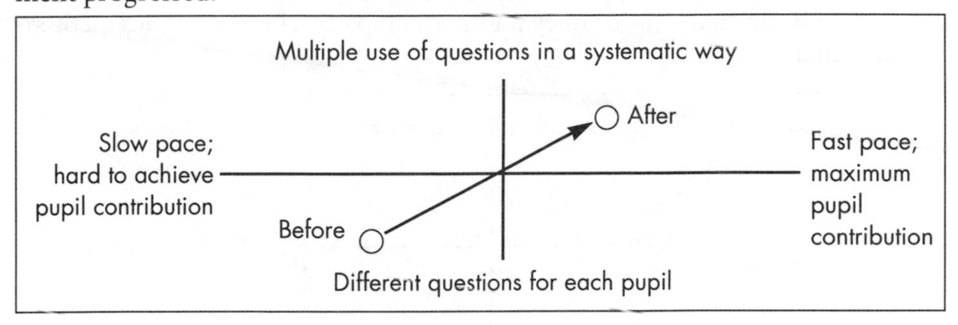

Diagram 2: Comparison between intensity of question use, and the pace of the lesson (including student participation) The result shown by the second descriptor is startling.

Result 2

The diagram shows that at the beginning of term, Mary was putting a different question to each pupil, and that the pace of oral practice tended to be rather slow, with pupil participation being somewhat difficult to obtain. As the experiment proceeded, and as Mary began to put the same question(s) to a number of pupils (2b, and her own technique), she noted that the pace of the lesson increased significantly, as did pupils' contributions.

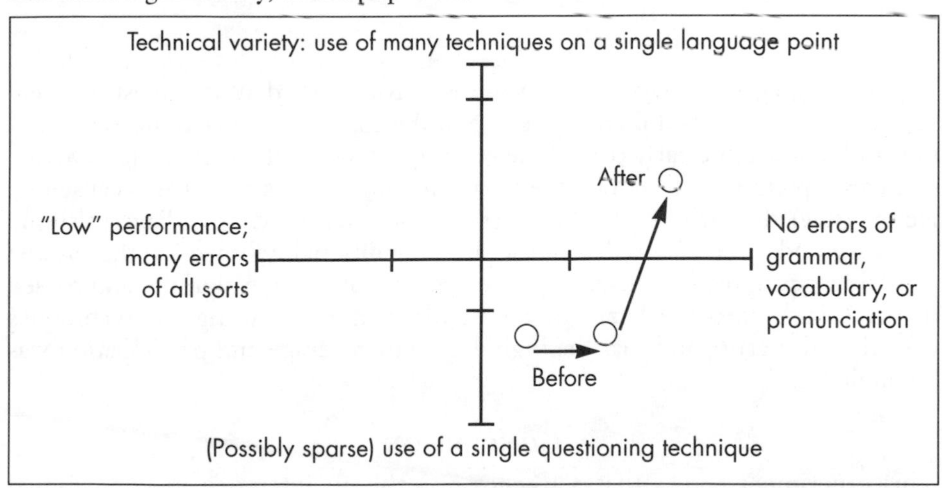

Diagram 3: Comparison of technical variety and incidence of error

Result 3

The horizontal direction of the first arrow, from left to right, indicates that Mary noticed the performance of her class was, as a whole, improving in accuracy. However, since she shows no upward movement along the vertical axis from the first observation to the second, the decline of mistakes has to be accounted for by factors other than technical variety.

The direction of the arrow between the second and third observation is simultaneously upwards and to the right. This shows that a further decline in the incidence of mistakes coincided with Mary deliberately focusing a greater number of questioning techniques than before on a single grammatical area. One should be wary, however, of seeing cause and effect here, if only because the initial improvement in accuracy was unaccompanied by a conscious methodological change.

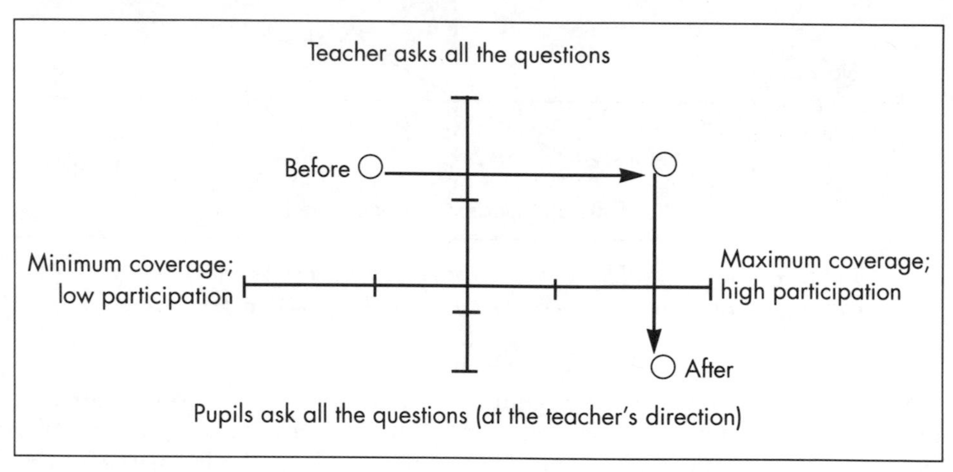

Diagram 4: Comparison of who asks the questions, and coverage of the class

Result 4

The above diagram shows that to begin with Mary asked all the questions herself, as many teachers do. Her coverage of the class nevertheless increased significantly during the early part of the project. However, the increasing coverage and participation, indicated by the horizontal line, shows that it was caused by factors other than who asked the questions. In other words, the diagram shows no cause and effect. The descriptor shows additionally, however, that as the experiment progressed, she relinquished control of the questioning, and passed it increasingly into the hands of the pupils themselves, using the techniques described in Part 6, and that the high degree of coverage and participation was maintained.

CONCLUSION

This experiment shows that a teacher was able to intervene in her habitual method of teaching in order to make principled changes of technique, and that the results of so doing could be described. She was able to accommodate these changes within her established, personal style of teaching.

Two factors enabled this to happen: the existence of precise descriptions of language teaching coming from observations of other teachers, and descriptive devices capable of being used by the teacher herself to record important aspects of her work in a reasonably accurate way.

The mentor in teacher induction and teacher development

Bart Van Thielen
CLT-Language Centre, Leuven University

◆

Inexperienced teachers know their colleagues insufficiently and often find it difficult to articulate their problems or negative experiences. Experienced colleagues often do not spot problems newcomers face or cannot spare the time to help them.

In order to remedy this situation, a coaching scheme paired each inexperienced teacher with a senior colleague, or mentor, who actively assisted them and provided support at all times. Teaching problems were extensively discussed, and experiences, teaching materials and aids were interchanged. Close collaboration between colleagues was strongly encouraged, and an open team spirit developed.

Characteristics of the inexperienced teacher

Awareness of the struggles of a inexperienced teacher is essential before meaningful guidance can be offered. Mentoring teachers need to recognise several problem areas:

- initial planning;
- designing basic classroom procedures;
- using effective language during instruction;
- balancing the whole instructional programme;
- evaluating students;
- integrating with the rest of the staff.

Initial planning

Planning is very important. At the first stage, a number of questions need to be answered. What am I going to teach? Why? To whom? How? What tools am I going to use?

The content of the course is largely determined by a syllabus, based on long and short term goals. The occurrence of a particular aspect of the course at a particular moment is not accidental. Therefore, it is of vital importance to formulate accurately and concretely the goals to be attained during a given lesson. Of course, in order to be able to achieve these goals one needs to know one's target audience and its already acquired knowledge, as well as its patterns of thought and learning strategies. An adequate knowledge of the target group is of the utmost importance in order to select the proper teaching method and tools.

It is striking that inexperienced teachers tend to emphasise the contents of the course: schemes and diagrams, word explanations, solutions to exercises (they focus on 'What shall I teach?'). Aspects such as goals, target group, method and evaluation (questions of why? to whom? how? with which tools?) receive less attention. Though quite understandable considering their lack of experience and insight, this misconception has far-reaching consequences for actual classroom procedures.

Classroom procedure

Classroom procedure is strongly dominated by inexperienced teachers' need for reassurance; they prefer to stick as closely as possible to the lesson plan and try to avoid venturing into unknown territory. If the latter does happen, they risk wandering off the subject, a problem lurking not only for inexperienced teachers. Yet, such teachers lack the experience to sense the usefulness and expediency of a digression. They try to avoid tricky questions by preparing their classes meticulously. If other questions do crop up, an inexperienced teacher will try to hide behind feigned self-assurance in order not to lose face.

Language interaction

Language is communication. The interaction between student and teacher is of crucial importance. The teacher needs to command an effective questioning technique. In the beginning, this technique often aims only at eliciting the expected answer. Consequently, the teacher listens only for the desired answer, whereas any answer enables the teacher to learn something about the students, about their ability to understand, patterns of thought, perception of a problem or their ability to comprehend a question.

Furthermore, inexperienced teachers fear moments of silence. If the answer does not follow the question promptly, a new question is added, possibly directed at another student. Therefore, it is essential for these teachers to learn to listen and to reflect on the answers and attitude of the students. Moreover, it is necessary to allow the students to talk as often as possible. Students require this practice, not the teacher. Yet, the 'teacher talking time' of inexperienced teachers is found to be very high. They talk during grammar and vocabulary sessions, they comment on reading texts, they explain more than is really necessary and they are easily tempted to participate actively in discussions instead of acting as listener or chair.

Programme balance

Learning to balance the total class programme is essential. The subject matter has to be clearly defined and well-timed. Offering learning strategies, selecting interesting material geared to attainable goals, limiting the amount presented during one lesson, distinguishing essentials from secondary considerations; this is a lot to ask.

Obviously, experience counts here. The fact that a good lesson consists of an introduction, a body and a conclusion is often only theoretically obvious!

The selection of a proper method and adequate use of teaching tools contribute largely to the success of a lesson. Inexperienced teachers, however, find it very hard to cope. Too often, they pay scant attention to what they see as trivial details. They attempt too often to use materials that have not been tested, and they use equipment without the necessary technical knowledge. However, the possibly negative results of all this can be turned into positive ones provided the necessary help is offered. 'Classroom management' is not a simple business, and yet a variety of rules of thumb can offer a solution.

Evaluation

'Is this clear?' A familiar question. And so is the affirmative student answer. Evaluation of the learning result needs to be an effective evaluation. After each part of the lesson, at the end of each session, it is essential to check whether the desired goals have been achieved. If one skips this evaluation, one is bound to start lecturing over the students' heads. This also holds true for assignments set in and outside the classroom; assignments must be simple and crystal clear, if the hoped for result is to be achieved. Inexperienced teachers must also learn to evaluate in the long term, starting from their objectives. The assessment of the skills acquired by the student in the course of a term or a school year is not an isolated activity but ties in closely with the above-mentioned aspects of problem analysis. Drawing this link again requires a lot of insight.

Integration with teaching staff

An inexperienced teacher should be able to integrate with colleagues as soon as possible. At The Language Centre (CLT), team work is a must; close collaboration marks each language team and the entire teaching staff at all levels. Our coursebooks are based on officially recognised curricula. Similar co-operation prevails when it comes to the organisation of written examinations. This requires substantial consultation and hence language teams meet regularly, sometimes even weekly, on their own initiative.

New colleagues find themselves involved from the very beginning. They receive existing coursebooks and during the first year their main task is to prepare their classes thoroughly. Although the inexperienced teachers have had a period of practical training and have taught a set of trial lessons, they now find themselves faced for the first time with the sole responsibility for an entire course. They find themselves powerless when confronted with numerous problems, partly because they are not familiar with them and hence find it hard to identify them. This is partly because they do not register certain signals emitted by the student audience.

Experience is an important criterion for critical self-assessment. Whereas experienced teachers are able to anticipate numerous stumbling blocks at an early stage, inexperienced colleagues often knock their heads against a brick wall, which is not only detrimental to self-assurance and job satisfaction, but also most unpleasant.

AN INDUCTION/DEVELOPMENT PROGRAMME

Although the CLT programme involved new and mentor teachers of adult learners in language instruction, many principles in this programme may apply to the mentoring process of teachers at various levels and in different subject areas.

At CLT, all students are adults. Their decision to attend classes is the result of careful consideration. Their motivation is very high and they assess the selected course solely with regard to their personal achievement. Their perception of the teaching behaviour of the teacher is based on high demands and expectations. They want to perform optimally in the chosen language and expect the teacher to stimulate their interest and effort. For this reason, they demand a thorough understanding of the target objectives and the required final result, a soundly structured organisation of course contents and classes, the necessary support and encouragement for their personal integration into the learning process, and an active and personal involvement in the classroom procedure.

These are high demands, especially when one takes into consideration the fact that 70% of the students are older than the inexperienced teacher and that they often have a higher professional or academic status than the teacher.

Objectives of the programme

1 To provide inexperienced teachers with special attention and the support of an experienced mentor.
2 To apply the experience of senior colleagues to the benefit of inexperienced teachers.
3 To encourage and reassure inexperienced teachers and offer them the opportunity to remedy possible problems efficiently.
4 To encourage junior and senior colleagues to reflect critically on teaching in all its aspects.
5 To teach junior colleagues to work toward attainable objectives.
6 To further the integration of inexperienced teachers within the teaching staff.
7 To instil a sense of responsibility in senior teachers towards their junior colleagues.
8 To encourage the whole staff to venture beyond their own field and to promote an open team spirit among all colleagues and language teams.

Procedure to recruit mentor teachers

At the beginning of the school year the new teacher is allocated a mentor, also called a godfather or godmother. The mentor teacher's recruitment is based on three criteria:

a the mentor possesses the required experience;
b the teaching timetable of mentor and new teacher allows them to attend each other's classes;
c the mentor teaches a language different from the beginning teacher's.

The last criterion arises from two considerations: first, the newly recruited teacher is assumed to be sufficiently expert in the target language, and second, the counselling and coaching must focus on the didactic approach rather than on specific, language-related subjects. In fact, a mentor belonging to the same language team is virtually impossible because of the constraints of school timetables.

The initial programme

The coaching scheme consisted of an observation and teaching part, and generally covered a period of two years until the new teacher received (promise of) tenure. If tenure was deferred for one year, the coaching was extended for that period.

The first coaching scheme consisted of a total of four lessons, two taught by the mentor teacher and, subsequently, two taught by the beginning teacher. Each teacher taught their own class. This set of lessons had to be completed by December.

The average teaching period at CLT comprises two or three lessons of sixty minutes each week. The mentor attended a minimum of one hour of it; the inexperienced teacher stayed for the whole duration of the teaching period. The written lesson plan covered the whole teaching period and both parties received a copy in advance. The idea was that the mentor stayed for at least one full hour. Later on she or he could watch different parts of different lessons to see how the inexperienced teacher was coping with suggestions made by the mentor, but this is on a free basis and although it happens frequently, it is not part of the official model.

An observation checklist was filled out for each lesson observed by the mentor. The following schedule applied:

Class I (mentor):

- extensive discussion of class preparation; agreement on special topics to focus on during class observation;
- the actual lesson observed by the inexperienced teacher;
- short debriefing.

Class II (mentor):

- lesson observed by the inexperienced teacher;
- extensive follow-up discussion.

Class III (inexperienced teacher):

- extensive discussion of class preparation; the inexperienced teacher is given ample opportunity to make modifications advised by the mentor;
- the actual lesson observed by the mentor;
- short follow-up with an outline of areas to focus on and concrete tips for the new teacher.

Class IV (beginning teacher):

- class attended by mentor and director;

- discussion of class by mentor and director;
  (The director now entered the situation and received feedback on the evolution of the counselling/guidance/coaching process. Beginners did not find themselves confronted with contrasting views during the ensuing deliberation and hence confusion was usually avoided.)
- extensive deliberation with mentor, director and new teacher.

During the second term/semester all support teachers met twice to assess the scheme. In general all participants felt that the experiment was positive. However, problems came to light.

First, two new teachers were unable to cope with their assignment. Consequently, the support teachers felt frustrated because all their efforts and positive attitude left them powerless and insufficiently armed to face up to the situation. A second problem ensued from the former. Although mentor teachers wished to reassure their junior colleagues and help them remedy their problems, they experienced their own role as a repressive and judgemental one. They had the impression that their junior colleagues-with-problems did not view them as experienced helpers but as executioners.

THE SECOND VERSION

Based on the assessment of the initial programme, a second variation was developed. The fact that junior teachers were allocated a different mentor during their second year under the scheme was a major alteration in the second version. The aim was to allow the junior teacher to share in the experience of several colleagues.

The junior teacher observed a minimum of three lessons taught by the mentor and used an observation checklist. For each session a different kind of lesson was selected (e.g. vocabulary, grammar, conversation, language laboratory). The observation checklist was aimed at helping the junior teachers to focus their observation on selected aspects of instruction and to recognise the underlying objectives. It was felt to be useful for the junior and senior teacher to discuss the lesson preparation prior to the lesson.

Then, after preparatory meetings, the mentor observed two classes taught by the junior colleague. The post-class conference included the director. Both the mentor and the director received a copy of the initial lesson plan. Dates for these lessons were fixed at least a week in advance.

Before the Easter holidays, another class was observed by the mentor and director. The junior teacher submitted all class preparations (lesson plans) of the second term to the director. These preparations were to comprise concrete objectives, teaching aids/tools, structure of the lesson and detailed procedure, exercises, questions and blackboard presentation.

After completion of the entire observation-teaching programme, the mentor compiled a final report on the coaching. This report was discussed with both junior teacher and director of studies and both parties received a copy.

Two meetings were held, the first for mentor teachers, the second for inexperienced teachers. The mentor teachers stated that in a number of cases it was hard to pinpoint or define the problems exactly. This was partly due to the fact that they had little experience in counselling and coaching new teachers; however, there was also a language problem. As the mentor teachers were coaching a colleague teaching another language, they found their insight into the learning process and their observations of the student-teacher interaction were hindered. They felt that certain problems were rooted in the very individual approach characteristic of each course.

The junior teachers seemed very satisfied with the existing format. They felt that their mentor could give them a comforting feeling and offer a rich source of inspiration. Feedback indicated that it would be useful for them to attend a lesson taught by a colleague belonging to the same language team and grade. They preferred a change of mentor for the second year and opted for a mentor belonging to a different language team but one teaching students at the same grade level. They outlined the task of the support teacher as not merely a didactic one, but also a practical one, of offering assistance when administrative, technical or other problems arose.

A two-day seminar on class observation was organised for the entire teaching staff and mentor teachers were given guidelines on lesson discussions.

THE THIRD VERSION

The observation of lessons by junior teachers was thoroughly altered. The number of classes observed was reduced again from three to two. The mentor and junior teacher attended two classes taught by colleagues teaching the same language at the same level.

Yearly, the counselling/coaching scheme is evaluated by everyone. Since 1991, the junior teachers have met without the director chairing their meeting. It is significant that junior teachers have suggested that their observations as well as their teaching should be extended, and that the number of visits by the director should be increased.

CONCLUSIONS

After some years, several conclusions may be drawn from this on-going mentorship project:

1 The overall feeling of participants in the project has been very positive.
2 This mentoring programme is not merely a duplicate teacher trainer programme. It is an in-service teacher development process focusing on the specific organisation and unique approach of each school. An elaborate didactic infrastructure has been integrated within a well-adapted method. It is based on the rationale that it would not be justified to make great demands of inexperienced teachers without offering them the tools necessary to meet these expectations.
3 Inexperienced teachers assessed the coaching positively. It was an instructive experience for them and facilitated their initiation into teaching. The support of a mentor offered them a comfortable feeling and reduced stress. The acquired insights into the learning process allow them to participate more actively when their language teams meet. They feel reassured and become inquisitive. This was exemplified in their demand

for more class visits by colleagues, which confirmed that the presence of observers was not perceived as an inspection or repression, but as an opportunity to be valued.

4 Experienced teachers were reassured because their experience and competence were needed. They felt jointly responsible for their junior colleague as well as for the quality of classroom instruction. They evaluated their own role in this learning process as constructive. Class visits and discussions with junior and other colleagues were an enrichment for them. They were stimulated to think beyond their own subject.

5 The director's assessment of inexperienced teachers is no longer based on chance, but on detailed data within a larger context. In this way, a more dynamic picture has been obtained of the development of a beginning teacher and it is possible to place a less proficient or untypical performance in perspective. Such performances came to be viewed as part of a growth process to be explored, and learning occurred from both positive and negative experiences.

6 The reaction of the adult students was not negative and the presence of 'inspection/control' seldom affected their attitude adversely. Many viewed this constant quality concern displayed by the school as mirroring their own demands for quality. They were offered opportunities to express their views on the CLT courses in a detailed evaluation questionnaire.

The CLT mentoring programme will continue to grow and change and attention must be continually paid to the area of tension between creativity and flexibility on the one hand, and the restrictive character of timing and planning on the other, while keeping in mind the maxim that 'learning is more important than teaching'. The programme is based on fieldwork, and practical experience contributes to it daily. New findings become premises for further practical research. In this way such a mentoring project can be considered a kind of 'action research': trying out ideas in practice as a means of improvement and as a means of increasing knowledge about the curriculum, teaching and learning. The result is improvement in what happens in the classroom and school, and better articulation and justification of the quality of educational practice. The CLT mentoring project is action research which provides a way of working that links theory and practice into one whole.

Introducing reflective practice: an experimental project in Silesia, Poland

Melanie Ellis
University of Silesia

◆

In a course to re-train teachers of various disciplines to be teachers of English, collaborative project work in school was introduced. Teachers identified and examined some aspect of their teaching, discussed this with their colleagues, observed each other teaching and finally produced a written account. The process of how reflective practice was introduced is described. Sample project outlines are given, together with extracts from the written accounts. Some comments from taped interviews with participating teachers and excerpts from an evaluation exercise are included. In conclusion, some guidelines for the introduction of reflective practice are suggested.

Introduction

This study reports on a project in the Katowice province of southern Poland. The subjects were a group of thirty-eight teachers, contracted and teaching English in school, who are not graduates of English departments. In the school year 1991-2 they were attending a course at the Regional INSET Centre (WOM) in Katowice to prepare them for the State Recognition Exam for teachers of English.

Background to the situation in Polish education

There is an urgent need for a large number of new teachers of English in Poland, following changes in foreign language policy. In 1991 Russian ceased to be obligatory and the choice of foreign language taught became open. At the same time the teaching of western foreign languages was extended to include all junior schools from 5th class (age eleven), instead of a small number as in the past (see Fisiak, 1992 for more detailed information). The PACE (Polish Access to English) Project was set up to train new language teachers in a three-year programme in new colleges (see Fisiak, 1992). In addition, permission was granted for 'unqualified' teachers (that is teachers who are not graduates of English departments) to teach, on the condition that they seek State Recognition.

The State Recognition exam

The results of the first State Recognition exam for teachers of English, held in 1991, were very disappointing. Out of 800 candidates who entered for the exam only thirty were successful. The stumbling block for most was the language paper, which only fifty passed. This paper was said to be a level approximately that of the UCLES First Certificate in English. Teachers who failed the written language paper were not allowed to take the orals or sit the subsequent papers in methodology and cultural studies (Sobolew, 1992). It was clear that any course preparing teachers for the exam needed a strong language component.

PLACEMENT FOR THE KATOWICE COURSE

In September 1991 a placement test was held at WOM Katowice, for teachers wanting to prepare for State Recognition. It was designed to screen out anyone who would have difficulty following a course which would be taught entirely in English. 120 people entered for the exam, 98 sat it and of these 68 were offered places. The rejected thirty were beginners or false beginners. Twenty-five of those placed were put into an extended two-year programme as they were of lower intermediate level. Their first year was to consist only of a language programme. They are not the subjects of this study.

Thirty-eight of the remaining 43 completed the programme and data is available on 35 of them. Nine of them were teachers of Russian. It is often assumed that re-training programmes in former Eastern bloc countries are exclusively for Russian teachers. In Silesia this is not the case. Amongst the others were five economics teachers, nine from various science-related subjects ranging from agriculture to architecture, one teacher of music, one Latin teacher, a Polish teacher, two graduates of the Police Academy and two graduates in primary education.

Participants range in age from 42 to 23 with an average age of 32 years. The group divides almost equally with eighteen participants under the age of 30 and seventeen over the age of 30. Work experience varies tremendously, from seventeen years to one year. Sixteen participants have one or two years' experience, ten have ten years or more and five have between four and nine years. Fifteen of the participants had already taught English for one year at the start of the course, ten were scheduled to start in September 1992 and the remaining thirteen had started in September 1991.

RATIONALE FOR ORGANISATION OF THE PROGRAMME

Above all, the course was to prepare teachers for the State Exam and this was a major consideration in designing the programme. In addition, there were other factors to be taken into account. 33 of the 43 teachers were already working in schools. The methodology component needed to address the day to day reality of teaching and to be related to the materials they were using in school. There was a strong need to ensure that what was taught on the course was applied and did not remain a theoretical subject to be learned and reproduced on an exam paper.

Provision for continuing support and supervision once a course is over is minimal. The Katowice Wojewodstwo (regional administrative area) is large, taking in the most densely populated areas of Poland and most of its heavy industrial belt. The LEA (Local Education Authority) currently employs one consultant for English language and one adviser, (a senior teacher who is released from twelve hours teaching a week to help teachers). This is the provision for in-service support and re-training. There are too many teachers and the geographical distances are too great to enable supervision of teachers in school and also provide a re-training programme and INSET workshops. Teachers have to become independent very quickly as support is simply not available.

Along with language, methodology and cultural studies, the group needed to learn how to cope with the problems of the classroom, with problem pupils, with their own limited resources in terms of materials and language. They also needed to develop a framework which would give them confidence and support for their own development once the course had finished. There needed to be some learner training, so that they could continue to study and develop their own language alone, and teacher education and development so that they had ways of looking at their own teaching and classrooms and the relationships between themselves and the learners, and the learners with each other. In this way they would be able to face problems practically and find solutions. The teachers' own language learning experience was almost exclusively from Polish secondary schools, where methodology is traditionally grammar-translation, with a great deal of teaching about the language in Polish and little opportunity for oral interaction. *'Ask me to describe to you what the present perfect is and what it means and I can recite it off,' said Bozena, 'but when I'm telling a story or writing a letter I have no idea which tense to use.'*

The teacher in a Polish school is traditionally the knower, the pupils empty vessels to be filled. The atmosphere is formal and at exam time the pupils are often expected to reproduce information they have learned by heart. The Ministry of National Education (MEN) now acknowledges that with new opportunities for using English, a greater emphasis must be placed on communication. Children need, above all, to be able to speak and understand English, rather than talk about it in Polish

The teachers needed an introduction to communicative methodology, enough theoretical background to give them a sound understanding of its basics and an introduction to a wide range of techniques to use in class. Course planning, lesson planning and materials preparation also needed to be included. It was expected that the methodology component would be a lecture course as this is how it is generally taught in departments of English at Polish universities. There was surprise and some resistance to the announcement of a programme which would integrate the methodology and the language programmes.

This decision was based on a survey carried out of 128 members of the academic staff of the University of Silesia. It was found that 85% of the participants had altered their attitudes to teaching and learning after following an English language programme. The factors most often mentioned were the relationship between the teacher and the learners, the active role the learners took in the lessons and the lack of fear or stress in the classroom. As the teachers involved in this study were from other disciplines, it was felt that with language teachers the effect would be greater (Ellis and Swiderska, 1991).

Feedback from summer courses for teachers at Pilgrims in Canterbury reflected this. Courses in language development for teachers often receive comments such as: *'I got a lot of new ideas to use in my teaching.'* (feedback form August

1991), while a one week methodology course in drama in the classroom was praised because: *'My English has really improved this week!'* (personal communication with Judith Baker). It seemed reasonable to expect that the language component of the course would unconsciously serve as a model for teaching behaviour. The plan was to make this more overt.

INTEGRATING LANGUAGE AND METHODOLOGY

At times during the language lesson we would stand back from an exercise and look at it as teachers, rather than as learners. For example, in terms of language analysis: 'What language have you been using to do this task?'; or organisation: 'In groups try to recall the steps we went through before we started the task.'; teaching theory: 'Why do you think we looked at those pictures before we listened to the cassette?' or 'Why did I choose those items of vocabulary to focus on before we listened to the tape?' and so on. On one level this was introducing the basics of communicative methodology and teaching theory, while at the same time the teachers were developing their critical faculties.

> *Becoming critical means that as teachers we have to transcend the technicalities of teaching and think beyond the need to improve our instructional techniques. This effectively means we have to move away from the 'how to' questions, which have a limited utilitarian value, to the 'what' and 'why' questions, which regard instructional and managerial techniques not as ends in themselves but as part of broader educational purposes.*
>
> (Bartlett, 1990:205).

There were to be exams at the end of fifteen weeks in language and British Studies and at the end of thirty weeks in language and American Studies. Methodology was to be assessed in the form of a 'project' which would be done in two three week blocks in school during the second half of the course. It is interesting that it was difficult to find an adequate Polish translation of the word 'project' and the concept seemed an unfamiliar one.

Little information was given about the precise nature of the project at the beginning of the course, as it was felt the teachers were not ready to cope with the concept of working independently of the tutor for a prolonged period and would begin to be anxious. The first steps needed to be building up the teachers' confidence and self-esteem, as these were very low, and encouraging them to take responsibility for their own learning. In other words, they first needed to grasp the concept of communicative language teaching through experiencing it as learners.

CLASS MANAGEMENT

Through unfortunate circumstances the teaching group was 43 and so it was fairly difficult to give adequate individual attention. In order to be able to develop closer relationships with individuals, classes included lots of pair and group work. In this way it was possible to move around the room to monitor or join in discussions. Slowly, teachers were persuaded, when unsure of instructions or procedure, to ask their colleagues, instead of always resorting to the tutor. Slowly, the concept of peer correction and collaboration on tasks developed. This was new, as their own learning experience seemed to have been competitive rather than co-operative, and the idea of working with a colleague to produce something together was strange. The option of working alone was always given and they were encouraged to recognise that people have different learning styles.

Discussion topics included work on the group's memories of their own teachers and their own learning experiences (inspired by the work of Ephraim Weintraub and John Morgan), to help the teachers become aware of influences and models. We tried exercises from *Inner Track Learning* (Lawlor, 1988) which focused on differences in learning style, and teachers discussed their preferred ways of learning and work environments. We talked about how teachers tend to use materials which suit their own learning preference and looked at how to provide for a range of learning styles (Rose, 1989).

INTEGRATING SCHOOL PRACTICE WITH THE COURSE

In early sessions teachers brought in the textbooks they were using in school. Language analysis tasks were taken from *English is Fun* (Zawadzka and Moszczak, 1991), as this was the book most widely used. Materials evaluation was done contrasting *English is Fun* exercises (grammar-translation) with exercises from *Discoveries* (Abbs and Freebairn, 1986) (communicative), the second most widely used book. Tasks on adapting *English is Fun* material to make it more communicative began early on. Homework tasks included lesson planning, language analysis of units soon to be taught, producing a listening task, producing pre-reading tasks, a task involving pair work and so on. Gradually resistance began to weaken and teachers who had at first refused to consider presenting new language without a Polish explanation, went away and tried it out. All practical tasks were followed by small group discussions, where teachers told each other what had happened in their classes and listened to each others' accounts.

In week ten, teachers were given an outline of the organisation of the 'project'. It was to take place in two blocks, each of three weeks. Teachers could work individually, but would be encouraged to work in small groups. The subject would be chosen by them and be based on work they did in school. There would be a deadline for submitting a detailed plan of what they intended to do and the aims were to be clear and achievable. The practical part of the work needed to be done mostly in the first block, with the second block giving more time for discussion and writing-up. The plans were to be written in English, at least 4 x A4 pages in length, and were to give an account of the aims of the project, what was done and what conclusions were reached. More detailed information about possible content would follow during a week's intensive session in the inter-semester break.

INTENSIVE COURSE

My hidden agenda in planning my contribution to the intensive course was to introduce the concepts of Action Research (Kemmis and McTaggart, 1982), without naming it as such, to introduce methods of data collection and basic principles of classroom observation and to establish the teachers in regional groups where they would be within reach of each other for collaborative work. In addition, I wanted them to experience micro-teaching to promote the idea of peer observation.

The course included language, methodology and cultural studies. For the language sessions I selected materials which matched the general theme, e.g. an extract from *Promoting Reflective Teaching* (Handal and Lauvas, 1987), which defined good teaching and a good teacher. Another language session looked at an extract from a lesson transcript from Nunan (1989). Focusing at first on the language used, discussion about the aims of the lesson followed and then teachers talked about how they would feel as learners in this teacher's class. The next stage was to watch videos of teachers teaching. Extracts from *Teaching and Learning in Focus* (The British Council, 1984) were used with a range of observation tasks.

In micro-teaching sessions very small groups (five or six) worked together. The reason for this was that many of the teachers were extremely self-conscious and ashamed of their English. It was felt the experience would be less stressful if the groups were very small. The groups were selected according to where the teachers worked, so that they were with people who worked in schools near them. It was openly suggested, after discussion of their schools and the materials they used, that they might like to go and visit each others' schools and watch each others' lessons to compare the levels of students and how students behaved. This idea was greeted very positively and even with enthusiasm. There was a strong need for some of them to feel they were doing the right thing and they welcomed the opportunity for confirmation. Micro-teaching focused on classroom techniques: drilling, eliciting, presenting new language using pictures or mime, and on the planning of lessons. The course feedback sheets reported that the majority had found it very helpful.

The final methodology session was to begin planning the projects. Emphasis was made that the projects should be on an area which would be useful to the teachers and not just an academic exercise for the course requirements. No-one was going to 'fail' and there would be plenty of opportunity for support and consultation.

Teachers sat in regional groups discussing their schools, their classes and the materials used. They then received a selection of 'starter questions' taken from Nunan (1989:19 and 53) and Kemmis and McTaggart (1982:18), which they discussed. I have found in previous experiences of introducing teachers to Action Research that problem focused questions, such as 'What is happening now? In what way is it problematic? What can I do about it?' (Kemmis and McTaggart 1982:18) can anger some teachers, who resent the suggestion that there is something 'wrong' with their teaching. I therefore gave a range of types of question, as giving the teachers a choice of questions seemed to circumvent this. Discussions of these starter questions went on long after the session was over. Teachers had a further ten days before the deadline for submitting their project outlines and consultation time was available if they wanted it.

Sample project outlines

Group A

I do too much talking, so I have to vary the amount of talking I do and give the pupils as many chances of speaking as possible. I'd like to encourage the pupils to speak by:

choral repetition
individual drilling
pair reading of dialogues
role play in a guided dialogue
group work.

Group B (3 teachers)

Speaking practice as a means to make lessons more interesting (pair work, group work, games, songs, role-play etc.).

Week 1:	Plan; compare our plans; discuss and prepare common plans.
Weeks 2 & 3:	Watch each other teach and take notes.
Week 3:	Summary and conclusions.

Group C (3 teachers)

Week 1:	We're going to target weak students and prepare materials especially for them.
Week 2:	Teach lessons with special concern for weak students. First impressions.
Week 3:	Visit each other. Discuss first results.
General aims:	Less teacher talking; more pair work; more real-life situations; help students listen to each other.

Group D (2 teachers)

Advantages and disadvantages of working with a small group (12 pupils) and the whole class (28 pupils) and teaching using different books.

Teachers who were not yet teaching English in school (ten participants) had a different task. They were asked to find out which textbook they would be using from September (or, if they could, select one), find a teacher who was using that book and discuss it with them and, if possible, visit two or three teachers, watch them teaching and note their impressions. Then they were to plan the first six lessons of their course which would start in September, either alone or with another teacher who would be using the same book. Again emphasis was laid on the project being something which would be of use to them when they came to start the new school year. It also meant that support could be given to help them through the difficult transition period, through the project, whereas support would not be possible at the actual time.

Evaluating the process

During the first block of project work each group or individual had a consultation with the tutor. During this thirty-minute session there was a chance to ask questions and raise problems. The tutor kept notes as a record. Participants were asked to include thoughts and feelings in their project write-ups. Some of the consultations were taped, if the participants agreed. The tutor kept a reflective tape diary during the project weeks — a practical measure as it was recorded in the car whilst commuting. There was also time for reading at this stage and several participants came to ask for references to areas of interest.

RE-ORGANISATION OF STATE RECOGNITION

The MEN dropped a bombshell in mid-February 1992 by announcing the abolition of the State Recognition exam. It was to be replaced by a series of steps, the first of which was the UCLES First Certificate in English. The second, beginning from 1993-4, a 'one-year course in methodology, approved by MEN' and the third, UCLES Certificate in Advanced English.

The writing-up stage of the project took place while a long process of negotiation began with MEN about recognition of the course. It is hoped to get exemption from the methodology component for the participants. This has not been resolved and negotiations continue.

The teachers completed and wrote up their projects, did their final language exams and completed the course.

EXTRACTS FROM PROJECT WRITE-UPS

Ewa prepared six lessons and submitted the plans together with an account of how they went:

> *In this lesson I used my hands to show the pupils how to make short forms. It was very useful because they didn't make mistakes when they could see how to do it …*
>
> *I decided not to teach them new words, because if they have too much in three lessons they don't learn it at all. … There was something strange in this lesson. There were three boys, who didn't want to sit in the circle with the rest of the class. I didn't pay any attention to them. They repeated all the sentences with the other pupils but they didn't want to sit with them. Nothing was important enough to them. But in this lesson they came and sat and learnt. It was surprising.*

Liliana had been interested by a video of a Total Physical Response (TPR) lesson and decided to try it out:

> *I tried a TPR lesson based on the article Activities with Robot Masks (Wingate, 1990). The children were really excited … The weak pupils were interested as they liked to be moving. They were surprisingly good at following the orders. It can even be said they were as efficient as the stronger ones.*

Grazyna and Ewa D. started with a bold statement:

> *Despite our awareness of the great value of group work our attitude to this was a little bit sceptical. We wanted to prove that it is rather impossible to work successfully using this method. Maybe it was because we were taught in a very*

traditional way. We were afraid of discipline and losing control under pupils' problems.

They tried it nevertheless and listed these advantages, among others:

All the pupils were involved in the activity and they were really interested in what they were doing ... Although this ... requires a lot of effort from the teacher before the lesson, the lesson itself is not very exhausting. These lessons are less stressful for the pupils and the class atmosphere is positive all the time.

Hanna had a difficult time:

In the first part of my project I tried out all forms of students groupings I had not tried before. Classwork [students doing a 'Find Someone Who' activity] was a failure in terms of: level of noise, behaviour of disruptive students, state of the classroom after the lesson, arousing some concern of the school authority and other teachers (because of the noise), not in terms of effectiveness, difficult to be proven in such noisy conditions. It is now clear to me that I should have introduced all new methods gradually. I should have given my pupils a chance to get used to one method and then introduced the next one ...

In the next part she goes on to list her solutions:

It can be necessary to write the most useful expressions on the blackboard or on a piece of paper. Very precise and clear explanation before the task, perhaps pre-display ... The teacher must ask the students to avoid hurry when competition is not necessary, or plan tasks which take advantage of their competitiveness ...

Marzanna observed four lessons in her school:

I talked to English teachers in my school about their problems with teaching English. They said that their big problem during the lessons is discipline, especially if the English lesson is the last lesson of the day. The lessons I saw confirmed this.

I think that planning the lesson the teacher must take into account when the class takes place. In my school pupils often have English when they are tired after a long day of study. In this case it is very important to make the lessons interesting for the children ... I think that there wasn't enough variety in the lessons I saw and not all parts of the lesson worked equally ... It seems true that perhaps the greatest single cause of indiscipline is boredom.

In terms of innovation few of the teachers have created anything which is very new. This was not the aim of the project. However what they report is new for them, as can be seen from the honesty and freshness of their comments. They are very willing not just to state problems they encountered, but to look for reasons for them and possible solutions. The seeds of reflective practice seem to have been sown.

EXTENDING THE WORK OF THE REGIONAL GROUPS

The final session was a meeting with teachers who will be starting a similar course in September 1992, to talk about the course and the project work. As the

MEN decision came too late for entry for the June 1992 FCE exam, most of the teachers will take the exam in December 1992. Distance materials are being prepared to keep them going. The regional groups, set up for project work, now take on a new form as study groups. Teachers will meet regularly to discuss the work in their regions. Once a month there will be a meeting for everyone in Katowice. In addition these groups will provide a focus for the new participants. They are willing to be contacted, to be observed and to assist the new teachers with lesson planning. Whatever MEN decides as to the required qualifications, these regional support groups are now in place and working.

POST-COURSE REFLECTION

Teachers received individual letters at the end of the course asking them to reflect, and in particular on the project work and its impact. Some extracts follow:

> *I am much more confident now. I've stopped controlling myself, (I was too tense during lessons) … and the pupils (like a good mother who seems to have very dependent children) — in fact they should be taught for their own good to be independent.*
>
> *I heard about group and pair work for the first time on this course. I was very sceptical at first, but after my project I found this kind of teaching very useful.*
>
> *I really understood that the teacher isn't the main person in the class!*
>
> *Project work helped me very much. We had a chance to talk about our teaching problems and I've seen how my friends prepare their lessons.*
>
> *My most important discovery was that I can simply enjoy using English in everyday life.*
>
> *Now I feel much better. I know that my pupils are making some progress. The most pleasant thing is that a lot of my pupils like English lessons very much — they are active, they work a lot (with pleasure!) they want to learn English next year.*
>
> *I feel better because I'm not alone any more.*
>
> *Now I realise what I know or what I still don't know and where I can find the solution to my problems.*
>
> *The most important thing for me is getting more self-confidence. I feel more confident … and more conscious about what I'm trying to teach, why and how.*

CONCLUSIONS: GUIDELINES FOR INTRODUCING REFLECTIVE PRACTICE

This project seems to indicate the strength of integrating methodology with language development. The teachers had first hand experience of the ideas expounded and this indeed seemed to act as a model for their teaching.

Here lies the second strength. These teachers were already teaching. They had everyday access to classes of their own to try out what they were hearing about. It was possible to take advantage of this, by designing practical tasks, to make sure that they did try things.

The project work acted successfully as an additional bridge between the course and the classroom and seems to have offered enough support to encourage even the more sceptical to take risks and experiment. There seems to be some evidence that a framework for reflective practice is in place and being used by many of the participants.

The steps to reflective practice seem to be connected with the development of independence in the learner. Just as language learners who are independent are aware of how they learn and what works well for them, so independent teachers seem not only to be aware of what they do, but also why they do it. Introducing reflective moments within the language development sessions can lay the foundations for this. The trainee teacher becomes accustomed to examining the process of activities, step by step, and to asking 'why' questions. Moving from here to their own teaching can be facilitated by short exercises on activity design, and reporting what happened when the activity was tried in class. Discussion with peers will help develop hypothesis-making skills: ('that might have happened because … ') and the posing of solutions: ('so if we change this, that might not happen again').

It is important that the learning/training process reflects the teaching/learning theory which is being offered. The Silesian experimental project seems to offer an example of this.

Teachers' classroom research: rhetoric and reality

Jill Burton and Peter Mickan
University of South Australia

◆

In this paper we will discuss some of the issues involved in teachers' undertaking research in their own classrooms. The major purpose of the paper is to examine the conditions under which teachers carry out research on their own teaching, and to relate this to an inservice programme in which language teachers carried out action research projects.

Issues for classroom research

Over the past ten years it has become commonplace to advocate teachers' involvement in research into the ecology of their own classrooms. The reasons for this include the closeness of teachers to the events being researched, the need for continual professional renewal through reflection on and evaluation of practice, and the importance of linking theory with practice by testing ideas in their classrooms. Although the teacher-as-researcher movement has many reported successes, and teachers' research has been applied in various programmes, it is significant that teachers' classroom research has not become widespread, nor has it been incorporated generally in mainstream teacher education programmes, whether pre-service, inservice or graduate.

A number of specific reasons have been put forward for classroom research which is carried out by language teachers:

1 Information from the front line: teachers are most familiar with the complex circumstances involved in the teaching and learning of languages; what they experience in classrooms is a direct source of information about language learning.

2 Learner as source of information: classroom researchers are interested in their students' learning and in the effects of their teaching on learning; classroom research suggests the possibility of students becoming co-researchers in finding out about the processes of language learning.

3 Research relevant to the teacher: teachers' classroom research relates directly to teachers' interests and concerns; teachers determine research areas pertinent to their professional life; classroom research is also of particular interest to other teachers, because it reflects their own experience.

4 Learning about language learning: classroom research is a significant source of information on language learning processes; it contributes to our

understanding of conditions for effective teaching and learning.

5 Learning through research: teachers' research promotes their own learning about what is happening in their classrooms, and their understanding of why it is happening; through research teachers hypothesise about their experience.

6 Research and decision-making: the knowledge gained through research in their classrooms influences teachers' decision-making; the process of research equips them with techniques for self-evaluation, and with the knowledge and skills for ongoing renewal of their teaching practices. (From Mickan, 1990:7)

Given an array of reasons such as these for teachers' classroom research, the case for promoting it seems strong. But is teacher research something which in reality is easier said than done?

In a review article on action research, Kemmis (1988:27) asked the question 'Why is it that the great army of teachers of Australian school children show little interest in educational research?' If we consider the number of publications advocating language teachers' classroom research, and conferences on the same topic, we might add to the question of Kemmis another which asks: why is it that they do not all undertake research themselves? It seems to us that the answers to these questions, at least in part, can be found in the conditions under which teachers work, which are not conducive to research, and in the purposes for which research is carried out.

There are significant differences between the conditions under which professional and academic researchers carry out research and those under which teacher researchers do so.

Academic research includes the following features:

1 The research role: academic researchers engage in research as part of their professional role, which means that resources and time are provided for their research, and promotion and credit are gained through research.

2 The application of research: academic research does not necessarily have immediate practical application and consequences; it is in a sense a theoretical activity, with the researcher free to decide what and where to research.

3 The research approach: the procedures of academic research include, for example, comprehensive literature reviews, and the documentation and publication of research, activities which require time and resources; the research approach encourages objectivity and distance from the object of study.

4 Research communities: academic researchers belong to research communities in which they can disseminate their research at conferences and through publications.

These features combine to support and encourage research. They enable researchers to choose from a range of research approaches. They give the researcher the freedom to decide what to research and where to carry it out. But these features also distance the results of academic research from the teacher —

through the language of research, through the tentative application of research findings and through a methodological concern with rigour.

Constraints on Teachers' classroom research

The role of the teacher is to teach, which is a practical and hectic activity. This role does not include research, so that the resources and time for research are not a normal part of teachers' working conditions. As a consequence teachers do not have time for writing extensive literature reviews, for constructing complex data-collection procedures and for detailed analysis of findings. It also means that the research does not contribute to professional rewards such as promotion.

Since research is not normally integrated into the role of the teacher, pre-service training does not include experience in research procedures for classroom research. The skills and methods have to be developed on-the-job in in-service programmes, which again are not geared for such activities.

The teacher-as-researcher movement promotes on-site research. The research carried out by teachers therefore arises out of the exigencies of their classroom experience. Like teaching it is a practical activity, so that the effects of the research relate in direct ways to what happens in the classroom. This imposes limitations on the kind of research teachers are able to carry out in their classrooms.

In contrast with professional researchers, teachers are not members of a community of researchers, who support and sustain research. Opportunities for publication are limited, as are events for reporting and discussing research. Not only are teacher researchers in environments which do not promote research, they are also subject to the criticisms of professional researchers. The very qualities for which teachers' research, such as action research, is advocated by teacher educators — contextualised, descriptive, applied and anecdotal in style — cause professional researchers to be critical of teachers' classroom research. As a consequence, the kind of research which is carried out by teachers is not valued or regarded as serious research, because it does not have the characteristics of formal academic research which is reported in journals and at conferences.

A further constraint on teachers' research is its promotion as a professional development activity. There is in a sense a contradiction here in that research is not considered part of teachers' professional role and yet teacher educators advocate it as a means for professional development. This imposes expectations of change or renewal on teachers' practice, which are not the same for professional researchers.

Taken together these constraints help to answer the question why there is not an army of teacher reseachers in classrooms. The implication is not that we should abandon the notion of teacher as researcher, especially when we consider the potential benefits for teachers and for research in general. But it poses a challenge for those who advocate teachers' research — given these constraints, how can we establish the conditions for research by teachers, so that it is valued, it is supported and it is do-able in a practical way? The inservice programme for language teachers, which is outlined below attempted to achieve this.

PROFESSIONAL DEVELOPMENT FOR LANGUAGE TEACHERS THROUGH ACTION RESEARCH

Between 1988 and 1991, a languages inservice programme for teachers (LIPT) was offered annually in South Australia (see Nunan, this volume). Formal Project involvement was for one or two terms. A systems initiative, LIPT aimed to help teachers of languages other than English (LOTE) analyse and extend their teaching skills. Organised support was provided each year through networks and conferences. Input focused primarily on the process of action research but also covered general aspects of the theory and practice of teaching and learning languages other than English. Over a four-year period, four different groups of LOTE teachers became members of a critical community. Together they learned about action research processes, conducted individual action research projects, and wrote up their research for publication (Burton, 1990, 1991, 1992).

Although LIPT was initiated by the three education systems in South Australia (the South Australian Education Department, the Catholic Education Office and the Independents Schools Board) and funded by the Australian Second Language Learning Program as part of a national languages development plan, the Project Management Team envisaged LIPT as a learner-centred process. The Project aimed to stimulate teachers to be active in their own professional renewal following training and experience in practical research-type processes. These were expected both to inform teaching practice and suggest directions for more formal research in which teachers might choose to be involved as co-researchers, as data-collection agents, as the subjects of research by other colleagues, and so on. Teacher participants were seen as reflective practitioners (see discussion by Carr and Kemmis, 1986:36-45).

The experience for language teachers was not one of neat progression through a series of logically sequential steps, since the opportunities for reflection sent participants backwards and sideways as well as forward. (It is quite logical in this context to talk of going backwards to go forward.) Though participants completed action research projects, a superficial topic analysis of the written reports reveals the twists and turns that teacher–researchers took, with them ending formal involvement in the Project, very often, with a question for the next piece of investigation. For many participants the process enabled them to refine their areas of concern, to prioritise action, to be realistic in their aims, and to go from intuitively held beliefs about important areas to develop or research to explicitly expressed, specific goals for action. The process established was based on the action research cycle as described by Kemmis, McTaggart et al., (1982). Fig. 1 identifies the phases of activity which participants experienced, the sources of input and their impact on the classroom and learners.

Input mode	Phase	Effect
Conference	Participants are introduced to the theory and processes of action research	Participants retrospectively apply theory in their thinking about their teaching
Networks/one-to-one	Participants determine individual action research topics and appropriate research methodologies	Participants identify aspects of their teaching to investigate
Networks/one-to-one	Participants collect data	Research activity involves participants' students in specially focused activity
Conference Networks/one-to-one	Participants analyse and reflect on data	Participants (and their students) are involved in scrutiny of classroom activities
Conference Networks/one-to-one	Participants write reports of their research for publication	Participants expose their teaching to peers
Conference Networks/one-to-one	Participants identify personal outcomes of their action research	Participants refine goals and articulate new directions

Fig. 1: The formal stimulus process

Fig. 2 characterises the reflection process set up by the Project. The diagram, which delineates the major components of reactive, reflexive (see Bartlett, 1990: 208) critiquing, suggests a neat chain of development, whereas the reality for many participants was closer to an interlocking mesh or net. We chose the chain metaphor because it implies progression and purposeful movement and because this is what teachers indicated they experienced.

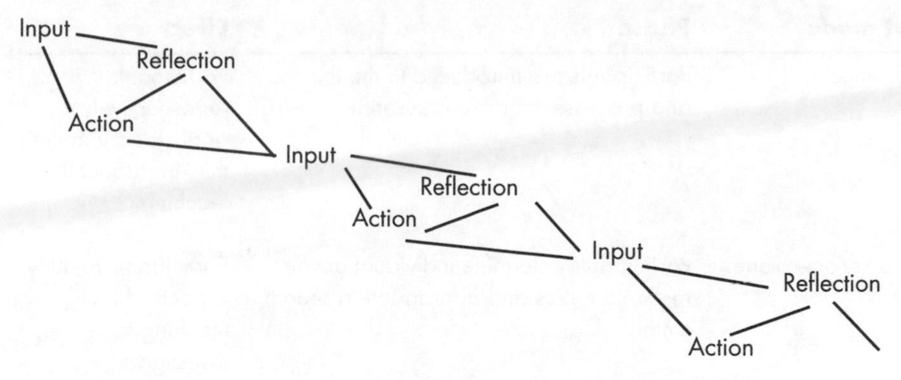

Fig. 2: The critical process

There were a number of features common to each of the four critical communities established.

Formal and informal input

Content was provided through conference presentations and through interaction with other participants at regular network meetings (see Fig. 1). For example, formal sessions were run on action research processes and writing for publication, and these and other issues were elaborated through network meetings. At network meetings, the agenda was often decided by members' immediate needs; these might be, for example, finding a manageable research topic, or planning the involvement of non-language teaching colleagues in a research project. Thus, the input used took account of participants' expressed needs as well as of the requirements of the Project.

Content resources were developed for participants and facilitators during the life of the Project. From year two of LIPT, there was a facilitators' manual, and in year three, input packages were prepared to assist content delivery through the networks rather than through conference presentations. However, the input packages for use in network meetings were found to conflict with the responsive, individualised nature of the Project; that is, it proved more effective to deliver general input formally in conferences and keep the networks free for self-determined, 'relevant' resource-sharing, which kept pace with the demands of participants' action research projects. This process was supported by a general resource bank of materials which facilitators and participants could access on demand.

Facilitators and networks

Network groups, usually of between four and eight participants, were run by facilitators. The facilitators, who included language advisers and experienced teachers, were given prior training in the inservice concept and opportunities to extend their knowledge and experience of action research. Their roles involved supporting participants at each research stage through the group process or in individual consultations. Facilitators also conducted their own research projects and documented their involvement in LIPT.

Sometimes, what the support participants required was material: where could a teacher find out more about a research methodology, or planning group work, for example? In the case of research methodologies, procedures and case studies which now form part of published material (e.g. Nunan, 1989, Allwright and Bailey, 1991, and Richards and Nunan, 1990) were used. Very often, the support required was sustained contact during the research process: for example, the facilitator might become active as a co-researcher in a teacher's research project. The level of involvement responded largely to the expressed wishes of the teachers concerned.

Membership of a network group was part of the contract of participating in LIPT. Discussion and informal feedback provided through peer interaction and team work were the basis of the critical community which formed each year for participants who were learning about and experiencing action research

Project-based

Exposure to the processes of action research (i.e. in this case, purposeful collection of classroom data and focused reflection on classroom practice) was central to LIPT. However, participants also engaged to complete a task. Involvement in LIPT included doing an action research project. In this sense, participation was both purposeful and product-oriented. Outcomes, however, were very often, as we suggested earlier, identifying another stage, another question to investigate.

Publications

Participants undertook to write a report of their action research for publication. The primary audience for the reports was other language teachers. Although the writers were initially diffident about their ability to write in what they viewed as an academic genre, they found that the writing process itself became part of the clarification of their ideas and the setting of further action research and professional renewal goals. Moreover, their own experience made them intensely interested to read about colleagues' action research experiences.

The experience of writing made teacher–writers more familiar with the processes of writing for a professional audience and more at ease with reading more widely. 92% of respondents in the final evaluation of LIPT said that they had continued to read professional publications since participating in LIPT (Burton, 1992). Since the evaluation surveyed and interviewed participants from the first three years of the Project, this response indicates that a professional renewal strategy had been successfully integrated in a number of teachers' normal routines.

Project management and modelling good practice

LIPT was organised by a small team of teacher educators chosen from the three education systems which supported the project and consultants and an evaluator from the tertiary sector. The Project Coordinator, Peter Mickan, the Project Evaluator, Jill Burton, the main Project Consultant, David Nunan, and one of the Project Officers, Rosemary Bigelli, were appointed for the full term of the Project. Each year, one or two teachers (depending on the size of the research community) were selected and seconded as project officers. The number of facilitators appointed depended also on the number of participants (this ranged from 26 to over 100). The Project Team also had a steering committee to report to. The community structure is shown in Fig. 3.

Much of the discussion which took place at Project Team meetings concerned the process of the project. The evaluation of LIPT 3 (Burton, 1991) describes a typical debate on the issue of structuring and streamlining experience in response to some participants' expressed needs compared with supporting them at identified stress points. The main concern of the Team, however, was to conduct the Project in a way which gave teachers the opportunity to experience professional renewal as they might want their learners to learn language.

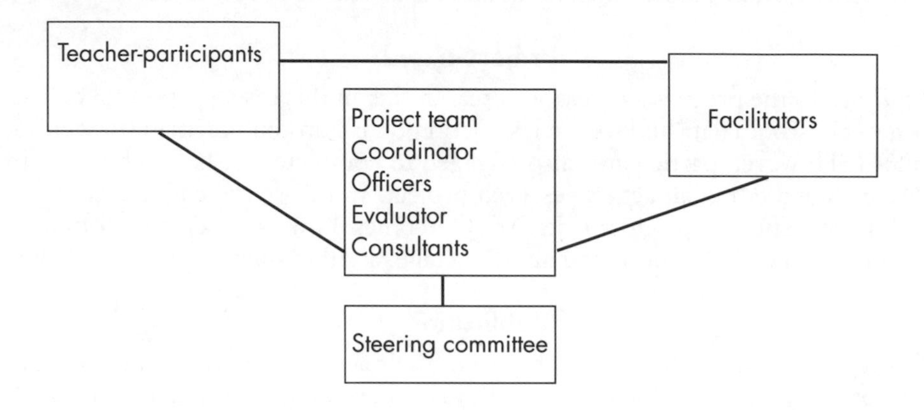

Fig. 3: The community structure

WHY INVOLVE TEACHERS IN RESEARCH?

The LIPT Project suggests that teachers become more interested in the more traditional kinds of research through employing action research processes in their own classroom. Investigating their own teaching stimulates their interest in reading formal reports of research and learning about more rigorous methodologies which will aid their own reflection. Organised projects, which have professional development as their explicit aim, create communities in which experiences are shared, joint tasks are undertaken, and participants become more confident and articulate about their own practice. Teachers become equipped to inform, shape, and contribute to traditional research.

The strength of action research is that it brings research into the classroom and into teacher education processes, thereby enabling research to be done, teaching and learning to be done, and professional development to be done (Allwright, 1992b).

What conclusions, then, can we draw from the experience in LIPT? The programme demonstrated the value and importance of teachers' classroom research, not only for the teachers involved in the programme, but for other language teachers and for research in language education in general.

Teachers who have read the published reports of the LIPT teachers have found them a rich source of ideas for their own practice. The reports are written in a narrative style which reflects the teaching context of readers and makes them comprehensible in a way which academic reports do not. Because the reports describe in detail the contexts and the steps of investigations, other practitioners have found them a practical guide to applying and trying out the ideas for themselves.

Our experience suggests that the classroom research of teachers in LIPT has wider implications as well. The outcomes of teachers' classroom research widen the research agenda to include questions and issues for professional researchers which have import for language teachers. Teachers' classroom research points to critical issues for a research agenda, and at the same time offers the opportunity to test and critique the results of academic research in different contexts. It reveals a shared interest between professional and teacher researchers in the processes of teaching and learning, which can be promoted through the collaboration of 'professional' researchers with teacher researchers.

What are the aims of research? They are generally considered to include increasing understanding, and more recently in a context in which knowledge is viewed as being personally and politically constructed, research is seen as empowering for the individual. Thus, there is, according to Cameron et al. (1992:22ff), ethical research (research 'on') and advocacy research (which adds research 'for' and 'with' to the 'on'). They suggest that research should be done collaboratively, that the subjects of research cannot be objectified, that subjects have their own agendas which research should address, and that *'if knowledge is worth having, it is worth sharing'* (ibid: 24).

It will be through this shared research process that the boundaries between the different research communities will be diminished. At the same time teacher educators must look to creating the conditions for teachers to engage in research as a valued and resourced professional activity, so the rhetoric of classroom research can be realised in practice.

TDTR: Conference as catalyst

Julian Edge & Keith Richards

Aston University

◆

PART 3

The papers in this section of the book are grouped together because of the writers' shared decision to respond directly to the invitation on the speakers' confirmation form:

> *In reporting on your investigations of your teaching context, we encourage you to highlight the personal discoveries and outcomes which appear important in your own development.*

These speakers reported on their own discoveries about themselves, as well as about their classrooms. In the previous section, this disclosure of self occurred only rarely. Rees, for example, refers in passing to a version of his observation template as 'the exasperated model' and Vanerman mentions his 'great relief' on evaluating his findings.

How would it be if we brought the relief and the exasperation to the foreground and investigated them, and wrote about them? It might be interesting, but would it be research?

Underlying the papers in this section is a dual claim which is only starting to be heard:

- Firstly, the data of the researcher's personal involvement, whether that be intellectual, emotional, ideological, or experienced on any other frequency, is valid and potentially important.
- Secondly, the exploring teacher must find a voice with which to record and communicate his or her development, whether or not that voice echoes the accents of academic discourse.

Some of the papers here are more concerned, and explicitly so, with the former claim. They already command the authoritative voice of members of the writing community. Joining this community by learning these accents is the usual way to written empowerment.

But some of the papers are more concerned with the latter claim, and their concern is frequently implicit. Among the volume of noise which surrounds us, individual statements can be lost in the hubbub. But when these unfamiliar voices come together, perhaps we shall start to discern the commonalities which will help us recognise a new way of speaking about teacher research and teacher development. And as we recognise each other's voices, perhaps we shall gain confidence in our right and duty to speak out.

The section begins with Allwright's workshop report. In some senses, we see this as a bridge between the two sections, linking as it naturally does with the concerns of Burton and Mickan. Allwright does not focus openly on his own personal outcomes, but his is the most explicit expression of this shared project to build '*...upon the articulated understanding of the people most closely involved: the teachers and the learners, working together to develop their own understandings of their own experiences.*' And arising from the workshop format, there is a palpable sensation of a shared experience being reflected on, and of learning taking place through articulation.

Rossiter reports on her work in teacher training, in which the empowerment of the trainees is clearly a strong element. What makes this report so central to our concerns, however, is that Rossiter writes as a teacher, investigating her teaching context as it is for her now:

> *I cannot be alone among my colleagues in feeling I know more about the classrooms where I no longer operate on a daily basis than about those in which I do work.*

Her teacher development is the development of herself. The outcomes are personal.

In a related way, Nakhoul reports on classroom research into learner empowerment. The particular depth of this report is achieved by the parallel insights she gives us into her own development as a teacher throughout this process. Emphasising the link between the growth of learners and of teachers, her conclusion is one of continuity rather than ends:

> *It is therefore in the best interests of learners and teachers to establish learner independence but, like any other learning process, it takes time and effort. Neither our own, nor our learners' slowness should be viewed as failure.*

This insistence on maintaining the perspective of a practising professional is a characteristic of all the papers here. The self-delusion of academic neatness is not on McGinity's agenda as she reviews her findings:

> *A few comments on these results are pertinent here. In the first place, they are probably artificial.*

Turner's paper seems to mirror the attitudinal changes felt in her working environment as she moves from the ironic contradiction inherent in:

> *There was a management decision that there were to be two SIGs to promote professional development amongst teachers...*

to the simply revealing:

> *There was satisfaction and pride at the end of the year...*

The practitioner's excitement, engendered by a deeper involvement with colleagues, students and self, is always close to the surface in Torres' account, as is the frustration endemic in her effort to clarify for herself and for others the nature of her multiple role in what she straightforwardly refers to as TDTR:

The research experience I had with them makes me look forward to going back, shedding the PhD researcher clothes and becoming a classroom teacher again.

In one important sense, of course, there is no going back; we carry our change with us. When the environment we discover is also in a state of flux, the interactions become unpredictable and deeper issues materialise without warning. Jenkins' writing bristles with the energy released by profound change:

Frankness is a new luxury in Estonia, and the truth has a new margin of safety that it did not have before. These are things that we foreigners take for granted and perhaps no longer value for their full worth.

In these accounts, then, the anxiety and the excitement, the frustration, the frankness, the pragmatism and the pride are openly expressed. They are expressed because they are important to the recording of these investigations. And there is another thread linking these papers, a thread which begins with the inverted commas which Allwright puts round the word 'academic' with reference to himself, and which runs through McGinity's questions about research and Torres' discomfort with herself as 'PhD researcher'. There is a desire to be taken seriously without necessarily having to assume the accepted forms of academic seriousness. There is a powerful request to be allowed to bear witness appropriately:

I would like to be informed about the consequences of my behaviour less by imagination and wishful thinking, and more by a sensitive witnessing of what is happening in me and in my relating with others.

These words are Underhill's, but they resonate throughout the following papers.

Integrating 'research' and 'pedagogy': appropriate criteria and practical possibilities

Dick Allwright
Lancaster University

◆

This paper reports a workshop whose discussions informed the text overall. These discussions are also reported, from memory, in separate sections. The paper begins, like the workshop, with possible forms for the relationship between research, teaching, and development. Next come ten criteria relevant to any proposal for teacher research, and a report of that workshop discussion. My own proposal for integration — 'exploratory' teaching and learning — follows, again with the workshop discussion on applying the criteria to that proposal. The paper concludes that 'exploratory' teaching and learning appears promising in respect of the stated criteria, and that hopefully the discussion will contribute to the continuing debates about the research-teaching-development relationship, and about the vital issue of 'quality'.

Introduction

Background

It seems to have become almost commonplace for people to advocate that teachers should become researchers in their own classrooms. However, teachers who are attracted to the idea in principle face the risk of discovering the hard way that research can be an unacceptable burden to add to those they are already suffering from in their daily lives as classroom teachers. What is surely (and sorely?) needed is a way, not of adding research to teachers' problems, but of fully integrating research into teachers' normal pedagogic practices. Elsewhere (Allwright, 1991; Allwright and Bailey, 1991) I have proposed 'exploratory teaching' as a potentially productive way of integrating research and pedagogy, and a very brief outline of that proposal may be helpful here. Broadly, it is that we should try exploiting already familiar and trusted classroom activities as ways of exploring the things that puzzle teachers and learners about what is happening in their own classrooms. For example, a teacher's puzzle about his or her learners' apparent dislike of group work might be initially explored simply by asking the learners to discuss it in class (rather than by conducting a questionnaire survey in the traditional academic way).

'Exploratory teaching' is being evolved specifically to deal with the problems teachers face in becoming researchers in their own classrooms. We already have a good idea of some of the major problems involved. We have also given considerable thought to the major aims that it is important to try to achieve. Together, the problems and the major aims constitute a set of criteria that it may be useful to apply to any proposal for teachers to become involved in research.

My aim in this workshop is to offer those criteria up for general discussion, and then to invite their application to my own proposal, for 'exploratory' language teaching and learning.

Before the discussion, however, it may be useful to fill in the background on the alternative possible relationships between research, teaching, and professional development.

The research/teaching/development relationship in principle

In terms of the potential types of relationship between research, teaching and professional development, advocates of 'the teacher as researcher' could in principle be interpreted as adopting any one of at least three major positions.

1 Research as an (optional) extra

'Teacher-researcher' advocates could be seen as promoting research as something that teachers should in principle simply add to their lives as teachers. They could be arguing that teachers should join in the overall research enterprise by undertaking research projects, in addition to all their pedagogic work, as an extra burden whose rewards will lie in the contribution to knowledge that the research projects will bring, and therefore the potential improvement in practice that such a contribution to knowledge should in time make possible. Such a view would not necessarily have any place for professional development at all.

I am not aware of any advocates of 'the teacher as researcher' who would explicitly argue in this way (although I am aware, unfortunately, of academic researchers who appear to think that they can call their research work 'collaborative' simply because they have found teachers who are willing to undertake academe-inspired research projects on such terms), but I am concerned, as I suggested in my opening paragraph, that this may be an understandable, if not entirely fair, message for teachers to find in the work of people like myself, academics whose applied linguistics teaching involves helping teachers develop research skills, and who may be communicating a model of the research process that is seen as hopelessly out of touch with the everyday realities and practical constraints of a teacher's normal working life.

2 Research as the driving force for development

An alternative view of the research/teaching/development relationship is to see the research element in a teacher's life, not as a contribution to some overall research enterprise, but as the driving force for that teacher's personal professional development. Following this view the research element can be seen as central to the pedagogy itself. It is there in order to enable the teacher to better understand what is happening in the classroom (and elsewhere in the overall pedagogic enterprise). In making possible this enhanced personal pedagogic understanding it becomes central to professional development.

This is probably the view that the majority of advocates of 'the teacher as researcher' would wish to convey, but there is a third position to consider.

3 Research as the driving force for development and development as the driving force for research progress

This third position, and my own preference, is to go one step further and suggest that if teacher research is made central to the pedagogy, and is in fact successful in enhancing teachers' understanding of classroom language pedagogy, then not only will the professional development aim be well served, but so will potentially an additional aim of general 'research progress'. By 'research progress' I mean a sense that the profession as a whole is developing its general understanding of classroom language learning and teaching.

My position here is based on the view that significant development in our general understanding of the relevant phenomena is likely to be dependent upon our ability to build upon the individual understandings of the various participants in the enterprise (principally the teachers and the learners). Prabhu, in a recent and very stimulating contribution to the debate (Prabhu, 1992) seems pessimistic about our ability ever to go beyond the notion of individual teachers developing their own personal theories of language pedagogy, but I see no reason in principle why individual understandings should be incapable of being brought together towards some sort of overall synthesis. Teachers' theories may perhaps be developable on a highly individual and personal basis, but it does seem at least arguable that the process might be assisted if teachers have colleagues to discuss their developing understandings with, and colleagues working together might surely be capable of developing a theoretical position of some generality, one not limited in relevance to just one teacher's experience. If that logic is accepted, then it seems also conceivable that someone in my position as an academic researcher, with potential access to the theory-building work of many different groups of teachers in many different countries (see, for example, the work of the English Language Teaching Community, Bangalore, in Naidu et al., 1991, 1992, Rao and Prakash, 1991, and also discussed in Allwright, 1991a) might be able to make connections that result in even more general theory-building.

The logic of my position with regard to the three possible research/teaching/development relationships outlined above is that the first position, putting research as a priority in itself, is clearly an obstacle to the other two, but that the second position is in an important sense a pre-requisite for the third. That is to say, if research is seen primarily as an extra burden then it just will not get done. If, however, it is seen primarily as a way of serving the pedagogy by helping teachers understand their work (and that of their learners) more adequately, then not only will the pedagogy be enhanced but the needs of professional development will also be well served. And, further, if professional development is secured through research then general research progress itself will become possible, through a process of building upon individual and group understandings.

The implications so far

I think it follows from the above that any proposal for teacher-research (especially any such proposal coming from an 'academic' like myself), must be extremely mindful of what it might communicate to the teachers it is addressed to. It must at the very least seek to present research, convincingly, as something that a teacher can reasonably expect to be able to integrate with pedagogy, at the service of the pedagogy, and therefore at the service of the teacher's professional development. It must also try at least to present convincingly the prospect that success on these two fronts will bring with it the potential for the development of a more general understanding of classroom language learning and teaching.

I have been trying for some time to develop such a proposal convincingly, and to make it work, under the heading of 'exploratory teaching' (for the first treatment in print see Allwright and Bailey, 1991b). Most of the development work has been done in Brazil, by people at the Cultura Inglesa in Rio de Janeiro (notably Rosa Lenzuen), and by people in the PIMEI project (a teacher association-based project for secondary school language teacher development, coordinated nationally by Vilma Sampaio in Natal). I will present later the broad outlines of the proposal, and illustrate the work done so far (see also Allwright, 1991b and c and 1992a for fuller accounts), but for now I wish to concentrate on the criteria that this work has suggested to be the most important ones for us to try to meet along the way.

APPROPRIATE CRITERIA FOR ANY PROPOSAL TO INTEGRATE RESEARCH AND PEDAGOGY

The criteria that have emerged from development work so far take two forms: seven things we have realised we are trying to achieve, and three sets of problems that we are consciously trying to bear in mind and to minimise. No particular originality is claimed for these two lists, rather I am presenting them here in order to find out if others also find them relevant and important.

The seven major aims

1 Relevance

The least to hope for from our work is that teachers bringing research into their own teaching will ensure that what they explore is relevant to themselves, regardless of what concerns academic researchers, and of course that it is also relevant to their learners, who may well have interesting puzzles of their own to explore.

2 Reflection

We can also, again at the very least, work towards ensuring that integrating research and pedagogy promotes reflection, by both teachers and learners, given how powerful reflection seems to be as a motive force for development.

3 Continuity

In addition it seems very important to try to ensure that integrating research and pedagogy is a continuous enterprise, not something that a teacher will try once and then drop for ever. Countless teachers on pre-service and in-service courses must have conducted mini research projects that have taken over their lives and convinced them that if that is what research means, then it is not for them. We must somehow encourage continuity.

4 Collegiality
Teaching is often seen as an isolating sort of job, and we could therefore surely aim to use the integration of research and pedagogy to bring teachers together more, to bring teachers closer to learners. Even more pertinently in the present context, we could (I am sure 'should') try to use the integration of research and pedagogy to try to heal the highly damaging rift that has frequently been noted between teachers and academic researchers.

5 Learner development
At the same time, it seems very important not to miss any opportunity to help learners develop as learners. Ensuring that the questions asked are seen as relevant by learners as well as teachers, and that learners, like teachers, are prompted to reflect on their experiences, should help learner development. We could of course take it much further, towards 'exploratory' learning as well as 'exploratory' teaching, as is already being done in, for example, autonomy projects in Europe (see Holec, 1988 for a valuable compendium of project reports).

6 Teacher development
I see little point in a teacher integrating research into his or her teaching unless it contributes to that teacher's own development, and to the more general professional development of the field (leaving aside for the moment any problems we might have about 'professionalisation' as a potential threat to some of our broader values). As noted earlier, teacher development, whether seen as personal or collective, across the professional community, is not necessarily the only ultimate aim, however. There remains the further aim of theory-building.

7 Theory-building
All of which should enable us to develop our general understanding of classroom language teaching and learning, by building upon the articulated understandings of the people most closely involved: the teachers and the learners, working together to develop their own understandings of their own experiences.

The major problems to be expected

This list is short, but the problems involved are extremely important.

1 The time commitment
Doing research in the language classroom is time-consuming, at all points. It will increase preparation time, for example, if lessons must be altered to accommodate a research activity, and it will probably also take up classroom learning time (both a practical and an ethical issue). Afterwards it will then be necessary to spend time sorting out what has been learned. We must be highly sensitive to this time issue, or teachers will simply find the burden unacceptable, and stop the research.

2 The skills-learning burden
Becoming a classroom researcher also seems inevitably to involve the learning of new skills — specifically the skills required to conduct research satisfactorily, skills lying outside the normal repertoire of classroom teachers. Acquiring them will take time, and intellectual effort, effort which will no longer be available to be put into more directly pedagogic concerns. Some of the skills involved may

be useful ones in any case (see the discussion of Steps 2 and 7 below) but many (for example perhaps the complex of skills required for the construction of successful questionnaires) may not be at all easily related to the other skill requirements for a classroom language teacher. Again this burden, particularly in regard to skills that are not likely to be more generally useful, needs to be minimised or it may prove fatal. 'Exploratory' teaching aims to achieve this minimisation by proposing, as already noted, that the investigative activities should be based on pedagogic activities that the teacher (and the learners) already know and trust.

3 Threats to self-esteem

Conducting research in and into your classroom means running the risk of discovering things that you would perhaps rather not have to face. It therefore poses a potential threat to your self-esteem. It may be much less of a threat than if an academic researcher comes into your classroom and produces a damaging report about you, but it is still a threat, and one that we need to work to minimise.

A further possibility in some work situations is that getting involved in research might actually endanger continued employment. One possible way this might happen would be if a teacher began research by identifying a 'problem' in his or her classroom, and was then him or herself identified as 'having problems' as compared to other teachers in the same institution who are careful to not get involved in research activity and therefore to not put themselves in a position to reveal whatever 'problems' they may actually be experiencing. 'Exploratory' teaching's suggestion is to start with 'puzzles', rather than 'problems', wherever this might help.

Workshop discussion of the criteria

The above text is to a large extent the product of immediate reflection on the events of the workshop itself. What follows is an attempt to capture at least some of the points that have not been incorporated already in some way.

Comments on relevance, redundancy, and omissions

The criteria (the seven aims and three sets of problems) were generally seen all to be relevant and important, with no major omissions or particular redundancies to be noted. It was, however, pointed out that the first three aims seemed to be of a different order entirely from the last four, and that the last four could perhaps be summarised (even collapsed) under the heading of 'learning development'.

It was also suggested that discussion was difficult, perhaps meaningless, without prior agreement on definitions of the central terms 'research' and 'pedagogy', but this was countered with the suggestion that a better understanding of what we might mean by the two terms could perhaps be expected to come from the work to integrate them, rather than be seen as a necessary input to that integration work.

'Horror' stories and 'success' stories

Participants had some 'horror stories' to tell about how in their experience the criteria had on occasions not been met. Typically these centred on situations in which classroom teachers found themselves at risk of official disapproval if they conducted research in their classrooms (for example, if they wanted to elicit learner opinion in a context where it would be considered a professional weakness to appear to need help of any sort from learners). Other participants, however, insisted that opportunities for teachers to conduct research in their own classrooms could be found in all circumstances.

'Success stories' were surprisingly, and gratifyingly, numerous, suggesting that at least some of the criteria (for example 'relevance', 'reflection', and 'teacher development') may represent entirely realistic aims in many situations, although 'learner development' seems less commonly achieved, and 'continuity' and 'collegiality' represent more distant aims. 'Theory-building' no doubt remains the remotest of them all, if only because we still need to do so much work to understand what we mean by it.

Comments on the three problem areas

Meanwhile, 'time' is clearly the great enemy for all, while the 'skills-learning burden' seems perhaps not as problematic as I have myself so far thought. In my own work with Brazilian teachers of English (see also the discussion of exploratory teaching's Steps 2 and 7 below), it appears that the principal skills-learning needs for teachers working within the 'exploratory teaching' framework lie in the areas of question formation and information interpretation, two key conceptual areas, it seems to me, both for any research enterprise and for any pedagogic enterprise. The issue of research representing a threat to self-esteem (and perhaps to a teacher's employability if classroom problems are not kept confidential) was discussed but not pursued in depth.

'EXPLORATORY' TEACHING AND LEARNING AS ONE WAY OF TRYING TO INTEGRATE RESEARCH AND PEDAGOGY

It is time to describe 'exploratory' language teaching and learning in more detail, before considering how it matches up to the criteria we have established for it.

The basic concept of 'exploratory' teaching and learning

The central concern of what I am calling 'exploratory' language teaching and learning, as noted in the opening paragraphs of this paper, is a wish to offer a practical way of bringing the research perspective properly into the classroom, without adding significantly and unacceptably to teachers' workloads, so as to contribute both to professional development and to theory-building within and across the profession.

The basic process

The basic process advocated for 'exploratory' work, again as noted above, is one of using already familiar pedagogic activities to investigate teacher and learner 'puzzles'.

The procedures

Work over the last two years or so in Brazil has suggested the following list of general procedures for teachers engaged in 'exploratory' work in their classrooms. (For a fuller discussion of these procedures, though inevitably at an earlier stage in the development of the ideas involved, the reader is referred to Allwright, 1991c.)

Step 1 Identify a puzzle area

This is the starting point, with the term 'puzzle' deliberately chosen in preference to the more usual 'problem' to avoid the potential threat to self-esteem that admitting to having 'problems' might represent, and to capture the important possibility that productive investigations might well start from poorly-understood successes just as much as from poorly-understood failures.

Step 2 Refine your thinking about that puzzle area

This is increasingly establishing itself as a key stage, and one for which people do not feel prepared by their previous experiences and by their prior training. For me it revolves around developing the ability to mentally 'explore' an issue, and not to accept a first interpretation of it. For example, a group of teachers in Brazil identified as 'puzzling' their perception that their learners insisted on knowing the meaning of every word in a text before they would feel that they understood it. In their first interpretation this 'puzzle' was clearly also a practical 'problem' (something they wished to change) and equally clearly a problem that they saw as located in the heads of their learners. It did not take much more thinking, however, to refine that position towards one where there were several possible locations for the problem — including the texts themselves, and the tasks that were typically associated with those texts.

Step 3 Select a particular topic to focus upon

This is also a key step, and one that workshop discussion at Aston suggested might be a terminal one for some teachers, who might feel paralysed by the complexities revealed at the puzzle refinement stage. My own experience has not yet produced evidence for such pessimism, but it is clear that choices of focus may sometimes have to be dictated by immediate practicalities, rather than by the centrality of the chosen subtopic to the overall issue at the origin of the work.

Step 4 Find appropriate classroom procedures to explore it

In my experience, teachers have not found it difficult to list a good number of classroom procedures, pedagogic activities they already know and trust, that they can imagine exploiting for investigative as well as for narrowly pedagogic purposes. The following is a selected list from the thirty or so ideas that different teachers' groups have offered. It is presented here by way of illustration, in the hope that it will not need further clarification:

1 Group work discussions
2 Pair work discussions
3 Surveys
4 Interviews
5 Simulations
6 Role-plays
7 Role-exchanging
8 Diaries
9 Dialogue journal writing
10 Projects
11 Poster sessions
12 Learner to learner correspondence.

Step 5 Adapt them to the particular puzzle you want to explore
This seems to be a relatively unproblematic stage, consisting simply of putting learning 'on the classroom agenda' by, for example, substituting discussion of the chosen puzzle for more traditional (but not necessarily more engaging) topics such as 'pollution', or 'holidays'. In retrospect it seems entirely bizarre, as well as unfortunate, that the language teaching profession should have taken so long to think of putting learning itself 'on the agenda', given the amount of agonising that language teachers, and textbook writers, must have gone through over the years in their efforts to find topics that might conceivably interest learners, and especially given their probable advantage over teachers and textbook writers for other subjects, who cannot so easily move away from the confines of their ostensible subject matter. The advocates of 'learner training' have of course been putting learning on the classroom agenda for some years now (see Ellis and Sinclair, 1989, for a thoroughgoing example of an entire coursebook devoted to the topic).

Step 6 Use them in class
Again this seems to be a relatively unproblematic stage, although I am not convinced that we have done nearly enough work on helping teachers develop the monitoring skills they will probably need if they are to use activities both for their pedagogic potential and simultaneously for what are essentially data collection purposes.

Step 7 Interpret the outcomes
This stage is seen as at least as problematic as that of refining puzzles in the first place. My only comfort is that effort expended in these two areas, as I have already begun to indicate above (see p 127), can be of real practical value to the teachers (and hopefully also to the learners) involved, since it is central to learning from any experience. At the moment this remains speculation, however, so future development work needs to focus on this stage, alongside Step 2 of course.

Step 8 Decide on their implications and plan accordingly
There seem to be four very different, though clearly related, possibilities for work following an initial exploratory investigation. The most obvious is that the original puzzle will have been refined in the process of investigation, and that it will now seem necessary to move on to some slightly different conception of it — a new puzzle emerging from the old one. The second possibility, but not a high probability, is that enough will have been learned to justify moving in some other direction with an entirely new puzzle. A third possibility is that enough will have been learned to justify trying out pedagogic changes in the classroom (if these are indicated). This will of course bring the enterprise much closer to the 'action research' model, with its focus on trying change as a way of investigating classroom language learning and teaching. The fourth possibility, compatible with any or all of the others, is that enough will have been learned, in some sense at least, for the teacher or teachers involved to want to share their work with others, most probably not as a set of findings, but more as a 'recruiting' measure, aimed at bringing more people into the investigation, for the very probable benefit of having more brains involved, and of therefore being perhaps

able to come to more convincing interpretations, and perhaps even more convincing contributions to general theory-building. The teachers at the Cultura Inglesa in Rio de Janeiro have approached this set of possibilities by converting their annual conference into a collective poster session, and by using their in-house newsletter (Views and News) to keep each other in touch with what they are all doing. There is an instructive parallel in the extremely interesting work of the English Language Teaching Community, Bangalore, also reported by poster, as well as by publications (see Naidu et al., 1991, 1992, and Rao and Prakash, 1991).

APPLYING THE CRITERIA TO 'EXPLORATORY' LANGUAGE TEACHING AND LEARNING

The workshop group was asked to address two questions, from their necessarily very limited exposure to the ideas and development work of 'exploratory' teaching and learning: 'Where are the major strengths?' and 'Where are the major weaknesses?'.

General comments

For at least one participant the suggested procedures for 'exploratory' language teaching and learning coincided almost exactly with those she had been using in her own work, but under the heading of 'action research'. Space precludes an adequate discussion here of the potentially important differences between the two concepts, differences which reside most obviously (but by no means exclusively or most importantly) in different views on how to achieve the major aims, but I would suggest that if the criteria set out and discussed above are met, then labels are in any case unimportant.

Potential 'strengths' and 'weaknesses'

The major strength of 'exploratory' language teaching and learning as presented, was seen (as I hoped, of course) to be its potential for offering teachers a minimum-cost way of integrating research and teaching. A potential major weakness was noted in that the suggestions for learner involvement seemed typically to rely strongly on learners having a well-established command of the target language. It was extremely difficult therefore to see how the suggestions for investigative classroom procedures could be employed with beginners, or even near-beginners. The counter-suggestion was made, however, that even beginners' opinions could be elicited successfully by means of checklists of isolated words (in the target language), with an agreement/disagreement scale.

FINAL COMMENTS

The workshop on which this paper is based was addressed to the discussion and further elaboration of a set of criteria for any proposal for teacher research, and to the application of that set of criteria to my own specific proposal for 'exploratory' language teaching and learning. The workshop took place in the context of a meeting devoted to the relationship between teacher research and teacher development. I hope this report will make a useful contribution to the continuing debate about that relationship. I hope that it also has something to say, given its focus on appropriate criteria, about another theme of the meeting, as emphasised in Bridget Somekh's plenary — the elusive but central issue of 'quality'.

Teacher educators and classroom research: practising what we preach

Anne Rossiter

West Sussex Institute of Higher Education

◆

This paper, while acknowledging the difficulties, stresses the value of teacher educators investigating what goes on in their 'classrooms'. It presents the results of an investigation into innovations in the professional component of an initial teacher training course. It examines in particular the use trainees can make of peer discussion of classroom events in the construction of pedagogical knowledge.

WHY SHOULD TEACHER EDUCATORS BE INVOLVED IN CLASSROOM RESEARCH?

I'd like to answer this question by explaining how my own interest in classroom research came about. In the course of my work on an in-service training programme a few years ago, I was asked to supervise the marking of the trainees' research projects. This proved an immensely distressing experience, wading through dozens of lengthy and ill-digested summaries of the ideas of well-known writers on 'group work' and 'communication games', in which the rare comments relating to classroom practice showed how far the writers were from seeing the relevance of these ideas to their own situation, let alone implementing them.

A colleague and I began, therefore, to consider how we could replace this theory-based and ultimately meaningless research with the trainees' own investigations into problems which actually concerned them in their own schools, and the steps they could take to cope with the very real difficulties they faced. Through circumstances beyond our control, our involvement in this programme came to an abrupt end, but what remained was firstly a very real interest in teachers' use of their own classrooms as a means of developing their understanding of teaching. Secondly, it seemed clear that there is a continuing need for teacher educators to examine their own practices in order to provide teachers, in training or on courses of professional development, with appropriate opportunities to learn what *they* need in order to become increasingly able teachers.

The more I learn from recent research in the language classroom, the more I become aware how little I know about the way learning takes place in my own. I cannot be alone among my colleagues in feeling I now know far more about the classrooms where I no longer operate on a daily basis than about those in which I do work. I am also aware of how large my 'classroom' is: the seminar room, the lecture room (occasionally), the one-to-one office tutorial, the TP supervision corner, the self-access area, the conference room, the journal ...

The need of all teachers to satisfy themselves that learning is taking place is especially felt now by teacher educators in Britain, where the training of teachers is the subject of very public scrutiny. The need to find out more about our teaching is obvious, but ...

- Where is the time to do so? New teaching contracts in higher education necessitate high contact hours. If time is allocated for research there is an equally strong pressure for academic publication to uphold academic standards.
- Where is the support group? Even more than teachers, teacher educators often work alone, developing an expertise or interest which may not be shared by other colleagues, for whom other commitments assume a higher priority.

Presumably we must follow the example of all teachers who have involved themselves in classroom research: make the time for it, show others what we are doing and gain their interest and support.

Investigating the use of peer discussion in the development of pedagogical knowledge

I didn't set out to find a research topic. As my reading of classroom research case studies showed me, the need makes itself known (if you want to listen).

Problem identification

Second year BEd (ESOL) trainees didn't seem to be getting much out of their 'professional' (i.e. practical) course. This is a thirty week course of two and a half hour peer microteaching sessions weekly. Dissatisfaction with the results of this course was especially worrying because the trainees have no teaching practice in English (their main subject) in this year of the course. The professional strand provides the major link between the one month teaching practice at the end of the first year and the three month teaching practice at the end of the third year.

Preliminary investigation

The course followed the traditional microteaching format. The students were required to teach 10-15 minute segments of a lesson. The teaching was filmed by a video camera placed on a tripod at the back of the class. Each student's lesson was recorded onto videotape which was then available for private study after the class. There was a brief class discussion of the points arising from the teaching. The tutor wrote notes on the trainee's lesson on a carbon pad. The top copy was given to the student, the bottom copy retained as a record. The focus of the practice was on technique, each trainee being required to teach the presentation and practice stage of a new structure. They were expected to produce a detailed plan of their teaching and their own set of teaching materials and visual aids. The course was assessed by the production of a course file.

Discussion with colleagues revealed a shared concern and the expressed belief that the trainees 'don't take the course seriously enough'. Further comments were: the trainees were very, very self-conscious about performing in front of each other, they didn't like being videoed, their teaching was in many cases quite weak and unimaginative.

Examining the trainees' course files revealed a considerable range of achievement. Some files were well presented with careful notes on the teaching. These focused, however, almost exclusively on descriptions of the techniques presented and judgements on their effectiveness. Other files were poorly presented, consisting of untitled, undated pencil jottings that formed no coherent record of the teaching presented, let alone an attempt to develop a personal theory of teaching.

Conversations with the trainees confirmed that they regarded the microteaching sessions as 'boring', something that they supposed 'had to be done', and above all, as having little to do with 'real teaching'.

Implementing a change

Reading about the development of the 'reflective practitioner' brought me to Wallace's analysis of the underlying concept of microteaching. He suggests that:

> *it is more valid to see microteaching as a technique for professional reflection rather than simply as a technique for shaping behaviour.*
>
> (Wallace, 1991:95)

I became interested, therefore, in considering ways in which the trainees could come to view peer teaching as an opportunity to develop their understanding of the nature of teaching, of 'what being a teacher is all about'.

My hypothesis was that the professional sessions could become a more valid vehicle for professional learning if the members of the group were encouraged to take a more active role as co-investigators of the teaching/learning process.

What did this mean in practice? — implications for action

The first implication was that the peer teaching should be made as 'real' as possible. It should offer the trainees experiences which they could relate to their real-life teaching situation. Secondly, they should be encouraged to make use of the multiple perspectives inherent in the situation and investigate teaching and learning as teachers, as students, as trainee teachers and as observers, through the eye of the camera.

Greater use should be made of the potential of video, its power to document the experience as an (apparently) objective event, enabling those involved to observe and reflect on situations in which they were the protagonists. It makes possible the re-examination of segments of experience in detail, through the accurate record of precise language used, gestures made, and the sequence of actions performed.

Above all, I was interested by the possibility of getting the trainees to use the videos of their own teaching to develop knowledge *about* teaching which will form the basis of future actions. Here I am adopting what Tickle (1987) defines as 'the interpretive view' of knowledge which:

> *assumes that knowledge is constructed actively and subjectively by the individual, and used in accordance with interpretations of problems and situations by the individual.*
>
> (Tickle, 1987:46)

In the context of my investigation, this suggests that as much time as possible should be set aside for peer discussion of the teaching videos and that the role of the tutor in the peer teaching sessions should be that of co-investigator rather than expert.

Action taken

Time was set aside for discussing with the trainees a different focus for the professional course for the second term. Proposed changes were outlined and the trainees' (slightly hesitant) agreement obtained.

The content of the peer teaching for the term was 'communicative activities' (this fitted in with the scheme of work). For each session, however, the peer teacher was required to plan and execute a complete 40 minute lesson, integrating this activity into a relevant sequence of work. The 'peer factor' could be faced either by devising tasks of appropriate complexity for the real-life abilities of their fellow trainees or by asking their colleagues to role-play the kind of class they would expect to meet in their home situation.

As teachers, the trainees were expected to exercise a high level of professionalism. They selected materials and made an outline plan of the lesson. They discussed their plans with the tutor. They produced and photocopied sets of teaching materials for their 'students', and sets of lesson plans for their peers at the discussion stage. They arranged the classroom in the way they wanted it, and discussed the filming of the lesson with the camera crew. During their teaching they had complete responsibility for the conduct of the classroom. After the session and the discussion of the video, they wrote their own reflections on the lesson as the teacher. As 'students' the trainees also had responsibilities. They were expected to remain in character throughout the session. After the discussion they were expected to reflect on the lesson, from two viewpoints, firstly as a student, and secondly as a trainee teacher.

Four of the students had expressed their interest in filming the sessions. This team filmed all the teaching, becoming highly professional in their use of the camera and also developing a clear understanding of 'where the learning was' at a given moment. They used this perspective in their evaluations.

The trainees were encouraged to see the peer teaching as a forum for trialling and evaluating teaching materials and procedures. They had the opportunity to build up banks of lesson plans and materials which they could adapt for use in their own classrooms. They had the opportunity to experiment with procedures which they had come across in their reading or seen used by others. Most importantly, however, in discussions of the videoed teaching, they were offered the opportunity to investigate the reasons which underlay decisions made in teaching.

To show that I really believed in what I was asking them to do, in the first session I was the teacher, and the resulting video was used as material for the first investigation. This was not presented in any way as a model, but as evidence that I was interested in investigating my own teaching and had a lot to learn from the trainees' questions, comments and suggestions. This session established some of the ground rules for subsequent discussions. It was agreed that, during the viewing of the video, the teacher-investigators should be in charge and control the video so that they could focus the discussion on the areas they were most interested in. How did the 'students' feel about being asked to do X? What do their peers feel about the decision to use material Y? Was that an appropriate way to handle situation Z?

The other trainees had the right to pursue their own enquiries into issues they saw being raised by the teaching, and could ask for the tape to be paused at any point for comments or questions. Words like 'good' or 'bad', it was agreed, had little meaning in themselves, although it was thought important for teachers to know which elements in their teaching their peers particularly liked and why. Questions as to *why* a particular decision had been made were considered most useful as they made the teachers think about what they had done and made the other trainees think too. Direct challenges were also seen as unhelpful and a more reflective form of comment was preferred: 'I wonder if ... ', 'Do you think ... ?', seeking the teacher's and peers' opinions on the idea proposed.

As the trainees became more and more confident in their roles, my role as tutor became important only outside the classroom, in the lesson planning conference, and as a resource in emergencies. When I was absent for ten days the class carried on as normal, and videos were made of the lesson discussions as well as the peer teaching.

Observation

As a course requirement, students were asked to submit course files. This time they were required to include their reflections on each lesson and their own assessment of what they had learnt from the course as a whole. I was, therefore, able to use these written assessments, supported by the students' spontaneous comments, and the formal evaluations made at their Programme Review Board, as well as an analysis of the recorded discussions and my own field notes, to establish where the innovations succeeded and failed.

Outcomes

The most encouraging outcome was that the trainees' perceptions of the professional course were more positive. Although the trainees were still conscious of the limitations of peer teaching as a replication of the real classroom, the predominant feeling was that the course was a useful one.

Although the trainees clung firmly to the word 'microteaching' throughout, one of the most appreciated features was the lengthening of the teaching:

> *I think that it is very, very good that the microteaching is done as a whole lesson instead of just a chunk or 5-10 minutes of a whole lesson, in that way we feel*

that it is a real lesson; full and complete, not 'hanging' from nowhere.

Encouragement to see the classroom from a variety of perspectives was also appreciated, although several found the switching of roles quite difficult:

> *Being both a student and an observer in a microteaching lesson made me more aware of things that are happening because I was a part of the lesson and not just sitting at the side — looking into a fish bowl.*

Those who filmed the teaching found that they had learnt more than techniques:

> *... most of my time would be focusing my attention to where the 'eye' of the camera is. Other students might be involved in the activities while I scrutinise how the 'teacher' is feeling, their reactions to what is going on in the class, and not to mention the anxiety to get the lesson over and done with.*

Most significantly, great importance was attached to the follow-up discussion. This was highlighted with reference to the course as a whole:

> *All in all I thought that the professional course is a very useful and helpful course. It helped to have the microteaching, and the discussions that followed were rich in ideas and comments from us. I suppose it highlighted all our fears which had to do with teaching as well as solving it in one go. I especially liked to see and experience all the other people's ideas and contributions because the range is wide and varied. It would have been torture if we had to come up with all the ideas individually.*

and to their own teaching:

> *The class discussion of my lesson was very useful. Although the word 'disaster' could sum up my lesson neatly, I'm glad because at least this was not a 'real' lesson and I have gained a lot through the classroom discussion.*

This recognition of how much they could learn from each other was repeated time and again in the trainee assessments. The stance of the tutor in discussions was also appreciated:

> *I felt that she didn't impose herself or her views on us. It seemed that though she is our tutor, she made it apparent to us that like us she is still learning.*

A major outcome, evidenced in the post-lesson discussions and in the assessments, was the trainees' willingness to theorise about their own teaching and to incorporate their own experience. For example:

> *On the whole my feeling as a teacher is that I haven't taught them enough of English. I feel like we're just having fun. But taking a closer look, I think they're getting a lot of input and practice from just doing the activity. This is what communicative language teaching does, making the students learn indirectly through interesting activities.*

Analysing the recorded discussions showed an increase in confidence on the part of the teacher, from the first firmly-controlled discussions where the tape was paused at regular intervals to ask: 'anything to say?', or 'anything else?', to a more open questioning in later sessions.

S1: */I feel that your warming up session was very good/that it was a good activity for that kind of ... /*

ST: */it's not/it's not silly you know?/because it was/on that low level?/*

S2: */no it's not silly/*

S1: */very challenging in fact/it picks up a lot of/because you need a lot of/um/specificness/and um detail/to get the picture right/in the instructions/*

Maturity and commitment to the aims of the course was shown by the serious approach to discussions videoed in my absence. These illustrate the effect, commented on by participants in other recorded discussions, of video-related work being more topic-centred than non-recorded discussion.

These video-tapes show the trainees' ability to articulate their ideas in sustained discussion of professional topics. There is frequent laughter but no off-task talking.

I would now like to analyse the transcript of one discussion in greater depth.

Analysis of peer discussion

The discussion can be analysed into thirteen 'episodes' or discussions of a single topic. The length and complexity of each episode can be measured by the number of 'turns' taken, and the number of different contributors. The episodes range from a three turn dialogue between the teacher and one trainee to a discussion of twenty turns with nine contributors. Although teacher-initiated episodes occur in the first section of the discussion, the final eight episodes are initiated by spontaneous comments from the trainees. One initiation is an opinion, giving a positive evaluation, the rest are in the form of questions. Six are put directly to the teacher, to explore and often, as in this example, to endorse his decision making:

S1: */(name)/did you say/er/'I made a mistake' then?/*

ST: */yes/*

S1: */yes I think that that's good because it tells people ...*

Two questions were asked of the group as a whole. In the following example, the repeated use of the modal 'should' appears to mark a search for principled behaviour on a topic interpreted both as a very real issue for the speaker, and one of collective concern:

/I just want to ask/um er/should we pick up all the words like that/I mean/I would sometimes/er/I was sometimes faced with things like that/do you think we should just say ... /

Here, I believe, we can see the dual focus of pedagogical theory: providing both principles of action for the individual and the development of a commonly-held body of knowledge.

Although their language contains the informal fillers: 'you know', 'sort of', 'stuff like that', of the trainees' usual speech, the turns are formally structured, with frequent use of logical markers, especially 'because' and 'so', 'if' and 'then'. The standard lexis of the world of education is used with some confidence as in: 'they tend to concentrate on', or 'it would modify the purpose of that exercise'.

The most notable feature of the trainees' language, however, is the determined attempt to establish and maintain an appropriate style for the presentation of their own, and acceptance of each other's, ideas. One very noticeable indicator is the prefacing 'I think' used by the trainees on twenty-five occasions to stress the non-dogmatic nature of their utterances. That this is a highly conscious decision is clearly seen in this reformulation:

/but it's not good to/I don't think it's good to put the students on the defensive/

In analysing the content of the discussion, the following topics were found to be covered:

Teacher's language:	clarity of expression pronunciation
Presentation skill:	use of visuals use of mime linguistic choices
Methodological procedures:	writing activities
Classroom management:	handling student questions giving instructions dealing with latecomers coping with teacher errors involving students in decision-making

The discussion contained many instances of trainees picking out examples of the teacher's performance and relating this to their own theoretical constructs of 'good practice'. In commenting on interpersonal skills trainees evinced most confidence in their own judgement; the need for fairness, clarity and a consideration of the students' own feelings can be seen to underlie many of the comments. In evaluating procedural skills, those which could be related most obviously to these criteria, were also clearly perceived:

/and you asking the students what can we do with it/it's like making the students/making the students feel that they are part of the lesson/and they can decide what to do/

There were fewer instances of trainees' questioning practice that seemed to be counter to what was seen as good theory, and most of these tended to focus on what McGarvey and Swallow (1986, quoted in Wallace, p 97) would recognise as 'performance skills', '... *the technical, observable behaviours which constitute the teaching act*'.

/when you ask/'what are these?'/instead of just holding it there/it's a good idea if you stick it on the board so everyone can see/

McGarvey and Swallow identify two more complex human capacities involved in teaching. The first of these capacities relates to 'cognitive processes' which underlie the ability to perform particular actions and to recognise when their performance is appropriate. The second relates to 'affective learning', and the teacher's desire to perform these valued actions well. In their attempt to construct theory as the basis for action it is clear that the trainees are involved with all three dimensions of teaching ability, as they blend principled belief and experience with their interpretation of the lesson data.

In the following extract the trainees are talking about giving examples in answer to students who ask what a noun is. The discussion contains a dramatic representation of her performance skill by S6, discussion by S2, S3, S4 and S5 of where and how examples can be appropriately used, and the demonstration by all the speakers of their commitment to providing students with the understanding they need:

S1: */you can't just leave it like that/*

S2: */you can just explain it to them/and give clear examples/*

S3: */it's better to give examples/it's going to be clearer to study them if you're going to say/this is the meaning/if you're going to give an explanation /then get students/to write/two or three examples/*

S4: */wouldn't that sort of/weaken the lesson/once you start giving two or three you're sort of ... /*

S5: */tangenting?/*

S4: */going off at a tangent/then OK/then you clarify/and then you come up with something else/*

S6: */I've done that before/but I didn't sort of only/Give me an example/OK nouns/Table/That's right/you go rapide/Adjectives/give me an example/*

In only one area did a discussion fail, both trainee and teacher finally echoing: 'I don't know'. This was when a determined, yet quite sensitive, attempt was made to probe the language rather than the pedagogic knowledge underlying the teacher's performance. The tone is set from the beginning of the exchange.

S1: */what about the use of/you know/where you say/'I'm walking'/and then you say/'I am walking'/and then/um/what else/some more structures where you say/'I am' instead of 'I'm'/ ... /why did you say 'I am'?/*

ST: */I can't think/*

S1: *(laughing)/I don't know/which do you think is better/'I'm'/or 'I am'?/*

ST: */I don't know/*

Reflection

I was impressed by the trainees' reactions and the interest and ability they showed in discussing teaching issues. I was especially pleased by the number of trainees who reported how much they felt they learnt from each other and at the serious and constructive way they talked through, at times quite personal, issues. I became very aware of the ways in which the tutor-as-expert can become a stumbling block to trainees trying to establish their own perspectives. I feel their discussions were much more successful the less I contributed. In comparing my notes on the peer teaching sessions with the points which the teacher-investigators raised I found that they diverged considerably. This again made me aware of how unhelpful and off-beam our comments often must seem. In considering the teaching of subjects where students' errors can be clearly identified, Ramsden writes:

> *Helping understanding does not mean correcting every mistake, often it is better to say nothing at all: time and reflection or discussion with peers may serve the purpose of correction of errors much better, as well as fostering the independence of thought that every teacher in higher education desires.*
>
> (Ramsden, 1992:170)

If we consider trainee teachers to be involved in the process of constructing their own knowledge of teaching there seems a clear need to ensure they have the 'raw materials' and then allow them the time and space to work.

One of the great weaknesses of the course was not giving more class time to the discussion of the videos. The time the trainees spent in watching and learning from their own teaching could have been several times as long.

It was perhaps an easy option to begin this investigation by focusing on form of teaching which demands less 'teacher fronting' and stresses motivating the students' language use through interesting and enjoyable activities. Several trainees have expressed their anxieties about being able to cope when more direct teaching of the language is called for. This anxiety, together with evidence from the analysed discussion, suggests that the next focus of learning should be the construction of what could be termed the 'linguistico-pedagogic' knowledge base. Trainees do not need to be confident only in the techniques of presentation of grammatical structures, they also need to know in what form and when to present elements of the language system, and to be confident in incorporating teaching on language form as well as encourage language use.

This seems an urgent area to focus on. At the same time, however, the problem of the lack of authenticity of the peer teaching session will inevitably become more acute. As competent English users, peers can not replicate the language knowledge and language learning skills and strategies of 'pre-intermediate' secondary school students.

PLANNING FOR FURTHER ACTION

The following guidelines for further action represent my current positions. I should welcome the exchange of suggestions and experiences from colleagues who have reached, or gone beyond, this point!

- Alternative ways of allowing trainees to investigate the language study element of their teaching need to be contrived.
- Ample time needs to be set aside for peer discussion.
- Consideration should be given to the use of peer discussion in assessment of the professional course.
- The recording and analysing of peer discussion should continue on a regular basis to discover how trainees consolidate their base of pedagogical (and linguistico-pedagogical) knowledge in preparation for their final teaching practice and their own research projects.

Letting go: preparing teachers and students for learner independence

Liz Nakhoul
University of Hong Kong

◆

This paper is concerned with learner training for learner independence in the context of a first year university (Arts Faculty) course in English for Academic Purposes. The weekly course timetable allows for two class contact hours and one hour for self-access language work. Learner guidance and feedback in the utilisation of this hour is at the teacher's discretion. The research described investigates student and teacher attitudes to the degree of teacher control implemented.

LEARNER INDEPENDENCE

Language teaching theory and practice has demonstrated an increasing concern since the 70s with the learner and the process of learning (see Oller and Richards, 1973; Rubin, 1975; Pickett, 1978). Ellis and Sinclair's *Learning to Learn English* (1989) is a logical outcome of teachers' increasing concern that learners should be able to assume responsibility for learning. Similarly, Dickinson's (1978, 1987 and 1988) work on self-instruction stems from the realisation that classroom teaching is not a language learning panacea.

Although Dickinson (1987:8-14) has defined the terminology of self-instruction meticulously in order to clarify discussion, I find I differ slightly in my own interpretations. With regard to learner independence I would suggest a scale of attitude to language learning ranging from dependent (i.e. teacher directed) to independent (i.e. learner directed). In my view, at any point on this other/self-directed learning continuum the learner may choose to take part in a class or work alone. The key to full self-direction, autonomy, or learner independence, is thus not the chosen learning mode, but the exploitation of that mode. Learner independence is revealed by the learners' awareness of their learning processes demonstrated in their ability to exploit the resources at their disposal, whether these are classes, self-access facilities, or counselling teachers, in order to fulfil their particular language learning needs and wants. Fully autonomous or independent learners are able to diagnose their learning needs, select the means of fulfilling them and assess for themselves when they have been satisfactorily achieved.

Allwright (1988a) reminds us that learner independence is not such an exotic flower as it may first appear; in any class, the differences in learner uptake of teacher input illustrate the powerful force of individualisation at work. It is inevitable, given learner variables, that this should occur and teachers know that the best way to encourage language acquisition is to get learners to personalise the learning experience and make it their own by forming their own hypotheses and making their own mistakes. Additionally, teachers seeking to individualise the learning experience successfully should ensure that learners are aware not only of their own learning strategies but of others they may like to use. In order to prepare learners effectively for learner independence, I would agree with Allwright (1981) and Banton (1992) that teachers themselves need preparing for what is in effect a deeper involvement with the people they help to learn.

SELF-ACCESS LEARNING FACILITIES

One way in which students can acquire awareness of learning strategies and thus begin to establish their independence as learners is by working individually, either at home, in a library, or in self-access learning facilities (SAFs). The latter may consist of a purpose-designed room or rooms, equipped with computer, audio and video hardware and language learning software and printed materials. A catalogue of materials may be available and other support systems, sometimes including a counselling teacher, to assist in the process from initial diagnosis of the learning need through choice of materials to assessment of the learning outcome. Class teachers seeking to satisfy the diverse needs and wants of students yet fearful of an 'anarchy of expectations' (Bloor and Bloor, 1988:65), will welcome the opportunity to include SAFs in the teaching/learning context, if they are available.

At this point, Dickinson's (1978) warning is opportune: whereas learner independence entails individualisation, individualised instruction can be the antithesis of learner independence. For example, homework and programmed learning are externally controlled — the former by the teacher, the latter by the materials. Nevertheless, I would suggest that if learners choose to do homework, since they have chosen to belong to a class, then they are not negating their independence. In the same way, learners may enter a SAF and independently select a programmed learning video or audio tape which meets their needs. Here I am in agreement with Sheerin (1992:5) who notes that SAFs *'facilitate — rather than impose — the development of learner independence'*.

CRAPEL (Centre de Recherche d'Application Pedagogique en Langues) at the University of Nancy, France, provides language instruction by means of such facilities and much can be learned from experience gained there. Henner-Stanchina and Riley (1978) remind us of Illich's (1970) tenet that classroom instruction teaches *'the need to be taught'*. CRAPEL therefore seeks to support personal growth by encouraging people to take charge of their own learning. This encouragement is given by a teacher working as a counsellor/facilitator in the SAF. On this point, Narcy (1991) has suggested that a SAF without learner support is useless.

Yet, the establishing of SAFs and related learning programmes is not without difficulty: Riley (1988) raises important questions regarding the possible ethnocentricity of such programmes. Accounts by those with experience of SAFs (Holec, 1987; Wenden, 1987; St John, 1988) suggest that both learner independence and the training which leads to it are subject for their success to influence from situational and personal variables.

LEARNER INDEPENDENCE AND LEARNER TRAINING IN PRACTICE

The language background

In the English Centre (EC) of the University of Hong Kong (HKU), first year Arts students take a compulsory one year, two semester, English language course. This is intended to 'enhance' the proficiency in English of these native speakers of Cantonese so as to enable them to benefit fully from tertiary education in the medium of English. Although all the students have passed Advanced Level English (grades A to D), very few students are exempted from the course after an examination, on account of major weaknesses in academic writing. Experience has also shown that the reading expected of first year students can be overwhelming in both quantity and level of difficulty for many students. Additionally, most of the students are for the first time listening and speaking to native English speaking subject teachers who cannot translate into Cantonese. There is consequently a wide range of needs among the students. In order to cater more specifically for individual needs, one of the three hours of weekly class contact was designated for self-access work in the 1991/92 academic year.

Self-access facilities

The EC shares with the Language Centre a SAF known as the Practice Laboratory where various kinds of self-access materials (including video, audio, computer) are available for use by all HKU students. Students who are not taking formal courses are encouraged to use the individual counselling/tuition facilities available at certain times of day. First year Arts students were expected to use the Practice Laboratory for at least the one hour per week released from class time during 1991/92.

Learner training

In order to facilitate the use of the Practice Laboratory, teachers were advised to spend a class session explaining and discussing the rationale behind the self-access work and then to organise a visit to the Practice Laboratory to see the materials and try out the equipment. Built into the regular coursework was a certain number of 'required' self-access assignments, which could be checked by the teacher in class or in tutorial groups. However, self-access work was intended to be self-directed so, to provide support other than the teacher's, it was suggested that students were grouped (variously — according to friends, major subjects, expressed major skills interest or weakness) and tutorials held to decide on specific self-access objectives and a study plan for the first semester. These details were to be recorded on a contract form signed by both teacher and student. Follow-up tutorials were to be planned at intervals during the semester to get feedback on the success of the materials used and to remedy any problems encountered. At the beginning of the second semester, a new contract was to be drawn up and follow-up tutorials planned.

The learning background

Students in Hong Kong secondary schools are used to rigid timetables and a rigorous study process controlled by the teacher, both for class and homework. It can be bewildering to find that tertiary education is quite different, with an emphasis on individual completion of the typical Western academic study cycle (conducting an information search, reading widely yet analytically, note-taking in order to cite sources, synthesising the information gathered into an original and relevant written or oral response to the topic set by the tutor). Those who have succeeded in secondary school by dint of the rote learning of notes provided by the teacher must revise their study expectations when they join HKU.

It must be stressed that generations of graduating HKU students have made the transition from dependence to independence without the benefit of overt learner training. Whether this occurs as a result of personal maturation, the acquisition of academic independence by virtue of tuition from 'content' teachers, or academic study skills courses (see Waters and Waters, 1992) offered by the English Centre is uncertain, but they did not achieve it without complaints from Faculty members about the difficulties experienced during the transition.

The self-access approach taken in the English language course was believed to encourage general academic independence by making students aware of cognitive processes while taking them through various language-oriented tasks, such as watching a video and note-taking, using a guided worksheet, then using the notes to respond to an essay question. In group tutorials, students were expected to discuss their learning at two levels: the learning experience itself which they had with the self-access materials and their metacognitive awareness of the learning process.

As described above, the responsibility for planning self-access study was shared with the teacher, but the responsibility for choosing materials and for achieving the tasks was the student's. The decision about the satisfactory achievement of specific objectives was intended to be a joint one. The overall objective was that learners would benefit from a semi-structured programme which would guide and support them on the path to learner independence, while satisfying their individual linguistic needs.

Problems perceived with establishing learner independence

I, like other new teachers in the English Centre in the first semester of 1991, was delighted to find self-access work an integral part of the English for Arts Students (EAS) curriculum. The Practice Laboratory, although still in a developmental stage, was satisfactorily equipped with both hardware and software. It seemed that self-access could be nothing but successful in establishing learner independence.

Before the first semester was over, my optimistic perceptions of self-access were somewhat dimmed as a result of poor feedback in tutorial sessions on self-access work completed. In discussion with other teachers on the same course, it became clear that both old and new teachers were experiencing misgivings about the dedication of one third of the timetable contact hours to independent study. The reasons for our doubts were varied. Some felt the students were not taking up the opportunity to learn English independently but were spending the 'free time' on other subjects which had greater pay-off in terms of credit-earning status. (EAS is a non credit-bearing, Pass/Fail course at present.) This lack of motivation was evidenced by the minimal completion of self-access objectives in many cases. Others felt that the students had speaking/listening needs which they could not satisfy in the Practice Laboratory. Linked to this was the perception that the students needed to spend more time together in class using English for social purposes and academic discussions. Some felt the Practice Laboratory was inadequately equipped. Whatever the cause, the problem was that the students appeared unwilling to take up this learning mode.

The problem was aired at an English Centre Curriculum Renewal Committee meeting, and issues such as the appropriacy of self-access work in the Chinese cultural setting, the dramatic change in roles expected of both teacher and student, the relevance of personality and attitudes to these role changes, were discussed. We had to consider why learner independence seemed to be slow to take root, given what we felt to be optimal conditions for early blooming. Furthermore, teacher morale was beginning to be as much of an issue as student achievement of learner independence. If teachers felt that self-access work was a waste of time, then this pioneering curriculum innovation would surely not be repeated the following year. We decided we had to consider the situation carefully, assess whether we had a problem and if so establish exactly what it was, then seek to remedy it. Action Research (AR) presented a user-friendly means of investigating the issues, which we took up as a group of concerned teachers at the end of semester one, 1991/92.

THE ACTION RESEARCH CYCLE

Reflection

After reflecting on the problem as a group, we planned a questionnaire to investigate the perceptions of all EAS teachers regarding the success of self-access work. Results showed that (amongst other things) teachers increasingly felt that self-access time could be spent more productively in class. We had thus established objectively that there was a problem; we then decided to set up individual AR cycles to investigate different aspects of the problem, and arranged to meet regularly to give each other feedback.

In personal reflection I felt that I had not 'pushed' students to be more productive in self-access work, since it was essentially their decision whether they needed to remedy individual weaknesses or not. Moreover, as a new teacher, I was afraid of overloading the students in their new educational environment. (Student suicide as a result of stress at school is a serious problem in Hong Kong.) However, in retrospect, I could see that my desire not to be a disciplinarian but to counsel and guide in the spirit of learner independence, might have been interpreted as failing in my duty in this context where students had been used to strict discipline in school.

In the light of results from the EAS end of semester questionnaire, which showed that 324 students felt positively about self-access work as opposed to 41 who had negative impressions of it, I also became interested in whether the perception by teachers of the lack of uptake of the allocated self-access time was caused more by overly high expectations than by real failure on the part of students. I wondered whether the lack of teacher control over self-access work caused a lack of teacher confidence in what students could do. In other words, did teachers have a self-fulfilling negative expectation of student achievement of self-access work and therefore of learner independence? I needed to find out what exactly my students were doing in self-access time and to assess whether this was in fact satisfactory at this stage of establishing learner independence. At the same time I wanted to consider my reactions to what students were doing.

Plan

I therefore established the following objectives for my research cycle:

1 To monitor more closely students' self-access work and compare their reactions to the teacher-controlled and teacher-free models by means of pre-control and post-control questionnaires.

2 To test reactions to the Practice Laboratory and self-access materials and to trial other types of self-access work, by offering a choice of activities in its place.

3 To find out if students wanted learner independence in any form (e.g. choice in selecting class materials).

4 To check students' reactions to my teaching style.

5 To monitor my own reactions to the controlled sessions by introspecting in a diary.

My plan was to conduct teacher-controlled self-access work over a four week period in the middle of the second semester, after students had established the second contract and had experienced the free (i.e. controlled only once a month) mode of self-access study again. I prepared a simple questionnaire (Appendix I) to use before changing the self-access study mode. As I taught two parallel classes I also devised a slightly different self-access plan for each: EAS 116 was to have more teacher control than EAS 109. Each class was divided into two groups (EAS 116 = 5+ 5, EAS 109 = 6+6). EAS 116 groups were to have a 45 minute session with me each week. During this they could choose to:

i do 'controlled' self-access work in the Practice Laboratory (i.e. self-directed, but monitored by completing a checklist (Appendix II) to be handed to me after each session);

ii stay in class and discuss topics chosen by me or them;

iii receive personal correction of written work.

EAS 109 would have the same choices but would meet me for one hour every other week. One regular class hour was scheduled, and the remaining timetable contact (one or one and a quarter hours) was still available to the students for 'free' self-access work. A second questionnaire (Appendix III) was prepared for use after the trial period.

Observation

After the completion of the trial period, I observed the results of the questionnaires, completed checklists and my diary.

The pre-questionnaire results (Appendix I) revealed that a large minority of the students were unclear about the official timetable commitment (Q1). A substantial minority felt a need for more tutorials (Q2) and a majority wanted to spend more time on oral skills in class (Q5). It appears from Q3 and Q4 that the majority had done self-directed self-access work and only a small minority wanted more control over it. Q6 and Q7 (intended as a cross check) reveal that the majority were not impressed with self-access work.

During the trial, the group work included discussion of personal, culture-oriented topics, such as customs practised in celebrating birthdays and marriages. According to Yang (1989), such discussions would be subject to behavioural restrictions imposed by Chinese cultural and social norms such as 'face protection' and the 'cult of restraint'. These would inhibit the learners so that they would be unwilling to share their individualistic feelings in a group. On the other hand, Chinese social relationships are intended to be 'harmonious' and so I included general academic topics following video viewings in order to measure the success of discussion on non-face-threatening topics. The checklists showed that three of the twenty-two students took up the Practice Laboratory option occasionally rather than the discussion. All expressed satisfaction with the interest or usefulness level of the choice. (Appendix II does not show the results, which are too copious to include.)

My teaching diary reveals in summary two main impressions:

1. I felt very anxious about the take-up of the optional discussion groups, as I knew that some students would be unwilling to desert me for the Practice Laboratory, and yet I did not want them to participate in discussions which were unpleasant for them. I tried to impress upon the students that I was genuinely interested in giving them a chance to spend more time in the Practice Laboratory. However, as the sessions progressed, students appeared to be choosing for the right reasons, i.e. to satisfy their needs rather than to please me. I felt less anxious and enjoyed the discussions, particularly when students contributed happily on cross-cultural topics. In fact, they seemed bored with the academic topics and preferred the cross-cultural issues.
2. I felt less anxious about the students' use of the Practice Laboratory when they were handing me completed checklists, although this could not be conclusive proof that they had actually done any self-access work there.

The post-trial questionnaire results (Appendix III) revealed that the group which had met in tutorial most frequently (EAS 116) showed slightly more interest in having a regular tutorial as part of the weekly timetable (Q1). Similarly, more students in this class expressed enjoyment of discussions (Q7), desire for more of them (Q9) and a preference for the use of English rather than Cantonese in class (Q8). All students had enjoyed the choice of activity available (Q3), and the majority felt that students and teachers should be involved in timetable and class activity decisions (Q2 & Q4). Reported reactions to the

Practice Laboratory indicated that there had been a movement towards knowing and enjoying self-access work (Q6), with the majority of EAS 116 expressing a desire for self-direction and the majority of EAS 109 expressing a desire for teacher control (Q5). The majority in both classes said they would use the Practice Laboratory in future (Q12).

With regard to my teaching style (NB questionnaires were anonymous), both classes expressed views which I interpret as positive, or at least uncritical (Q10). It is interesting to note that EAS 116 expressed greater happiness, interest and confidence in my classes.

Reflection

Reflection on the implications of the above results with regard to my AR objectives reveals that the students in this study:

1 can direct their own learning process and wish to do so, despite initial confusion for some in organising their study timetable. It could be that teacher expectations of self-access study take-up were too high for all students to achieve in the short space of one fifteen week semester. However, it does seem that the more controlled sessions increased the awareness of what self-access work is and that familiarity with the Practice Laboratory bred content. Hence, EAS 116 were ready for 'letting go' after their intensive control, whereas EAS 109 were not yet ready. It is axiomatic that learners cannot make suitable choices unless they are suitably informed and the information process will take time.

2 enjoy and want discussions and are not overtly subject to cultural inhibitions in discussing personal topics. One can speculate on whether EAS 116 reported greater happiness, interest and confidence in my classes as a result of the closer interchange in group discussions.

3 would like to exert learner independence in classroom issues such as choice of materials.

4 do not need discipline even if they expect it initially.

5 The teacher in this study felt anxious when undertaking the innovatory discussions and felt relief at their success. Similar relief was felt when students appeared to complete their assigned self-access tasks, in other words, when teacher control seemed to be in force. Anxiety thus stems from two possible causes: innovation and accountability. Both of these are present in the self-access project and therefore indicate a need for greater support to be given to teachers in their preparation for learner training.

Group reflection

None of the group advocated giving up on self-access work. Some members came to similar conclusions about the need for more learner and teacher support during the learner training period. It was decided therefore that the 1992/93 self-access induction process would be more thorough, in terms of both teacher and student preparation, including an induction workshop for teachers, a record book with objectives, timetable blanks and self-assessment checklists for students. This new process will be the subject of the continuing AR cycle during the 1992/93 academic year.

CONCLUSION

It seems that there is a direct relationship between teacher and student readiness for learner independence: the more preparation that is done, the better equipped the students are to cope with learner independence and the more secure teachers will feel that they can loose the reins and let the students go free. Neither a 'guilt trip' nor 'ego panic' is necessary if we remember that the teacher's role does not become superfluous when learners become autonomous. The teacher is still necessary as counsellor, adviser and expert and these roles are more, rather than less demanding, open-ended and deeply committing as they are.

The attitudinal or personality implications of letting go are clearly important for both learners and teachers. For learners, learner independence or learning maturity cannot be achieved suddenly, after one session of preparation. Preparation should be built into the learning programme, so that cognitive and metacognitive awareness is fostered in, rather than foisted onto learners. The length of time needed for this depends on the individuals concerned: their previous learning experience, age, language level, personality, social level and cultural background. However, we should beware of falling into the trap of 'cultural camouflage'; what may seem to be averse to a culture, and innovatory in terms of educational experience can nevertheless be implemented provided the necessary adjustments to role are made slowly, learners' awareness of the process they are undergoing is awakened and acceptance of change is agreed. Also, only when learners have been successful in learning independently in small ways will they be able to grow to full learner independence with confidence.

For teachers, similar adjustments are necessary in role, awareness and acceptance of change. Class teachers cannot hope to process instantaneous and continuous feedback from learners in order to fine-tune the learning process in the way learners can individually. It is therefore in the best interests of learners and teachers to establish learner independence, but like any other learning process, it takes time and effort. Neither our own, nor our learners' slowness in uptake should be viewed as failure. We must beware of creating negative self-fulfilling prophecies.

The AR project was in itself a reassuring endeavour. Simply looking at the problem objectively gave me the impression that I was getting onto firmer ground and took away some of the anxiety I was feeling. Similarly, the AR project gave our group an opportunity for sharing feelings and discussing our projects, which increased our solidarity and helped us to look more objectively at ourselves. Within a collaborative group (see Underhill, 1992) our individuality was fostered. The AR project thus mirrored in some ways the learner independence training I was investigating, revealing that individuals (both learners and teachers) can be empowered professionally and personally if they can let go of inhibitions and work in a non-competitive environment of mutual trust, respect and support.

Appendix I: Results from Questionnaire I, pre-trial. (Students' responses expressed in %)

1 The EAS official timetable is:

a	3 hours of class and 1 hour self-access	36
b	2 hours of class and 1 hour self-access	64

2 There should be:

a	more classes	0
b	more self-access time	9
c	more tutorials	32
d	no changes to the timetable	55
e	no answer	4

3 In Semester 1, learners did:
(more than one answer possible)

a	some optional self-access in the practice lab.	77
b	some optional self-access in the library	36
c	some other type of self-access (English TV, newspapers)	68
d	only the required self-access practice lab. work	27

4 Self-access work should be:

a	more tightly controlled	14
b	as it was organised (contract tutorial + follow up)	41
c	left to the individual to handle alone	45

5 Discussion/oral presentation skills should be given:

a	more time (between 1/2 and 1 1/2 hours per week)	68
b	the same amount of time as at present	32
c	less time	0

6 To date:
(more than one answer possible)

a	benefited more from class work	41
b	benefited more from self-access (and project) work	27
c	benefited more from corrections of written work	36
d	did not benefit at all from any of the above	4

7 To date:

(more than one answer possible)		
a	benefited least from class work	32
b	benefited least from self-access (and project) work	55
c	benefited least from corrections of written work	9
d	did not benefit at all from any of the above	0

Appendix II: Checklist of Self-Access Activity

1 Today I would like to:

a go to the Practice Laboratory

b get personal correction of written work

c take part in discussion

2 Today in the Practice Laboratory I worked on:

3 Today's session was:

		1	2	3	4	5
a	useful and interesting					
b	useful but boring					
c	not useful but interesting					
d	not useful and boring					

4 Next week I would like to:

Appendix III: Results from post-trial Questionnaire, arranged by class. (Students' responses expressed in %)

EAS 116 = 8 respondents EAS 109 = 12 respondents

1	The EAS weekly timetable should be:	EAS 116	EAS 109
a	2 hours class and 1 hour Practice Laboratory	25	42
b	2 hours class and 1 hour tutorial	12.5	0
c	1 hour class and 2 hours Practice Laboratory	0	25
d	1 hour class and 2 hours tutorial	25.5	8
e	1 hour class, 1 hour tutorial, 1 hour Practice Laboratory	37.5	25
f	other suggestions	0	0

			EAS 116	EAS 109
2	The timetable decision should be made by:			
	a	teachers	25	0
	b	students in each class	12.5	0
	c	teachers and students	62.5	100
3	Regarding the recent tutorial groups:			
	a	I enjoyed having a choice of activity	100	100
	b	I prefer the usual class.	0	0
4	Class/tutorial work should be decided by:			
	a	teachers	12.5	17
	b	students	25	0
	c	teachers and students	62.5	83
5	Practice Laboratory self-access work should be:			
	a	controlled on a daily basis	0	17
	b	controlled on a weekly basis	12.5	33
	c	controlled on a monthly basis	12.5	25
	d	controlled every 3 months	0	0
	e	free of control	75	25
6	After regular visits to the Practice Laboratory, I feel:			
	a	I know the Practice Laboratory better than before	50	25
	b	I enjoy the Practice Laboratory more	37.5	42
	c	the same as I did before	12.5	42
	d	I like the Practice Laboratory less than before	0	0
	e	other feelings	0	0
	[* see comments at end]			
7	In tutorials, I:			
	a	feel embarrassed discussing personal topics	0	0
	b	felt embarrassed at first, then got used to it	12.5	8
	c	didn't feel embarrassed, but my English is not good	12.5	50
	d	enjoyed discussing personal topics	62.5	34
	e	would rather discuss more formal topics	12.5	8

		EAS 116	EAS 109
8	In EAS classes/tutorials, I think:		
a	English only should be spoken	87.5	58
b	Cantonese can be used sometimes	12.5	42

		EAS 116	EAS 109
9	In EAS classes I would recommend:		
a	more discussion	87.5	58
b	more oral presentation	12.5	8
c	no changes	0	34

10 I think your teaching style was:

relaxed ... strict	1	2	3	4	5
116	12.5	37.5	37.5		
109	17	58	17		

informal ... formal	1	2	3	4	5
116	12.5	12.5	75	0	
109	0	42	50	8	

appropriate ... inappropriate	1	2	3	4	5
116	37.5	50	12.5		
109	42	58	8		

11 In your classes I usually felt:

happy ... unhappy	1	2	3	4	5
116	62.5	25	12.5		
109	8	75	17		

interested ... bored	1	2	3	4	5
116	25	62.5	12.5	0	
109	8	25	58	8	

confident ... nervous	1	2	3	4	5
116	37.5	50	12.5		
109	0	50	50		

12 In future, I'll probably:

		% EAS 116	EAS 109
a	come to the Practice Laboratory sometimes	87	75
b	come to the Practice Laboratory often	0	25
c	never come to the Practice Laboratory	0	0
	[zero entry]	12.5	0

Comments

EAS 116 No comments

EAS 109 3 positive comments, 3 constructive suggestions, 1 complaint about heavy workload

[* One student marked two answers: (a) and (b).]

Come together: the search for practical answers to specific problems in ESP

Margaret McGinity
University of Badajoz

♦

This paper outlines specific problems faced by teachers of ESP in Spanish universities. It presents some personal experiences in the ESP classroom which, as I attempted to confront these problems, have helped me to develop as a teacher. They include devising and testing techniques for specific teaching problems and getting together with colleagues to improve classroom performance.

The background

ESP specialists working in Spanish universities tend to suffer from inferiority complexes where research is concerned. Rubbing shoulders as we do daily with scientists, we find that our attempts at data collection tend to be belittled by our colleagues: our sample is not sufficiently objective, our results are not statistically valid, and we are constantly made conscious of our lowly position in relation to the 'genuine' research being carried out by other departments. Yet we make up a fairly numerous body of 'do-it-yourselfers' par excellence. What happens in ESP? Most of our time is, in fact, spent researching, studying the particular needs of our students, thinking, reappraising, evaluating, learning new facts and testing ideas. Purists could and do argue that what we are doing cannot be called research, but if not, it is uncommonly like it.

In Spanish universities students of economics, science and technology have to study a compulsory foreign language. In the majority of cases this language is English. This fact creates a series of very specific problems for the ESP teacher. First and among the most important is the size of classes. In many universities there are groups of up to 300, and the average is well over 100. Secondly, of that 100 some 50% will have studied English at school for seven or more years while the rest will have studied French. Student motivation is yet another major problem since the majority consider English to be what is known as a 'Maria', something to be passed with as little effort and with the highest mark possible while they dedicate their efforts to more worthy subjects like Mathematics. In addition, the language courses which most English teachers have studied have normally left them fairly ignorant of the subject matter of the material being used in their ESP classrooms.

To these specific problems can be added those common to most teaching situations where teachers feel the need to be accepted as professionals and given the social prestige which they are normally not awarded. They need to develop a capacity for what Stenhouse (1975) called '*autonomous professional self-development*'.

Thinking teachers are constantly asking themselves questions like: What am I doing? Am I doing it right? Are my students really learning anything? Are they learning what I want them to learn?

Within Spanish universities there exists a system of teacher evaluation aimed in principle at discovering the answers to these questions, at encouraging improvement in teaching and at highlighting areas where in-service training could be useful. I say 'in principle' because, as always, the reality falls far short of the theory. The system is based on questionnaires to students, in which they are asked to grade:

- the extent to which teachers do what is required of them as regards lectures, seminars and tutorial groups;
- whether teachers know their subject;
- teachers' capacity for communicating that subject;
- the adequacy of teachers' methodology;
- the quality of teachers' relations with, and attitude to, their students.

If a teacher passes, apart from a feeling of well-being, of superiority over less fortunate colleagues and a pay rise every five years, some questions remain:

- Does the system actually tell us if the students are learning anything, never mind what we want them to learn?
- Does it tell us if we are teaching well or whether we could be teaching a lot better?
- May it not occur that although the overall result is satisfactory, many smaller points may be highly unsatisfactory?
- May it not simply mean that the teacher concerned is kinder, more generous, more understanding than other members of staff?
- Does it not merely measure the level of students' satisfaction with their teachers, students' attitudes towards the subject, their psycho-social needs and the personality of the teacher but not the teacher's effectiveness, quality of teaching or output (c.f. Wittrock and Lumsdaine, 1977)?

Of course, there are other means of evaluation. Students' exam results can tell us something about whether we are being effective as teachers, but even that is limited by the fact that if we set our own exams they will undoubtedly follow our teaching system, and if we use outside examiners, poor results do not necessarily mean poor teaching or learning, simply a difference in focus.

So we face up to three questions:

1 What is happening in my class?
2 Is what is happening problematic?
3 If so, what can I do about it?

And at the moment of asking, we are into teacher research. I now turn to a personal example.

TEACHING ORAL SKILLS

Our department, together with the Faculty of English at the University of

Evora in Portugal, has, since 1990, organised a specialist LSP conference where representatives from the majority of universities in Spain and Portugal, as well as from the UK, France and Germany, get together and talk about their research, their teaching techniques and their problems. One of the recurring comments heard during the 1991 conference was the 'impossibility' of teaching oral skills in our LSP classes and it was suggested that we should concentrate on reading skills and forget about the rest until such time as the University authorities begin to take seriously the whole question of LSP.

I agree that the problems are acute and that, as teachers of LSP, we should be using every weapon in our power to force our authorities to address them. But what do we do in the meantime? Do we, as has been suggested, teach reading skills and forget the rest? Can we sit back and say it can't be done well, so we won't do it at all? Shall we pack up and go home?

I argued that, in spite of all the problems, admitting that at best we can expect mediocre results, we have to try and develop oral skills with our students. We cannot opt out and wait for better days which we all know may never come. So I found myself more or less committed to looking at the problem seriously, examining what I was actually doing about teaching speaking skills, seeing whether I was achieving anything at all and then preparing the results to present to my colleagues at a future meeting.

I began by trying to define what I mean by speaking skills. In the widest sense it is the ability to express ideas orally. It includes knowledge of the phonemic system, the sequence of sounds, the lengths of pauses, stress and intonation patterns as well as having something to say, knowing how to say it and having the confidence to break the sound barrier and say it in English. ESP students need the same basic skills as any other English speaker; they differ only in what they have to say.

With the problem identified, I then set about collecting information on what I was actually doing in the classroom. I decided on this occasion to use my Industrial Engineering students, partly because it is the largest group I have and partly because they are well motivated, being conscious that without a good level of English their possibilities on the job market are greatly reduced. The majority of the students had studied English, although there was considerable difference in level because some 30% had received vocational training where the hours given to English are greatly reduced.

I used two methods of data collection: field notes and audio-taping. During two periods of one hour I kept a notebook open on the desk and noted down whenever I talked (TT), asked questions (TA), whenever students answered me (SAn), or whenever they talked among themselves (SS).

After the first hour I realised that the original four headings were not giving me enough information. I needed to know which of the students talked, where they were sitting within the classroom, whether they volunteered information without being specifically asked and the length of time they talked. So for the second hour session I added: student asks (SA) and student informs (SI). I also included position in class: front (F), middle (M), back (B), left (L) and right (R). I marked each with a tick as before but initialled SA, SAn and SI wherever I knew the student's name.

I also audio-taped the two lessons. This was not particularly time-consuming because I did not transcribe the tape but merely used it to back-up the field notes and to give me the length of time of each intervention.

As was to be expected, I discovered various points, none of which surprised me greatly:

1 I talk too much.
2 Quite a lot of oral work went on in my class, as all exercises were done orally either in question and answer, or in pairs, but not much spontaneous English conversation was present.
3 The speaking was dominated by a nucleus of very able students except when I directed questions at a specific individual.
4 I tended not to direct questions to the students at the very back because I invariably had to direct them to repeat their answers several times as I could not hear. This not only slowed up the class but caused embarrassment to all of us, so subconsciously I avoided the issue.
5 I was pleasantly surprised at the overall level of pronunciation. I felt this to some extent justified my insistence throughout the years on the importance of teaching phonetics as a tool to all students, especially those in ESP, where incorrect pronunciation of technical vocabulary can cause a complete communication breakdown.

A few comments on these results are pertinent here. In the first place, they are probably artificial. There is nothing more inhibiting than seeing a long list of ticks under 'teacher talks', so under normal circumstances I probably talk even more.

It is also possible that there was more talk than usual during these classes because we were concentrating on that aspect only and students were aware that I was recording what was going on. In the same way, some students who are normally more receptive could have been inhibited while others talked in excess precisely because they were being taped. Nevertheless, the results provided some interesting insights and specific problems to which the next step had to be to find some solutions.

I established two areas of action. Firstly, I drew up a list of improvements that I could make to the problem of questioning. These included moving round the class when asking questions so that if I was asking students at the back they were near enough to avoid the problem of my not hearing their answers. I also increased the use of specifically directed questions or demands for information so that the best students did not dominate the lesson. Cutting down on teacher talking is more difficult, but at least I am trying, which is a step forward. At some future date I will have to tape a lesson for comparison to see what improvement if any there has been in these aspects.

My second course of action was to draw up a list of oral activities which I hoped would increase students' participation. One of the advantages of teaching in universities is that students are used to and prepared to take part in experiments. I explained the problem to them and received their full support in trying out the activities which they later evaluated.

This is not the moment to describe in detail the different activities, which can be seen in McGinity (1991), but they ranged from simple question and answer through meaningful drills, structured conversation, open discussion and debate. I found that using students' technical knowledge orally during the presentation stage of the lesson was a good way of getting them to talk. They invariably have some interesting information to contribute, especially when it comes to explaining how electrical circuits work to someone as unscientific as I am.

We used a lot of pair and group work, with, for example, information gap exercises using pie charts or graphs which are particularly suited to ESP classes where visual forms of communication are very common. At this point I was able to use more effectively the students who had emerged as outstanding orally during the taping sessions. On some occasions I moved them into different groups so they were able to help their companions and on others I grouped them all together so that they were working at their own level.

Group work was used about once a month to prepare topics chosen by the students themselves for general discussion and we did some fun exercises, such as role-play based on a television sketch viewed with the sound off, or inventing dialogues round newspaper cartoons.

When asked to evaluate the experiment, students were enthusiastic. A few felt the fun exercises were not suitable — they take learning English very seriously — but all felt their spoken English had improved. Many raised the following research issue: the main problem is not so much talking as understanding. Patricia Edwards (1991) discovered that 90% of her students at the Business College at the University of Extremadura considered 'listening' to be the most important skill needed. At the moment, my students and I are embarking on a project to develop listening skills. We have begun by buying 20 personal stereos and are now involved in taping suitable material to begin implementation.

In conclusion

These are a few of my personal experiences in what could possibly be called Teacher Research. My methods seem to be a little more systematic than they were, though I am sure there is room for improvement in that area. My enthusiasm for a particular project tends to make classes more interesting. Students certainly respond well, but I sometimes find that most of my energies are being devoted to the particular group doing the project and the rest are perhaps being short-changed. I hope after the summer break to solve this problem by using all the groups which, while being more work because of the variety of material to be written or taped, will provide a wider and therefore more valid sample.

We are still left with the vexed question of whether this is research in the strictest sense of the word. In teacher research the answers to our questions tend to be qualitative rather than quantitative, which makes them suspect to our scientific colleagues although, in fact, they are much more appropriate to the particular situation being studied than purely statistical methods. In quantitative methods the selection and organisation of data can be isolated from, and ignore, the social and cultural context in which they are obtained. Researchers limit their study to the observable and measurable aspects of the teaching/learning process, while the need to quantify and submit to statistical analysis forces them to renounce all information which cannot be adapted to this treatment.

Qualitative research, on the other hand, argues that education is a social, not natural, phenomenon and must take into account different parameters, including perspective, intention and context.

We begin with a problem, from which we form a hypothesis, collect data, draw up and execute a plan of action and evaluate the results. In this sense, what we are doing meets the requirements of contemporary research criteria and falls within the definition of research. As Hopkins (1985:21) says, quoting Stenhouse (1979), *'I'm not sure if I'm doing research. I am testing hypothesis by experiment as systematically as a busy job allows'*.

Teacher Research has a vital role to play in improving not only classroom performance but, more important still, teachers' awareness of their professional role. We will get little help from outside. We need to become what Stenhouse calls *'autonomous in professional judgement'* and stop accepting the role that society, professional researchers and materials writers give to the teaching profession as a whole.

Diary of a Special Interest Group

Anne Turner

British Council, Thessaloniki

◆

This paper will follow the development of a Student Centred Learning Special Interest Group (SIG) which was set up amongst teachers of the British Council in Thessaloniki. It will cover: the conditions under which the group was formed, its evolution, some of the problems involved in running a SIG and the effects on teachers and students.

=

Genesis

In the beginning, there was a management decision that there were to be two SIGs to promote professional development amongst the teachers of the Direct Teaching Operation (DTO) of the British Council, Thessaloniki: the Young Learners SIG and the Student Centred Learning (SCL) SIG. There were many protests from the teachers, but to no avail. Two hours per month were to be devoted to SIG meetings.

And so it happened that each month there was a SIG meeting, where the teachers were made to rack their brains. Occasionally the SCL co-ordinator beat her breast and at other times she jumped for joy. The teachers showed their disapproval in many ways (arriving late, pursuing other interests, giving priority to other matters, taking time out for coffee and sandwiches) but they did not dare miss a meeting, for this arrangement had been negotiated by the Teachers' Union in return for a pay-rise.

The idea of having two special interest groups arose because management wanted to concentrate on areas which would be relevant to all teaching levels as opposed to being level-specific. The themes, Young Learners and Student Centred Learning, were chosen by a majority vote from amongst other proposals, but then teachers had to join either one or the other. It was a new concept to all of us and no-one knew what direction the groups would take or how they would operate. Apart from the directive that SIGs would have a two-hour meeting each month, the rest was up to us.

Evolution

The Student Centred Learning SIG had its first meeting on 1 October 1991. There were thirteen members, about half of the teaching staff. Obviously, as this was an extra morning at work, their attitude was polite but negative and they felt reluctant to contribute anything outside 'SIG time'. As SIG co-ordinator, I was apprehensive; this was no class of students awaiting pearls of wisdom but my peers, wizards of classroom management and teaching techniques. The first task was to decide what the SIG was about, what SCL was, and how it related to our classes.

So at the first meeting we talked; people aired their views in groups and then reported back. Gradually a list of students' needs in the area of SCL began to take shape. This formed the basis for future work.

Areas suggested by the SIG group for improvement (related to SCL)

1 Student Assessment
Encourage more self assessment. Regularly assess what students feel to be their strong/weak areas.

2 Self-Access Centre (SAC)
Encourage more use of SAC. Create tasks for students to complete in SAC which are related to coursework.

3 Learner Training
Create more worksheets/OHTs on how to use textbooks, grammar books, and dictionaries.

4 Learner Awareness
Give students reasons for the tasks they are asked to do. Give more information about methodology to students.

5 Organising Learning
Many students do not know how to organise their notebooks. Give students help to organise notes: for homework, lessons, vocabulary etc.

6 External Speakers
Invite English speakers to give talks in areas of interest to students.

For the next meeting I decided most of these areas could be covered by four working parties, and SIG members were given the choice of which group they would like to join from the following: Learner Diaries, Self-Access, Learner Training, Testing. The decision to split into four working parties was perhaps one of the most crucial factors in contributing to the success of the SCL SIG. It meant that teachers had the opportunity, albeit limited, to follow their own interests, and that several projects were in progress at the same time. Also, in small groups people find it easier to express their ideas and they gain a group identity.

Other projects arising from the list were: an external speaker programme, for which I took responsibility, and student counselling; there was to be a 'tutorial week' in January and another in June.

There were seven two-hour meetings of the SIG after the initial one and these usually consisted of some time for working parties and a meeting of the whole SIG to discuss progress or view a short presentation. However, there were problems, so first let us take a look at these before going on to view the SIG's achievements.

PROBLEMS

1 Attitude: teachers had a negative attitude because of being pressurised into attending SIG meetings. They also had a fear they would be further imposed upon to 'produce' outside SIG time.
2 Timekeeping: meetings were often late in starting. This was frequently due to other meetings over-running and, in some cases, individuals arriving late.
3 Shifting aims: some working parties lost track of their original aims and the continuity with the work they had been doing. This was because of the infrequency of meetings and the lack of 'blocks' of time for group work. If there was a presentation or extended discussion among the whole group, this left only half an hour to an hour for the working parties.
4 Distraction: members were easily distracted from their group work by anecdotes, albeit often to do with teaching, by other tasks or by being interrupted by other members of staff.

Most of the problems occurred as a result of lack of motivation and, in all fairness to members, it became apparent that the SIG was not a special interest group in the true meaning of the word. In the beginning choice was limited to joining either the Young Learners SIG or the Student Centred Learning SIG. Also, within the SCL SIG, the working parties were formed as a result of the students' needs as defined, and not as a result of special interests. People were interested in SCL but time was limited, and they had a heavy teaching programme and in many cases family or other commitments.

ACHIEVEMENTS OF WORKING PARTIES

Some working parties were more successful than others. We should bear in mind that the amount of time allocated to this work was very limited i.e. less than two hours a month for seven months.

Aims of the working parties, from minutes of meeting 5 November 1991:

1 Learner Diaries — 2 members
Aim: to experiment with the use of learner diaries in class in order to monitor developments in learner training and learner awareness.
2 Self-Access Centre (SAC) — 4 members
Aim: to try and link up coursework with material available in SAC.
3 Learner Training — 2 (+2) members
Aims: to try and integrate existing learner training materials into courses and to create more material; to build up a Learner Training File.
4 Testing — 3 (+1) members
Aims: to investigate students' attitudes and preferences in relation to testing and methods of testing; to investigate ways of helping students assess themselves.

Learner diaries

This group did some research on how learner diaries could be introduced into the classroom and experimented with the use of learner diaries with a class. Unfortunately, after an enthusiastic beginning, the class did not maintain their interest in diaries because the project was badly timed (it was interrupted by the Christmas break). The group's findings were presented to SIG with advice on how and when to introduce learner diaries and a package of information on the use of learner diaries was displayed on the SIG noticeboard. The group asked for volunteers to try out the use of diaries so they could research the results but we were three-quarters of the way through the academic year and no-one felt it was a suitable time. The project was shelved until further information was available and the two members joined the Learner Training group.

Self-access centre

Despite being overwhelmed by its over-ambitious aim, this group did produce a general list of extra work and materials available in SAC for each level, and a more specific list of vocabulary work for two advanced levels. Members also discovered a wealth of video material for which there were no worksheets, made several worksheets, and compiled a subject index of video materials available which was topic linked to existing syllabi.

Learner training

Again the task was overwhelming, and in the beginning the group spent time reading around the subject of learner training. Because the area is so large it was difficult to know how to tackle it: level by level or one Learner Training File for all levels; advice for teachers on how to incorporate learner training or organisational skills for students. The end result was the integration of a learner training programme into the course outline of one level plus a Learner Training File of materials for the same level. Existing learner training materials were also integrated more systematically into another level. It was not possible to do this for some levels where coursebooks were going to be changed for the next year.

Testing

Strange to include testing in an SCL SIG — but the initial idea was to find out how students felt about testing and whether they would be receptive to more student-centred methods, i.e. student-authored tests or 'take home' tests. As there was already an indication of difference of opinion within the group on this matter, it was felt necessary to investigate teachers' attitudes towards testing also. Therefore two questionnaires were compiled and distributed: one to all the teaching staff and one to a hundred of our students (10% of all students representatively spread over all levels).

The Teachers' Survey — 26 respondents

Opinion was divided as to whether teachers actually liked testing, and comments showed that the main problem was the validity of in-house tests administered on courses. Apart from that, all teachers deemed tests necessary at some point, the main reasons being as a checking device and to set standards. 76% of teachers felt that at some time students could construct their own tests.

The Students' Survey — 91 respondents

Students were overwhelmingly in favour of testing (99%). The reasons given were mainly as revision of work covered and as practice for external exams. (Most of us were already aware of students' preoccupation with testing, which is a reflection of their previous learning experience.) Here only 15% believed that students could construct their own tests compared with the teachers' relatively positive view on this question. This may be attributed to the fact that in most cases our students have had no experience of designing tests or even exercises for each other.

However, I decided to ask two of my classes, both young learners at the same level and using the same coursebook, to write tests for each other on different units of the coursebook. I must admit I was surprised how quickly and easily they did this and how little correction I had to do. They tested grammar, vocabulary and some pronunciation from the units. After administration and marking of the tests I asked the classes to fill in the students' questionnaire, mainly to see if their views on student-constructed tests would be different from the representative survey. Over half of the students believed that some tests can be constructed by students.

Personal development

As the SIG co-ordinator, I probably gained more than anyone else from the SIG. Primarily I learned about handling people and getting them to co-operate; basically it is the same as handling classes, but you can hardly tell your peers what to do, so you need to find ways of suggesting they do things. Apart from that, I increased my knowledge in several areas, particularly learner training as I gave a presentation about this. I learnt a lot from other presentations in the SIG meetings and from the research going on in the working parties.

I became quite interested in the research on testing and would like to do some further exploration of the use of student-constructed tests. Also, very importantly, I learnt to type and use a word-processor — I had to, to type up the minutes.

I wanted to try using learner diaries with a class but didn't quite get round to it. Maybe next year?

There was my satisfaction and pride at the end of the year on reviewing the achievements of the SIG, and seeing the change in attitude towards SIGs. But the nicest part was when I got an unexpected round of applause at the end of the last meeting.

Solutions to problems

1 Attitude: if teachers are going to be more motivated then they should be free to choose their own areas for development.

2 Timekeeping: I still don't know the answer to this one. Strong directives to others to stop previous meetings on time? One suggestion was to let people put in their 'SIG time' when they wanted to.

3 Shifting aims: more time should be given to working parties and less time spent in whole group meetings.

4 Distractions: monitoring by co-ordinator. Asking groups to report progress to whole SIGs at intervals.

I feel it is important to mention the co-ordinator's role in circulating between groups to offer advice and encouragement instead of being part of a sub-group.

FOLLOW-UP

Next year SIGs will continue but in a different form, and I have been re-appointed as co-ordinator. Some things were obviously wrong and need changing. Small working parties are successful and more time should be given for their work and less time spent in whole group meetings. Next year the SIG will have to fit the interests of individuals/groups instead of vice-versa. So it will be a 'Group of Special Interest*s*' rather than *a* Special Interest Group. This may result in chaos, who knows? My job will be to try and co-ordinate the groups and keep them informed of what other groups are doing, and where possible ask them to co-operate with each other. If people are not allowed to follow their own interests then the problems will continue.

A fish's story: insights from investigating use of a fisheries-based ESP textbook in classrooms

Eunice Torres
University of the Philippines in the Visayas

◆

This paper describes some insights from my classroom research experience investigating teacher and learner use of a fisheries-based ESP textbook in the Philippines. As the research was project-based, and as I had already established what I perceived to be close 'insider' relationships with the teachers, I had hoped to combine research with pedagogy, to go beyond academic research into the area of 'teachers develop teachers research' (TDTR). My TDTR experience, though full of surprises, was difficult because:

1 researching with teachers is a highly complex social process, a process learned while doing and not planned out in a research proposal;
2 researching with teachers works out only with 'teacher-initiated' (and not 'researcher-down') decisions and agendas and in a 'teacher-teacher' research relationship.

Some initial thoughts — what's the fish's story?

In this paper I would like to describe my classroom research experience and share some thoughts on this experience of investigating teacher and learner use of a fisheries-based ESP textbook in the Philippines. One major concern I had in this classroom research was teacher development, the possibility of making the research a part of the pedagogy. In other words, I had hoped I could be more than just the traditional, objective, nearly invisible, researcher making as little input as possible into the classrooms of the three teachers and seventy-two learners from a state fisheries college with whom I worked for one semester.

Thus, in the teacher development concern of my research, I had hoped that I could be perceived as another teacher, a colleague or perhaps a mentor, who together with the other teachers, was interested in looking into the classroom process to understand and learn from it. This sharing is therefore my story, the 'fish's story' in the title of this paper, which also happens to be the title of the first module in the coursebook used in the study. At this point, I would like to emphasise that my sharing focuses on this research experience 'story' not on my research results.

Seeing the potential

Why did I think it was possible to make doctoral study and pedagogy work together in my research? I had three reasons that made me feel, at the proposal stage, that I could do it. Firstly, my research was project-based. That is to say, I already had 'insider' status with the teachers with whom I was working. I did not just 'rush in and then rush out' of classrooms as academic researchers are generally perceived to do. I had been working with the teachers and learners during the whole four or five years of the project before I actually began my research, working closely with them at all stages of the project — from the initial contacts, to needs analysis, to the development of the materials and finally to the piloting of the materials.

The topic content of the materials was provided by both the language and content teachers of the fisheries colleges and the language possibilities of the different modules were worked out by the language teachers themselves. We shared the difficulties and problems in implementing the project. I thought of these teachers both as friends and as colleagues and I could sincerely say that I was more insider than outsider when I started the research.

Moreover, the presence of a British Council English Language Teaching Officer in the project (I was the project's local counterpart) who was perceived as the project head further reinforced my insider status in the project. I was perceived as not the 'boss' and therefore the local ally, 'one of us'.

Secondly, before I started my actual classroom observations, I had involved the teachers in the research itself during a project seminar. They helped me with ways to pilot the questionnaire and work out the guides to diary writing. Since I was investigating the use of the textbook they had helped develop, they were more than willing to help me with my research. They even helped me to gather the questionnaire data, and had recorded their lessons as they taught one module. There was the general feeling that if it was for the project network, then we all help.

Thirdly, I was researching the use of a textbook that I had helped to develop and was therefore given the opportunity of seeing the textbook used in actual classes. I had had no chance to do this during piloting of the textbook, because we did not use classroom observation, but relied upon teacher reports and questionnaires. Working with the learners and teachers using the textbook was, I thought, a good opportunity to develop a relationship between teachers, learners and a materials writer.

For the above reasons, I sincerely felt at the beginning of the research that the teachers and I could be colleagues. I hoped that the close working relationships I had established with the teachers would lessen their fear of me as being evaluative or judgemental in their classrooms. To this end I had reassured them several times that I was not in their classroom to judge or to evaluate their teaching but to see what role the textbook had in their lessons.

In my study, the use of the project textbook posed potential risks and changes to the regular classroom practices of the teachers as it was the first time they had had a textbook to use; the fisheries content was different from the usual language-focused or literature-focused content and most activities required the teacher to change from teacher-fronted activities to more learner-centred ones.

To cope with these potential risks and changes. Teachers A and C tried as much as possible to fit their use of the textbook into their repertoire of classroom practices, fitting its use into their usual methods of teaching. Teacher B did this, too, but because she opened herself more to the changes posed by the use of the textbook, her lessons somehow became somewhat different from those of the other two.

Teacher C was most successful in using the textbook to fit into his usual teaching because of his long experience in teaching with minimal resources. In the Philippines this usually means teaching without proper textbooks. He had regularly used textbooks only as the reading or writing sources for his lessons — to be copied onto the blackboard — or for his lectures, and not to be used by learners in class at all. He placed emphasis on learners using the new textbook as a resource to be used outside the classroom. Whether the learners used the textbook on their own I could not say, because Teacher C hardly used it at all in his lessons.

Teacher A's experience with a textbook both as learner and teacher had been its use as the main source of content for lectures, and any activities were teacher-managed. And this was how Teacher A used the new textbook. Thus, suggested group work and pair work became whole-class work, and suggested classroom talk became mainly teacher-talk with learners giving one-word responses. In the classes of both Teachers A and C, the learners hardly talked at all; if they did it was to read from the text or to react, in one-word responses, to teacher questions.

Teacher B's lessons were also mostly teacher-fronted, but she was more accepting of the difficulty of the textbook content, and of the sometimes confusing instructions and visuals it contained. Also, only Teacher B openly admitted to not knowing much about fisheries, with perhaps her learners knowing more. While transcribing the taped lessons, I was often surprised to hear most of Teacher B's supposedly declarative sentences ending up as questions, with her throwing back the content to the learners to elaborate further or discuss. She also worked closely with content teachers and even asked them to use some of the activities in the textbook. It was her lack of fisheries knowledge that started the lengthy interactions between her and her students and among the students themselves. In addition, Teacher B, perhaps due to her ELT training (compared to the other two who were not initially trained in ELT), had more confidence to try out other ways of doing things even if this meant complicating the lessons for her. It was because of this openness that Teacher B paved the way to the theorizing about her teaching we did together during my research.

Working with these three teachers who used textbooks differently, I thought about how we teachers could possibly become more reflective and questioning about classroom practices. The security of familiar classroom practices hinders us teachers from reflection.

REALISING THE POTENTIAL: DASHED HOPES

Armed with the anticipation of doing something more than traditional research in the classroom, I was not prepared for the dilemma that confronted me in the actual research. It was easy writing about combining research with pedagogy in the research proposal but very difficult doing so in actual research. What are the reasons for this difficulty?

Firstly, even though I had already established close relationships with the teachers I worked with, the fact that I was 'PhD researching' gave that relationship with teachers another dimension, different from the one I had with them during the fisheries project implementation.

For me, the reasons for my hope had become my doom. It was precisely because I already had the close relationship that I became apprehensive about combining pedagogy with research. The teachers trusted me and I was uneasy about our talking about the teaching in a way that might possibly destroy this trust. The objectivity of academic research was for me a good way to maintain that trust. Because of this, even at the early stage of my research, I was ready to give up the pedagogical concern.

Still, even if they were not researching for a degree, academic or professional researchers who come to classrooms to do research using their own agendas and hoping to help teachers in their teaching would still face the dilemma I faced. 'Researcher-down' (to borrow from 'top-down') research is, I think, inevitably problematic because it depends for its success on the maintenance of cordial relationships with teachers, not to mention ethical considerations, in a research methodology that involves close personal relationships with teachers. Thus, I have doubts about academic research that claims to be teacher-centred.

Secondly, though the teachers were very supportive of my research during the piloting stage when my presence was thought of as temporary, doing the actual classroom observations of the teachers' lessons was another thing. I had made myself a permanent fixture at the back of the classroom and I was not sure that either teachers or learners were happy or comfortable with the situation. I had to now and again reassure them that my presence in their classroom was not evaluative. During the first few lessons when I observed them, I had to reassure them regularly that they should do what they wanted/planned/needed to do and not mind my presence, as I was there to investigate use of the textbook and not judge their teaching. Though the teachers did not complain, I was very conscious of the fact that I may have intruded into their lessons, so I tried as much as possible to minimise this intrusive feeling by making myself as invisible as I could manage. Thus, again, at this early phase of research, I had to shelve the idea of helping in the pedagogy, of helping teachers be aware of their teaching.

REALISING THE POTENTIAL: LITTLE SURPRISES

But, despite my early decision to abandon hope for making research and pedagogy work together, there were surprises as the research continued and, looking back, some small successes. What were these surprises? How and why did they happen?

Surprise one. Teacher B, after my second observation in her class, expressed her '*interest and desire to know more with my presence… to take the opportunity to learn from me*' and inquired whether she could ask me to help her in class if she wanted or needed to. To quote her again: '*I'm tempted many times to ask you to help me in class, can I?*'

This was the opening I was looking for and in my notes for this session I wrote the following:

> *Suggested to [Teacher B] that we meet as a group and go over the [audio] tapes, so they can listen to their lessons — [Teacher B] was excited over the idea!!*

Unfortunately, this suggestion was not taken up by the other two teachers, so nothing came of it. From Teacher B's openness to learning from my presence we can see that teacher-initiation is crucial in academic research that also wants to be TDTR.

Surprise two. Four more lessons passed before Teacher B gave in to the 'temptation' to involve me, and my participation in the lessons is shown in the transcripts of this and two subsequent lessons. I had gone beyond merely observing to actually participating in her lessons either as teacher, learner or as materials writer. Specific instances when this came about involved situations when Teacher B had difficulty with the lessons (caused by her inability to ask the right questions, for example) or with the textbook (i.e. unclear instructions or confusing visuals).

My participation and our subsequent informal talks after these particular lessons, according to Teacher B, helped her to understand and resolve 'critical moments' (Wright, 1992) in her lessons. These informal sessions, when I behaved and thought more like another teacher than researcher, were few but still they were unplanned instances of researcher and teacher working together to understand classroom teaching. The other two teachers, though they encountered similar critical moments in their use of the textbook, did not give me this opportunity; in both their classrooms I was mostly the researcher-observer.

Surprise three. Taking their cue from Teacher B, the learners in her class also allowed me to join in their lessons either by asking me directly or looking at me for help (like Teacher B) when I was to join in. Again, these were sources of after-lesson sharing with Teacher B and, looking into the transcripts, I can see instances of similar situations which Teacher B resolved in the way we had discussed.

Surprise four. Video-recording of two lessons by each teacher was another source of informal theorising. The learners were keen to see the videos of the lessons I recorded, so we arranged for the classes of Teachers A and B to watch them. I watched their video-recording with Teacher B and her learners and I was witness to an informal, noisy, full-of-laughter, talking-about-their-lesson session. Admittedly, the learners focused most of the time on how they looked or what they did, but there were beginnings there of the potential of video-recording for learner development or for TDTR. Both Teacher A and Teacher B admitted that they could not stop thinking for days of what they had learned about their teaching from the video. Certainly, the learners talked about the video, in and out of their classes, for days.

Thus, despite my giving up hope for teacher research, despite my seeming inability to help the teachers and learners, despite my apprehensions and a nagging feeling of guilt as an intrusive researcher, despite my wondering how we — teachers, learners, myself — could have managed, we all somehow survived the four-month long classroom research encounters. And now when I look back, when I look into my field notes, listen to the tapes, go over the transcripts, remember the many small events in the classroom relating both to learners and teachers that sadly do not get into the collected research data but happily are part of my collected memories, when I try to find meaning in it all, to understand these complex encounters we call language lessons, I find myself sad that the classroom experience had to end just when bonds had become stronger, just when learners and teachers had become more open to and accepting of me, just when I was getting to know the classroom a bit more, just when I was forgetting I was doing this for a degree... then I had to come back to Lancaster to finish the PhD.

LEARNING FROM THE EXPERIENCE: 'LOOKING BACK'

Looking back on my data-gathering experience and looking into my data, the audiotapes and transcripts of lessons especially, I come upon small surprises that made my attempts at TDTR not entirely lost. It was indeed a learning experience amidst the many accepted difficulties of working with people, me with them (the teachers and learners) and them with me — all people with differing agendas. The experience has certainly helped me become more understanding of teachers, learners, researchers and of the research process.

As my research experience shows, it is only on the basis of teachers' own decisions and will to theorise from their classroom experiences that teaching and research can work together (c.f. Day, 1991). This is the real beginning of teacher-initiated TDTR, when teachers make themselves and their development the top priority in the research and development process. To this end, Allwright's proposal for exploratory teaching (1992a and this volume) is indeed welcome, as are other approaches to teacher theorising from the classroom, such as those of the Bangalore ELT community (Ramani, 1987 and Naidu et al., 1992).

LEARNING FROM THE EXPERIENCE: 'LOOKING FORWARD'

One of the regrets I had upon completion of the data-gathering phase of my PhD research was that I had to leave just when the beginnings of possible TDTR could be seen among the teachers and learners I worked with. The research experience I had with them has certainly made me look forward to going back, shedding the PhD researcher clothes and becoming a classroom teacher again.

Estonia: self development for teachers and pupils

Pauline Jenkins

School 16, Tartu, Estonia

◆

Innovations were started by practising teachers in schools: weekly meetings enabled teacher development mainly initiated by teachers. Learner autonomy has been pursued through contacts with Oulu University, Finland and Danish schools. This incorporated co-operative teaching methods. After six months, the change in our pupils' attitudes was significant. Teacher exchange and research presentations are planned in Finland.

Born again EFL!

Straight after the Soviet coup I began in-service training and teaching in a school in Estonia. Communication problems are numerous: in everyday life, between teachers, and with English speakers.

In an authoritarian society, the extreme suppression of ideas and literature, and the rigidity of rules for teaching, will force the trend towards the opposite extreme. There will be an explosion of self-expression, talk and innovation. Teachers all want change, and are often not sure how to achieve it. There have been no new guidelines for the past three years. Soviet style textbooks are obsolete, new literature is urgently necessary.

Learner autonomy

In Western societies, learner autonomy is regarded as the development of the individual; in Scandinavia, it is often used with co-operative teaching. Extensive studies of co-operative teaching have been made during this century and its benefits have been proved. Then why is there so little of it? Many of us favour group teaching (I prefer to use the word learning rather than teaching), but co-operative learning is more than group work. The group cannot be successful until its weakest member succeeds in understanding and completing the task. It is a wonderful response to mixed ability classes.

Weekly meetings for Tartu teachers

Since January, when two of us visited Oulu University and its school in Northern Finland, a group of about twelve Tartu teachers have met weekly. We talked about what we had seen there, the theory and practice of learner autonomy. The first hour of each meeting was devoted to theory, presented by different teachers, usually in English but sometimes in Estonian. We discussed cognition, learning strategies (Wenden, 1991), communication strategies, co-operative teaching and classroom research methods.

The second half of our meeting was occupied by small group discussions about recent incidents in our classrooms. Problems were viewed positively and constructive help given. Discussion of the lack of buses, petrol, heating, and various foodstuffs quickly passed. Some weeks it was hard work to get discussions going in some of the groups. Some teachers felt more comfortable with Estonian. After several months they were confident enough to express their ideas in English.

A BASIS FOR CLASSROOM RESEARCH

From these informal discussions questions arise, initially on a very small scale. With the collection and analysis of data a more scientific approach will evolve. It is beginning with a raising of awareness of what really happens in the classroom as opposed to what we imagine is happening. Building trust and raising self-esteem are very slow processes but very rewarding. Teachers are encouraged to keep diaries of their thoughts and developments in the classroom, even if only for occasional days.

Encouraging teachers to begin thinking and to put thoughts into writing takes time. It is what classroom research grows from: analysing what is really happening in our classrooms. It is not always a pleasant realisation: after recording some of my lessons it became evident I was spending too much time eliciting correct answers. I realised how much better the time would have been spent in encouraging groups to correct their own answers. Recently a school teacher of 20 years' experience commented that this was not teaching. True, but it is learning.

Already we have been visited by two Finnish teachers, from Oulu, keen to exchange with Estonian teachers in Tartu. In turn, several of our teachers are eager to exchange. It is a wonderful boost for self-esteem, to know that their teaching skills measure up to those abroad, and exchange provides a much richer experience than merely going 'to observe'. The best way to learn is by teaching.

Professor Irma Huttunen, who has been working on learner autonomy for over a decade (Huttunen, 1983), said that, locally, she knows of one teacher per school practising learner autonomy. Our School 16 has four. A teacher of Russian, and of chemistry also belong to our group. They began seriously studying English last September and have taught English when School 16 was a teacher short. EFL Conferences are no longer composed solely of EFL teachers. Learner autonomy is not restricted to languages and teachers of other subjects add a richness to the group; it is good to have a mix from other academic disciplines. In Estonia, some subjects, such as geography, are being taught in English because there are no textbooks on world geography, and the history books have to be rewritten.

Our weekly meetings have discussed the in-service training courses provided for Danish teachers by Breen et al. (1990). During the early 80s they presented new theory, but within several years teachers rejected such workshops and held their own preliminary workshops where they discussed and decided what would be the subject of the theoreticians' workshops. Teachers later networked the innovations to further groups of teachers. Theory was applied to practice and practice to theory.

This to-ing and fro-ing is the basis for classroom research. How much easier to generate research from such a workshop involving teacher development rather than from in-service training. There is a tremendous amount of feedback, and it is from the feedback/data/research fodder that we can learn for ourselves and from each other.

Pupils' change in attitude

Some teachers complained that some groups were too difficult to change; they would not work without strict supervision; they were not interested in anything; they were only interested in the mark at the end. The pupils' attitude has to be changed first and unless their teacher is convinced enough to be patient and persistent there will be failure. Resistance must be viewed positively; it is a method of reviewing and questioning, far more promising than no response.

Over the last six months we noticed a significant change in the attitudes of our English pupils in School 16. At Christmas I visited other schools' English shows. Our school also staged one. The difference was that our sketches and monologues were written by the pupils, and the latest pop songs were brought in with requests from the pupils for 'all the words, Miss Jenkins'. An impossible task! Estonians, like many people, like to be word perfect; and the nervousness of the children in other schools was uncomfortably evident. Ours were not word perfect; any mistake they made was accompanied by a wide grin at one of us teachers. We encouraged them to think what they were saying (they had written the lines) and improvise when the script failed them. Visiting teachers were impressed by the acting and said how much the children seemed to enjoy it. One group was even invited to perform at another school.

Pupils who at first did not like English and made no effort, gradually came eagerly to class, their writing became legible, they actively participated in peer group discussions, initiated conversations with me and took more care over their homework. When they were no longer in my group they still said 'Hello' or exchanged a few words around school. It was as though we all shared a lovely secret. As for our Russian and chemistry teachers, they told me I had changed their lives. I have not of course, but they are finding a way to be in control of learning English and are able to test it out on me, and on their pupils. They are systematically applying learner autonomy to their own teaching. Alar, our chemistry teacher, found that autonomy could not be achieved in the first lesson. Pupils did not know how to work together, and they did not know how to take responsibility initially. These realisations came back to our weekly discussions and everyone was able to benefit from them. Frankness is a new luxury in Estonia, and the truth has a new margin of safety that it did not have before. These are things that we foreigners take for granted and perhaps no longer value for their full worth.

CONTINUING TOWARDS CLASSROOM RESEARCH

Rigmor Eriksson, a secondary teacher in Sweden, found that some of her groups took two years before they fully adopted learner autonomy. Some groups put up strong resistance and want 'to be taught' passively (Eriksson, 1990). I am returning to the same school in Estonia for another year. Many comment, 'Isn't it a waste having a native speaker in school rather than at the university?' I don't think so. If we are to develop classroom research it is important that teachers constitute many of the researchers, and that teachers co-operate.

Just before leaving I congratulated my adult student group for arranging a meeting in my absence, without my knowledge, on becoming autonomous. They crossly accused me of making them so autonomous that they would no longer need me.

When I return, another teacher and I have planned a course for teachers of Third Grade classes, eight year olds. Russian is to be replaced by English as the first language in many schools, and we have invited teachers from other schools to join us. Four teachers are involved from School 16. The course will follow the lines of the Danish workshops, and will initially be activity based — upon materials production. Some of us will go to an EFL Workshop in Helsinki, and one or two will give a paper there. It is important for us to move from 'Please help us!' to 'Look, this is what we are doing, can we talk about it?'

We think of classroom research not as an end in itself but as a tool to use in teacher development, the personal development of each of us. In a fast changing world we must constantly adjust. Nowhere is it changing faster than in the former Soviet Union. Analysing our classrooms is a big step. Once we have recovered from the initial shock we begin thinking 'What if I change this a little against those variables — a little to the right, to the left?' We begin fine tuning in a much more sensitive way than before. We discuss our findings with colleagues and learn more about ourselves and more about our colleagues. We gain a deeper understanding and probably become more tolerant.

There are many ways theory could be introduced regularly. In Estonia our group plans to network with teachers in other areas, just as soon as some reliable transport is available. By becoming autonomous in a co-operative way we can introduce new theory to ourselves without having someone bring it to us.

Awareness: the instrument and the aim of experiential research

Adrian Underhill
International Language Centres, Hastings

◆

The aim of this short workshop was to focus on the kinds of question we can ask ourselves when engaged in experiential enquiry or action research. We first discussed the proposal that awareness is both the instrument as well as the aim of such research, and we then tried to discriminate between those questions we can ask ourselves that are likely to have a higher yield in terms of awareness and those that are likely to have a lower yield. I suggested a simple model for discriminating between questions, and we then applied this discrimination to some of our own questions.

=

My subjective reality

I am confined to a version of reality that has been filtered through the subjectivity of my perception. I am immersed in my own subjective experiencing, and others around me are immersed in theirs. There are areas where we overlap with each other and areas where we don't. One thing that disturbs me is the discrepancy between my experience of myself and my learners' experience of me. There is constant evidence that the effect I think I am having on my learners or on my trainees is different from the effect I am actually having on them. How *I* think I am coming across to others seems to be different from how *they* think I am coming across.

The aim of asking questions in this area would be to raise my awareness of my own role in the complex human equation of teaching and learning, and to try to reduce the discrepancy between what I think is happening and what is actually happening. I would like to be informed about the consequences of my behaviour less by imagination and wishful thinking, and more by a sensitive witnessing of what is happening in me and in my relating with others.

Some questions about our own practice

I asked workshop participants to write down some of the questions that they had asked themselves concerning their own teaching, or some questions they would like to ask. Participants shared some of their questions, and here I should like to share some of mine:

1 Why won't my students work on their own?
2 Why do they make so many mistakes?

3 Why do they sometimes shut down and not listen to me?
4 Why do they have such a low interest in listening to each other?

These questions are personal, and in this form may not mean much to you, but they are real to me, and I'm going to use them to illustrate the remaining steps in the workshop.

STATEMENTS BEHIND THE QUESTION

I then asked participants to write down some of the statements behind their questions, or some of the assumptions that seemed to be contained in their questions, or some of the emotions concealed beneath their questions. I shall refer to all these 'lurking assumptions'. Again these assumptions are personal, and the aim is to bring to light unconscious biases. Here are some of my 'lurking assumptions' behind the same questions. Don't expect them all to seem logical to you. They may not all seem logical to me.

Question 1:
Why won't they work on their own?

My lurking assumptions:
Anyone can see this is a good way to work.
It is the right thing to do so they ought not to resist it.
The problem is to do with them.
There is something wrong with them.
If I was in their shoes I'd work on my own.
This coursebook is useless.

Question 2:
Why do they make so many mistakes?

My lurking assumptions:
They don't listen.
They don't care, they're not trying.
It's too hard for them.
They have poor memories.
They're not very bright.
The syllabus is too steep.

Question 3:
Why do they sometimes shut down and not listen to me?

My lurking assumptions:
They are wasting my time and theirs.
It's a drag.
They don't see how important this is.
No one can work in a room like this.
I hate the first lesson after lunch.
I'm not paid enough.

Question 4:
Why do they have such a low interest in listening to each other?

My lurking assumptions:
They aren't trying.

This method isn't all it's cracked up to be.
What can you expect?
If only they realised how important this is.
I'm wasting my time being progressive.

There are lots of statements behind questions like these, and as we delve into them some can be quite revealing. This brings us to my distinction between High Yield questions and Low Yield questions. The aim here is to transmute lower yield to higher yield questions, to release them from the grip of my unconscious prejudices and biases.

Here then is a characterisation of High and Low yield questions. Of course it is not a straightforward polarity, but a long continuum, where the variable is the degree to which I am willing to involve my own attitudes, behaviours and habits in the overall equation.

HIGH YIELD QUESTIONS AND LOW YIELD QUESTIONS

	High Yield questions:	**Low Yield questions:**
1	Open me up to change.	Confine me within my status quo.
2	Try to fathom or get to the bottom of my experience.	Explain my experience in terms of what I already know.
3	Lead to other finer questions.	Are extinguished by the answer.
4	Lead me into new territory.	Keep me where I am, give me more of the same
5	Value uncertainty.	Value certainty.
6	See problems as being both 'in here' and 'out there'.	See problems as 'out there'.
7	Are sensitive to the relativity of my own viewpoint: I am part of the human circuitry that shapes the problem.	Contain assumptions that my viewpoint is absolute: the problem and the question exist independently of me.
8	Are a high risk to my status quo.	Are a low risk to my status quo.
9	Expose preconception.	Leave preconceptions hidden.

Neither kind of question is superior to the other as long as I am using each question to do the job it is best at. However when I overdo the low yield questions I may suffer from 'development-that-goes-nowhere'.

EXAMPLES OF MY LOW AND HIGH YIELD QUESTIONS.

Again these are personal, and one person's Low Yield question could be another person's High Yield question, and vice versa. But here is my attempt to transmute the same four questions into higher yield ones by progressively excavating my lurking assumptions.

Low Yield:

- Why won't my students work on their own?

High Yield:

- In what ways might I be standing in the way of their self-direction?
- Do I offer them self-direction intellectually but resist them taking it emotionally?
- Am I projecting an assumption that they would be better off guided by me?
- Do I really trust their capacity to direct themselves?

Low Yield:

- Why do they make so many mistakes?

High Yield:

- Am I accepting my students as they are, or wishing them to be different?
- How can I turn their mistakes to advantage?
- Am I working with my learners from where they each are, or from where I am?
- Am I afraid of their mistakes?

Low Yield:

- Why do they sometimes shut down and not listen to me?

High Yield:

- What is the quality of my own talk?
- What else am I transmitting while I am talking, e.g. through my body language, posture, and gaze?
- Am I behind my words, or do my lips just waggle?
- Am I present as myself, or am I role playing?
- Am I sensitive to their moment by moment needs, or am I carried away with my own?

Low Yield:

- Why do they have such a low interest in listening to each other?

High Yield:

- How interested am I in listening to them?
- What is the quality of my own listening?
- Do I listen to the content of what they say, or to the person who says it?

Conclusion

As I see it, underlying all valid subjective enquiry is the aim to become more aware of myself and of my manifestations as they affect others, and those of others as they affect me, so that I am more able to respond creatively to situations out of choice, rather than react mechanically to situations out of habit. Awareness is the only instrument I have that can drive this enquiry, so as I said at the beginning, it seems as if awareness is both the instrument and the aim.

How can I frame questions that can unhook me from the limits of my present perception, rather than keep me where I am? It's rather like trying to lift myself up by my own bootstraps, except that I know it's possible.

TDTR: Conference as catalyst

Julian Edge & Keith Richards

Aston University

◆

Part 4

Spontaneously, at the start of the final plenary discussion, the decision was made to move from the main lecture theatre to what throughout the conference had served as the coffee bar. It was Saturday morning, the university was quiet and there were armchairs for all. We sat in a large circle and talked. Sometimes, with luck and the right people, things will come together in a way that no amount of planning can achieve; sometimes a group will find its voice.

What brought us together at the end was a question raised by Dick Allwright about 'the teacher as researcher'. It is at the heart of his paper here — a paper which is at the heart of the collection — but its articulation at the end of the conference had particular power. What was significant, and apparent, was that the question was *personal*. Its application may have been universal but it expressed a personal and genuine need to find something out. It encapsulated the theme and the mood of the conference, and the response was worthy of the question. Nobody sat at the feet of anybody else, nobody presumed to offer answers or advice from on high: we explored together in a spirit of harmony, and in that spirit the conference closed.

So where is our development in all this? What story do we have to tell? It is a story with three themes: professional, personal and social.

Professional

We began with a belief that the relationship between teacher research and teacher development was worth exploring seriously, but we had no preconceptions about the nature of the relationship. Hence the conference title.

We naturally expected to learn something about that relationship, and we think we did, but there were two specific outcomes which now influence our intellectual responses to the development/research relationship.

The first arose from the conference itself and the sense that new ways of thinking are emerging. For example, in his paper, Nunan explores the relationship between action research and more traditional conceptions of the research process, and Allwright offers a new and exciting way of describing the relationship between research and teaching. In the same way, what interests us is the relationship between personal and public outcomes and the ways in which these might be explored. It is in our ability to pose and respond to this new set of questions that we see our own development.

The second outcome was not fully apparent until we came to read the papers submitted for publication. The voice of the papers in the first group in this collection is recognised and sanctioned by the academic discourse community to which the writers belong. The voice is public and a source of confidence to the user. But many of the modes of expression in the second group, including our own, are less sure, not because they have less to offer but because there is no recognised public voice in which to express personal insights. We feel that the development of such a voice is of fundamental importance. The move from 'voices' — varied, noisy, ephemeral — to 'voice' is a journey we must make if the personal is ever to be more than incidental (see Somekh, p 28, Burton and Mickan pp 117f, in this volume).

Personal

> There is a Zen *koan* (Reps, 1971) which tells of a monk called Tozan who, when weighing flax, was asked, 'What is Buddha?' His reply:
> 'This flax weighs three pounds.'

Our own enlightenment came in the weighing. We had lived with the Buddha-question and seen practicalities as a source of necessary but unpleasant distraction: the sidetrack to a world of blankets and vegetarian lunches. There would inevitably be 'Why do I get myself into things like this?' questions, but we would survive them and live to explore higher things.

What we discovered on our return to 'higher' things was that higher and lower were reflections of our own idiosyncrasies. The quality of our engagement in the ideas-world of implementation had introduced us to subtleties and intricacies with an innate value of their own.

How do we explain this? How do we respond to the publisher's fully justified request for us to 'restate this in less general, abstract terms to make its significance clearer'?

We might take an example. To know that, as a result of your actions, a person who was cold has received a blanket is, of itself, qualitatively no less satisfactory an experience than to know that an educational insight has been well received in a workshop. The quality lies in your involvement in your act.

We might look at the mutually shaped effects of different influences on the individual. A person who knows that someone has taken the trouble to arrange welcome food and warmth is a person who is likely to want to invest available energy in personal and professional development. The cognitive and the affecttive do not function separately from our material world.

We do not feel that our attempts at clarification have been very successful. What is clear to us is that the process of 'doing the mundane' changed us: when we opened our ears to that teaching, the return to our own ideas-world was enriched. Perhaps in trying to explain this we have also taken a small step towards understanding the need for koans.

In all this, the history of the conference and collection found a natural rhythm. We began with the enthusiasm of the idea and settled into the business of making it real; moved to reflection again when all arrangments were made and back into administration when the conference began; gathered ideas for the collection, pieced it together, then returned to our thoughts.

This is our contribution to the conference: our own recognition (perhaps obvious to others but new to us) that the process of research, including its most minute and tedious aspects, is not set apart from the ideas we seek to illuminate — these aspects are part of the illumination. If we are truly present in *all* aspects of our work, we become the best teachers and researchers we can possibly be.

> Another *koan*. Banzan became enlightened through overhearing an exchange between a customer and a butcher. 'Give me your best piece of meat,' said the customer. 'But they are all the best,' replied the butcher. 'You won't find any piece of meat in my shop that isn't the best.'

Social

The extent to which we were dependent on others for the success of 'our' conference taught us a lot about ownership. Who are we? First there was 'The Conference Secretary'. Participants arrived expecting to find one person and found three. It was strange to be Alison Birch, Julian Edge and Keith Richards again, but we pulled it off without too many people noticing the ragged edges.

Working together on something that was completely new to all of us brought us close together and made the assumption of a single title all the more natural. There were times when individuals were ready to throw in the towel, but never the Secretary. In working together we developed trust, and through trust confidence. We add this experience to the examples of collaboration described in the papers in this collection. But ownership of the conference was not ours. It belonged to the participants and this collection is our — inevitably inadequate — reflection of its presence. We restate our opening dedication.

Postscript

Just before publication of this volume, we were happy to discover in Schecter and Ramirez (1992: 203) a comment on the development of, '*the double narrative, that is, a narrative of the research process interwoven with a narrative of self, in public forms.*'

So, a link with literature is forged. We proceed.

The Limerick Competition

A highlight of the alternative conference proceedings was a limerick competition. With due gratitude to Oxford University Press for contributing two books as a prize, we are proud to present the winning limerick.

A Collaborative Limerick

Publicity widespread said 'Come
To a challenging conf'rence in Brum,
'Cos research without action
Brings no satisfaction:
Start puzzling — and get off your bum!'

Bateman St. Enterprises & Friends

References

Aardman Animations Vol. 1. 1989. *Creature Comforts*. A Connoisseur Video release from Argos Films and the British Film Institute.

Abbs, B. and I. Freebairn. 1986. *Discoveries*. Harlow: Longman.

Argyris, C. and Schon, D. 1974. *Theory in Practice: Increasing Professional Effectiveness*. Palo Alto, California: Jossey-Bass.

Allwright, R.L. 1973. Prescription and description in the training of language teachers. *Applied Linguistics: Problems and Solutions*. AILA Third Congress, Copenhagen 1972. Proceedings, Vol. 3. Heidelberg: Julius Groos Verlag.

Allwright, R.L. 1981. What do we want teaching materials for? *ELT Journal* 36/1:5-18.

Allwright, R. 1988a. Autonomy and individualization in whole-class instruction. In Brookes and Grundy, 35-44.

Allwright, D. 1988b. *Observation in the Language Classroom*. London: Longman.

Allwright, D. 1991a. Exploratory Teaching, Professional Development, and the Role of a Teachers Association. Invited paper for the Cuban Association of English Language Specialists (GELI), Havana, Cuba. Available from Lancaster University as CRILE Working Paper N°7.

Allwright, D. 1991b. Understanding Classroom Language Learning. Plenary talk given at XI ENPULI, São Paulo, Brazil. Forthcoming in the Conference Proceedings. Also available from Lancaster University, as CRILE Working Paper N°. 8.

Allwright, D. 1991c. Exploratory Language Teaching. A description and report on a mini-course conducted at XI ENPULI, São Paulo, Brazil. Forthcoming in the Conference Proceedings. Also available from Lancaster University, as CRILE Working Paper N°. 9.

Allwright, D. 1992a. Exploratory Teaching: bringing research and pedagogy together in the language classroom. Plenary talk for the first Encontro em Ensino das Linguas Estrangeiras, Viseu, Portugal, May 1992. Accepted for publication in a special conference issue of the Revue de Phonétique Appliquée. Pre-publication version available from the author at Lancaster.

Allwright, D. 1992b. Teachers Develop Teachers Research. University of Aston (personal communication).

Allwright, D. and K. M. Bailey. 1991. *Focus on the Language Classroom*. Cambridge: CUP.

Altrichter, H., P. Posch and B. Somekh. 1993 in press. *Teachers Investigate Their Work: an introduction to the methods of action research*. London: Routledge.

Bannister, D. 1970. *Perspectives in personal construct theory*. Kent, England: Bexley.

Bannister, D. and F. Fransella. 1986. *Inquiring Man: The Theory of Personal Constructs*. London: Croom Helm.

Bannister, D and J.M. Mair. 1968. *The Evaluation of Personal Constructs*. London: Academic Press.

Banton, A. 1992. Successful self access through learner development. *Learner Independence* 8:20-22. (IATEFL SIG Newsletter).

Barker, R. 1968. *Ecological Psychology*. California: Stanford University Press.

Barnes, D. 1992. The significance of teachers' frames for teaching. In Russell, T. and H. Munby *Teachers and Teaching*. Lewes: The Falmer Press.

Bartlett, L. 1990. Teacher development through reflective teaching. In J. Richards and D. Nunan (eds.), 202-14.

Ben-Peretz, M. and S. Katz. 1980. Curriculum perception profile of language teachers. Paper presented at AERA Conference, Boston.

Bennett, N. and C. Desforges. 1984. *The Quality of Pupil Learning Experience*. London: Lawrence Erlbaum.

Benson, M., E. Benson and R. Ilson. 1986. *The BBI Combinatory Dictionary of English*. Amsterdam: John Benjamins Publishing Company.

Biddle, B. 1967. Methods and concepts in classroom research. *Review of Educational*

Research 37/3:337-57.

Bloor, M. & T. Bloor. 1988. Syllabus negotiation: The basis of learner autonomy. In Brookes and Grundy, 62-74.

Breen, M., C. Candlin, L. Dam and G. Gabrielsen. 1990. The evolution of a teacher training programme. In J.K. Johnson (ed.), *The Second Language Curriculum*, 111- 135. Cambridge: CUP.

Brookes, A. and P. Grundy (eds.). 1988. *Individualization and Autonomy in Language Learning*, ELT Documents 131. Modern English Publications in association with The British Council.

Brumfit, C. and R. Mitchell. 1989. *Research in the Language Classroom*. London: Modern English Publications and the British Council.

Brumfit, J. and A. Rossner. 1982. The decision pyramid and teacher training for ELT. *ELT Journal* 36/4.

Burton, J. 1990. Languages Inservice Program for Teachers: LIPT 2 Evaluation — Discussion Paper (LIPT Training Practice and the Resulting Professional Renewal). Adelaide: National Curriculum and Resource Centre.

Burton, J. 1991. LIPT: Where Next? Aims and Achievements from LIPT 1 to LIPT 3 (A Case-Study Evaluation of LIPT 3 with Reference to the Evaluations of LIPTs 1 and 2). Adelaide: SA Education Department.

Burton, J. 1992. The Languages Inservice Program for Teachers of Languages Other Than English 1988–1991: An Evaluation. Adelaide: Centre for Applied Linguistics, University of South Australia.

Cameron, D., E. Frazer, P. Harvey, M.B.H. Rampton and K. Richardson. 1992. *Researching Language: Issues of Power and Method*. London: Routledge.

Carr, W. and S. Kemmis. 1983. *Becoming Critical: Knowing through Action Research*. Victoria, Australia: Deakin University Press.

Carr, W. and S. Kemmis. 1986. *Becoming Critical: Knowing through Action Research*. London: Falmer Press/Taylor and Francis.

Chalmers, A. 1990. *Science and its Fabrication*, 21. Milton Keynes: Open University Press.

COBUILD Dictionary. 1987. London: Collins.

Day, C. 1991. Roles and relationships in qualitative research on teachers' thinking: a reconsideration. *Teaching and Teacher Education* 7/5:537-47.

de Bono, E. 1969. *The Mechanism of Mind*. London: Jonathan Cape.

Desforges, C. 1989. Understanding Learning for Teaching. *Westminster Studies in Education* 12:17-29.

Dickinson, L. 1978. Autonomy, self-directed learning and individualisation. In ELT Documents 103: *Individualisation in Language Learning*, 7-28. London: The British Council.

Dickinson, L. 1987. *Self-Instruction in Language Learning*. Cambridge: CUP.

Dickinson, L. 1988. Learner Training. In Brookes and Grundy (eds.), 45-53.

Dunkin, M. and B. Biddle. 1974. *The Study of Teaching*. New York: Holt, Rinehart and Winston.

EAR (1993 -) *Educational Action Research: an international journal*. Oxford: Triangle Press.

Easen, P. 1985. *Making school-centred INSET work*. London: Croom Helm.

Ebbutt, D. and J Elliot. 1985. Why should teachers do research? In Ebbut, D. and J. Elliot (eds.), *Issues in teaching for understanding*. London: Longman.

Edwards, P. 1991. A Motivation Study of ESP in Business Studies. Paper presented at the II Congreso Luso-Hispano de Lenguas Aplicadas. Universidade de Evora, Portugal.

Elliott, J. 1976, *Developing Hypotheses About Classrooms from Teachers' Practical Constructs*. North Dakota Study Group on Evaluation, University of N.D., Grand Forks ND 58202.

Elliott, J. 1988. Educational Research and Outsider-Insider Relations. *Qualitative Studies in Education* 1/2.

Elliott, J. 1991. *Action Research for Educational Change*. Milton Keynes: Open University Press.

Ellis, G. & B. Sinclair. 1989. *Learning to Learn English: A course in learner training*. Cambridge: CUP.

Ellis, M.J. and M. Aniskowicz-Swiderska. 1991. Teaching as a subversive activity: changing thinking through methodology. Paper presented at the Second National ELT Conference, Vienna, Austria.

Engels, L.K., B. Van Beckhoven, Th. Leenders and I. Brasseur. 1981. *Leuven English Teaching* (LET) Vocabulary-list. Leuven: Acco.

Eriksson, R. 1990. Report: Språhl arason och språhinl armugsfarshimgen. Sweden: Högskolan i Karlstad.

Fisiak, J. 1992. English language teacher training in Poland: the past legacy and the present challenge. *English — A World Language* 2.

Freire, P. 1972. *Pedagogy of the Oppressed*. London: Penguin.

Fullan, M. 1982. *The meaning of educational change*. New York: Teachers College Press.

Galton, M. (ed.) 1978. *British Mirrors*. Leicester: University School of Education.

Gardner, R. 1984. Discourse analysis: implications for language teaching with particular reference to casual conversation. *Language Teaching* 17/2:102-17.

Ginzburg, C. 1990. *Myths, Emblems, Clues*. London: Hutchinson Radius.

Goffman, E. 1959. *The Presentation of Self in Everyday Life*. London: Penguin.

Gregory, R.L. 1966. *Eye and Brain: The Psychology of Seeing*. London: Weidenfeld and Nicolson.

Grellet, F. 1981. *Developing Reading Skills*. Cambridge: CUP.

Gump, P. 1974. Operating environments in schools of open and traditional design. *School Review* 82:575-93.

Handal, G. and P. Lauvas. 1987. *Promoting Reflective Teaching*. Milton Keynes: SRHE and The Open University.

Harri-Augstein, S., M. Smith, and L. Thomas. 1982. *Reading to Learn*. London: Methuen.

Harri-Augstein, S. and L. Thomas. 1991. *Learning conversations: The Self-Organised Way to Personal and Organisational Growth*. London: Routledge.

Henner-Stanchina, C. & Riley, P. 1978. Aspects of autonomous learning. In ELT Documents 103: *Individualisation in Language Learning*, 75-97. London: The British Council.

Holec, H. 1987. The learner as manager: Managing learning or managing to learn? In A. Wenden & J. Rubin (eds.), *Learner Strategies in Language Learning* , 145-57. Cambridge: Prentice Hall International.

Holec, H. (ed.). 1988. *Autonomy and self-directed learning: present fields of application*. Strasbourg, Council for Cultural Cooperation, Council of Europe.

Honeyfield, J.G. 1987. Word frequency and the importance of context in vocabulary learning. In H.M. Long and J.C. Richards (eds.).

Hopkins, D. 1985. *A Teacher's Guide to Classroom Research*. Bristol: Open University Press.

Hopkins, D. 1986. *In-service training and educational development*. London: Croom Helm.

Horton, M. and P. Freire. 1990. *We Make the Road by Walking*. Philadelphia: Temple University Press.

Huttunen, I. 1983. Dissertation on Learner Autonomy. University of Oulu.

Illich, I. 1970. *Deschooling Society*. New York: Harper & Row.

Kelly, G. 1955. *A theory of Personality; The Psychology of Personal Constructs*. New York: W.W. Norton.

Kemmis, S. 1988. Action research in retrospect and prospect. In S. Kemmis and R. McTaggart, *The Action Research Planner*, 27-39. Melbourne: Deakin University Press.

Kemmis, S., R. McTaggart, M. Fitzpatrick, C. Henry and C. Hook. (eds.) 1982. *The Action Research Reader* Geelong, Victoria: Deakin University Press.

Kemmis, S. and R. McTaggart. 1982. *The Action Research Planner*. Victoria: Deakin University.

Kemmis, S. and R. McTaggart. 1988. *The Action Research Planner*. Third edition. Geelong, Victoria: Deakin University Press.

Kruse, A.F. 1987. Vocabulary in context. In H.M. Long and J.C. Richards (eds.).

Lawlor, M. 1988. *Inner Track Learning*. Canterbury: Pilgrims.

LeCompte, M. and J. Goetz. 1982. Problems of reliability and validity in ethnographic research. *Review of Educational Research*, 52/1.

Lewin, K. 1946. Action Research and Minority Problems. *Journal of Social Issues* 2:4-46. Reprinted in Kemmis et al., 1981.

Lewin, K. 1951. Formalization and Progress in Psychology. In D. Cartwright (ed.), *Field Theory in Social Science: Selected Theoretical Papers. New York*: Harper. Reprinted in G. Lindzey and Hall (eds.), *Theories of Personality: Primary Sources and Research*.

Lewis, C. 1992. Action research with French immersion teachers: a pilot study. Unpublished monograph, University of British Columbia: Canada.

Long, H.M. and J.C. Richards (eds.). 1987. *Methodology in TESOL*. New York: Newbury House Publishers.

Long, M.H., L. Adams, M. McClean and F. Castaños. 1976. Doing Things with Words — verbal interaction in lockstep and small group classroom situations. In J.F. Fanselow and R.H.

Crymes (eds.), *On TESOL '76*, 137-53. Washington: TESOL.

Lukes, S. 1974. *Power*. London: Macmillan.

McGinity, M. 1991, Motivación en IFE. Proyectos Interdisciplinarios. In M. McGinity and R. Alejo (eds.), *Lenguas Aplicadas a las Ciencias y la Tecnología*, 99-104. Badajoz: Universidad de Extremadura, Spain.

McGinity, M. 1992. So How Do We Teach Them To Talk? Paper presented at I Jornadas Internacionales del Inglés Académico, Técnico y Profesional. Madrid University of Alcala de Henares, Spain.

Mickan, P. 1990. Languages Inservice Program for Teachers (Manual). Adelaide, South Australia: State Print.

Mickan, P. 1991. LIPT: Languages Inservice Program for Teachers Stage 3 1990. Action Research Reports Volume 6, March 1991. Adelaide: Languages and Multicultural Centre.

Mitchell, R., B. Parkinson and R. Johnstone. 1981. *The Foreign Language Classroom: An observational study*. Stirling University: Stirling Educational Monograph N° 9.

Naidu, B., K. Neeraja, E. Ramani, J. Shivakumar and A. Viswanatha. 1992. Researching heterogeneity: an account of teacher-initiated research into large classes. *ELT Journal* 46/3:252-63.

Naidu, B., K. Neeraja, S. Devi, E. Ramani, U. Shankar, X. Sashikala, S. Jayagowri, & V. Vanamala. 1991. The Classroom Interaction Group of the English Language Teaching Community, Bangalore, India. Poster presentation prepared for TESOL '91, New York City.

Narcy, J.P. 1991. Education as a pre-requisite for independence. Paper presented at the IATEFL Conference, Exeter.

Nation, I.S.P. 1990. *Teaching and Learning Vocabulary*. New York: Newbury House.

Nation, P. and R. Carter (eds.). 1989. *Vocabulary Acquisition, AILA Review*. Amsterdam: Free University Press.

Nattinger J. and DeCarrico. 1989. Lexical phrases, speech acts and teaching conversation. In Nation and Carter (eds.), 118-139.

Nisbet, J. and J. Watt. 1978. *Case Study*. Rediguide 26: Guides in Educational Research, University of Nottingham, School of Education.

Nunan, D. 1989. *Understanding Language Classrooms: A Guide for Teacher Initiated Action*. London: Prentice Hall.

Nunan, D. 1992a. *Research Methods in Language Learning*. Cambridge: CUP.

Nunan, D. (ed.). 1992b. *Collaborative Language Learning and Teaching*. Cambridge: CUP.

O'Hanlon, C. 1992. Testing Out Development Psycholinguistics. *English in Education* 26/1:48-57.

Oller, J.W. & Richards, J. 1973. *Focus on the Learner: Pragmatic Perspectives for the Language Teacher*. Rowley, Mass: Newbury House.

Peck, A. 1988. *Language Teachers at Work*. Hemel Hempstead: Prentice Hall.

Peck, A., M. Davies and M. Davies. 1990. Autonomous experimentation in language teaching: a case study of question and answer. *The Language Teacher* 3/1:9-20. Linguistics Institute of Ireland.

Pickett, G.D. 1978. *The Foreign Language Learning Process*. London: The British Council.

Prabhu, N.S. 1992. The Dynamics of the Language Lesson. *TESOL Quarterly* 26/2:225-241.

Ramani, E. 1987. The ELT community, Bangalore: an experiment in human resources development. Paper presented at the international seminar on Language Education and Human Resources Development, RELC, Singapore.

Ramsden, P. 1992. *Learning to Teach in Higher Education*. London: Routledge.

Rao, Y.R. & C.L.N. Prakash. 1991. The English Language Teaching Community, Bangalore: Five Years On. Historical Postscript to Ramani and Joseph (eds.): *ELT in India: the dynamics of change*. Lancaster University, CRILE Occasional Report Number 1:83-90.

Rees, A. 1988. Classroom Observation. In A. Pincas (ed.), *Themes in ESOL: Past, Present, Future*. Proceedings of the ESOL Department 40th Anniversary Celebrations, 35-36. London: University Institute of Education.

Rees, A. 1989. Developing a Segment Based Survey of L2 Classrooms. London: University of London Institute of Education unpublished PhD dissertation.

Rees, A. 1992. Research and the Language Teacher: What's the use? In A. Van Essen and E. Burkart (eds.), *Essays in English as a Foreign or Second Language* (Homage to W.R. Lee), 85-92. Berlin: Foris Publications.

Reps, P. 1971. *Zen Flesh, Zen Bones.* Harmondsworth: Penguin.

Richards, J. and D. Nunan (eds.). 1990. *Second Language Teacher Education.* Cambridge: CUP.

Riley, P. 1988. The ethnography of autonomy. In Brookes and Grundy, 12-34.

Roberts, J. 1986. *Action Research: An Introduction.* Teachers Development SIG Newsletter, IATEFL, N°. 4.

Rose, C. 1989. Accelerated Learning: The State of the Art. *Multi-Mind* 1.

Rubin, J. 1975. What the good language learner can teach us. *TESOL Quarterly* 9:41-51.

Schön, D. 1983. *The Reflective Practitioner.* London: Temple Smith.

Sehecter, S.R and R. Ramirez. 1992. A teacher-research group in action. In D. Nunan (ed), *Collaborative Language Learning and Teaching*: 192-207. Cambridge: CUP.

Sheerin, S. 1992. Self-access: A practical path towards learner independence. *Learner Independence* 8:5. (IATEFL SIG Newsletter).

Simon, A. and E. Boyer. 1970. *Mirrors for Behavior: an Anthology of Classroom Observation Instruments.* Research for Better Schools. Philadelphia: Temple University.

Sinclair, J. and R. Coulthard. 1975. *Towards an Analysis of Discourse.* Oxford: OUP.

Sobolew, L. 1992. Panstwowy egzamin dla nauczycieli jezyka angielskiego: wyniki i wnioski. *Jezyki obce w szkole* 1/1992:176.

Somekh, B. 1990. The Evaluation of Teaching with Computers. *CTISS File* 10:32-39. Computers in Teaching Initiative Support Service: Oxford.

Somekh, B. 1992. Supporting Teacher Educators in Adopting an Innovation in the Training of Beginning Teachers. Paper presented at the annual meeting of the American Educational Research Association, San Francisco, April 1992.

St John, M.J. 1988. Attitudinal changes to self-access in EAP. In Brookes and Grundy, 126-35.

Stenhouse, L. 1975. *An Introduction to Curriculum Research and Development.* London: Heinemann.

Stenhouse, L. 1979. Using Research means doing research. In H. Dahl et. al. (eds.), *Spotlight on Educational Research.* Oslo: University Press.

Stern, H.H. 1983. *Fundamental Concepts of Language Teaching.* Oxford: OUP.

Tickle, L. 1987. *Learning Teaching, Teaching Learning.* Lewes: Falmer Press.

Underhill, A. 1992. The role of groups in developing teacher self-awareness. *ELT Journal* 46/1:71-80.

Underhill, A. 1986. Editorial, Teacher Development SIG Newsletter, IATEFL, N°.1

Vanermen, U. 1985. Collacmatics: an interim report. IATEFL Newsletter, Issue N°. 88.

Vanermen, U. 1990. The making of a lexical ladder. In Reports of the 24th IATEFL Conference, Dublin 1990. IATEFL Newsletter, Issue N°. 108.

Vanermen, U. 1991a. CTP: A CALL programme for intermediate and advanced EFL learners. In Reports of the 25th IATEFL Conference, Exeter 1991. IATEFL Newsletter, Issue N°. 112.

Vanermen, U. 1991b. Eerste bevindingen i.v.m. het gebruik van het experimenteel computerondersteunend leerparkket CTP. In Proceedings of the symposium on Differentiation in Language Learning and Teaching, 7-9 November, 1990. Leuven: Institut voor Levende Talen.

Van Lier, L. 1992. Not the nine o'clock linguistics class: investigating contingency grammar. Unpublished monograph, Monterey Institute for International Training, Monterey: California.

Wallace, M. 1991. *Training Foreign Language Teachers: A Reflective Approach.* Cambridge: CUP.

Wardell, D. 1991. Collocations: teaching word pairs in EFL classes. *English Teaching Forum* XXIX/3:35-37.

Waters, M. & A. Waters. 1992. Study skills and study competence: Getting the priorities right. *ELT Journal* 46/3:264-78.

Watts, P., A. Miller., N. Frederickson., M. Myers and D. Hart. 1988. Planning Professional Development for Educational Psychologists. *Educational Psychology in Practice.* 4.

Wenden, A. 1987. Incorporating learner training in the classroom. In A. Wenden & J. Rubin (eds.), *Learner Strategies in Language Learning*, 159-68. London: Prentice Hall.

Wenden, A. 1991. *Learner Strategies for Learner Autonomy.* London: Prentice Hall.

Wingate, J. 1990. Activities with Robot Masks. JET 1/1.

Winter, R. 1989. *Learning from Experience.* Falmer: London.

Wittrock, M.C. and A.A. Lumsdaine. 1977. Instructional Psychology. *Annual Review of Psychology* 28:417-59.

Wright, A.D. 1992. Critical Moments in the Second Language Classroom; Towards an Understanding of Second Language Culture. PhD thesis, Lancaster University.

Yang, C.F. 1989. A conception of Chinese consumer behaviour. In Yang, C.F. et al. (eds.), *Hong Kong Marketing Management at the Crossroads: A Case Analysis Approach*. Hong Kong: The Commercial Press.

Zawadzka, A. and E. Moszczak. 1991. *English is Fun*. Warszawa: Wydawnictwa Szkolne i Pedagogiczne.